Will Jones is from Oxfords   , and of pig
farming stock.

He decided that adorning a suit and commuting were not
for him very shortly after the end of a glittering education
career. The sixteen years since have been filled with
global travel, ski bumming and the occasional bit of work
to top the coffers up.

After ten years of radio presenting and telemark skiing
each winter in Val d'Isère, he is now a full time
professional sailor.

Will is forty going on seventeen, and has no possessions
of note or savings.

A View From The Cheap Seats

The Art of The Gap Decade

Many thanks to my parents Alec and Jane for being so understanding and supportive, and to all the people I've met and travelled with around the world.

'Radio' Will Jones

A View From The Cheap Seats
Seats
The Art of The Gap Decade

AUSTIN & MACAULEY
PUBLISHERS LTD.

A CIP catalogue record for this title is
available from the British Library.

ISBN 978 1 84963 171 6

www.austinmacauley.com

First Published (2012)
Austin & Macauley Publishers Ltd.
25 Canada Square
Canary Wharf
London
E14 5LB

Printed & Bound in Great Britain

Introduction

You're going to die soon. Don't worry though, I'm not thriving on your misfortune. I'm going to die soon as well. So is everybody else for that matter. Each of us has got a hundred years on this planet at the outside, and no more than three quarters of that as a fully active person. In relation to how long this planet has been around, we are all going to die comparatively soon. Morbid but true. The question is, what are you going to do in the mean time? In the time you've got to make a mark before you buy the farm? Before you turn up your toes? How are you going to use the time you spend on this planet? About a third of it is going to be spent sleeping, and you've got to do some of that, even if you're a three-hours-a-night woman like Maggie Thatcher or bulletproof Keith Richards, who once allegedly stayed awake for nine days. That bit doesn't require any imagination because it's compulsory. What about the other two or so thirds though? What do you do with it? You have a couple of choices.

Are you going to go for Option A? Option A is to settle for the accepted norm of birth, school, work, death. Option A is spending your whole adult life staring at a computer screen for eight hours a day. Option A is spending three hours a day sitting alone in your Ford, in a traffic queue full of other Fords with one person in them, so you can get to your computer. Option A is spending two hours a day getting to your computer on some underground system, and jostling for room in overcrowded carriages, looking glumly at your feet to avoid interaction with those in the same sordid mess. Option A is filling in forms. Option A is following everyone else, toeing the line, using the beaten track. Option A is working for forty eight weeks a year to pay to unwind for the other four. Option A is living to work.

Option B is working to live. Simple as that.

As the saying goes; if you can piss, you can paint. So there I was painting this wall. It was just before smokeo sometime in September 2004 and my seventh day on the job. My thoughts over the week had broached a lot of subjects and insanity loomed large as yet another wall slowly turned white. I can think of better colours to paint a wall, but it's not my wall and it's not my contract, so I'll just do as I'm told. White is such a missed opportunity, don't you think? Boring colour but luckily, the boringness of the colour was inversely proportional to the beauty of the location. The flat I was painting has a grandstand view of the 1992 Olympic men's downhill ski run, and there was only one of them that year; in one of the world's best ski resorts, Val d'Isère in France.

While leaning there on the balcony looking at what normal people would consider a cliff, but which Austrian man mountain Patrick Ortlieb hurtled down in a seriously courageous and death defying minute and 50.37 seconds, to win Olympic downhill gold, I decided to write a book.

'Who does he think he is, writing a book?', you may rightly enquire. The answer is no one special. I'm just another inhabitant of the planet like you. Also like you, I'm existing on what Hendrix called the third stone from the sun, and having a great time. I'll tell you something for free as well; if you stick with it you'll find more out in this book than in some footballer's 'story so far'.

As an Option 'B' earth dweller I haven't got a lot of money, don't own anything apart from a twenty-year-old motorbike, two pairs of Salomon skis, a pair of Telemark boots and this here laptop. I also have no savings, but I do have a lot of spare time though. That's because I work when I have to and spend the rest of the time wandering around the planet spending the proceeds. At the moment that wandering has brought me to room 305 of the New Wellington Hotel in Tunbridge Wells, Kent, England. In mid-November. Yippee. Oh well. Admittedly I have penned parts of this book in more exotic locations but that's all part of the ups and downs, the peaks and troughs, the highs and lows of a low budget lifestyle.

Welcome to life in the cheap seats.

Travel bugs

'Where have you two been on holiday this time then?' It's the 3rd of June 1998 and my brother Charlie and my good self are in our local drinking establishment in the sunny West Oxfordshire village where we grew up. The question comes from one of the other villagers at the bar, who is occupying approximately the same territory as he was on the 13th of November previous, the last time either of us two had set foot in the place. 'South America, Pete' is the stereo reply which we emit simultaneously. And with that they're all off, firing questions at us about our latest far flung adventures, and we're giving answers as quickly as the pints are going down.

A few things are worth mentioning at this juncture. Firstly, the only reason I got bladdered that night was that I hadn't had a pint of cider for six and a half months. I only had three but that was enough to get me lashed. Secondly, I would , considering that Dry Blackthorn cider is the elixir of life itself, have had a few more but for; Third, when you come home you get to choose what's for dinner. That, without fail, is the old dear's roast shoulder of lamb with all the trimmings, one of the few things in life which takes precedence over 'West Country champagne'.

Apart from thoughts from the stomach, the other thing worth considering in all of this is the use of the word 'holiday' in Pete the local's initial question. It is fair to say that a lot of the people who frequent our village boozer look on Charlie and I with a variety of expressions. Some are of wonderment, some disgust, and others vary from interest and amusement through to total bewilderment at the way we operate and live our lives.

I suppose that it is fair to assume, once you've established that somebody hasn't done a day's work in 6 months, that they've been on holiday. A long one but a holiday all the same. But when you're one of the people who's lived that six months in South America, as opposed to just imagining what it must have been like in your mind's eye, you don't quite think of it like that. Pete was probably thinking of a sunny afternoon on Copacabana beach in Rio de Janeiro when he used the word holiday. I don't know what memories it triggered in Charlie's mind, but it took me back to Bolivia for about half a second. You know , in a sort of 'your life flashing before your eyes' moment of clarity.

More specifically, it evoked a trip down into the jungle and to a town called Rurrenabaque, 300 kilometres north of La Paz. Great place, but a right bummer to get to in those days. The easy option was to fly down there with the Bolivian airforce; hardly luxury personified, but good enough. That is of course as long as the airstrip isn't grass, it's not an El Niño year and the plane can land at the other end. Unfortunately, it is, it was, and the plane couldn't. El Niño was in full swing and there hadn't been a flight down to the jungle for 10 days.

Not to worry, we thought, we'll take the bus. That'll be the bus which goes uphill out of La Paz, through a customs checkpoint, and then plunges a full 4000 metres in 300 kilometres into the Amazon Basin. The 'road' (really a wide goat track) is very aptly named the 'road of death' or the *calle de la muerta* as it's known to folk in those parts. The reason for this catchy name? The fact that an average of a bus a fortnight takes the fast track to the bottom, and no one ever survives. That is the sort of experience that being on 'holiday' is all about sometimes, but not the actual part of the trip I had in my mind's eye in the pub a couple of months later.

By that stage of the trip I was travelling with a chap called Cockney Bastard who we'd met in Ecuador. CB, aka Nick from Bethnal Green, was a salt of the earth Londonian chef who was about as sane as most chefs on this planet, as in not very. Nick never shut up, except for the time it took to search our bus at the checkpoint on the heights of La Paz. It is essentially for the searching of vehicles coming up from Amazonia and potentially carrying narcotics, but they do a lot of downward traffic as well. 'That was lucky,' said CB through his seedy Sid James-like cackle of a laugh as we cleared the checkpoint, 'I've got three grams of coke in my bag.' I was just about to explain to him with the use of a bevvy of sexual swearwords what a prick he was when we got to the top of the 'road of death'.

It really is hard to describe the horror of it all as the front of the bus swings round the first of a thousand hairpins. Watching the last twenty minutes of the *Italian Job* doesn't even come close. In the Michael Caine version, a steep rocky slope or at worst a cliff awaits you. In the Bolivian version this is replaced by nothing. A void. Should you wish to see your next point of contact with the planet, you have to stand up, turn your face sideways and compress your cheek hard against the window while trying to focus with your eyeball stuck to the glass. At any given point on the road you're inches from taking a thousand metres worth of bus-plunging free-fall before dying. It is not overly surprising to learn that no one ever, ever survives should their bus or truck turn out to be that fortnight's lucky winner. It gets even worse when you meet your first piece of oncoming traffic, fully conscious that Hino coach plus Scania truck does not equal 8 foot 6 inches which is the approximate width of that muddy scar of a brown goat track on a hillside which locals call a road. The two vehicles somehow inch past each other and you're off again. After contending with driving through El Niño induced waterfalls and listening to the blaring Latino music for what seems like days, you may be lucky enough, as we were, to survive and make it to the bottom of 'the road of (not quite certain) death.' At the bottom I celebrated life by sinking a couple of valium, and looked forward to a bit of shut eye. It was getting dark and we had another good 8 hours of Bolivian public transport to endure.

Digression no 1 – Diazepam

Being prone to digression, here is the first of what is sure to be a regular straying from the path.

I didn't fully appreciate Valium, or Diazepam as it is known professionally, the first time around. That was in 1988 when I'd been on morphine after a really badly haemorrhaged spiral fracture in my leg. Morphine really is great. It's the .44 Magnum of the pharmaceutical world, the big boy on the block. After an hour of waiting for the GP and then an ambulance in a world of pain, and then a load of happy gas which had no effect, someone in A&E stuck a needle in my arm and the world took on a different meaning. I could feel the total bliss of numbness spread all over my body, eventually shutting down my vision as if I were looking the wrong way through binoculars. The last thing I remember is someone saying, 'It's illegal to slipstream an ambulance Mrs Jones!' Good old Mumster! Forever the psycho-pilot, she'd been tailgating the blood wagon.

One operation and a few days later, I was on Ward 5C in the house of pain, aka the John Radcliffe hospital in Oxford, complete with leg scaffolding. I had found out what morphine was and had since taken the rash decision to pursue a career as a drug addict as soon as I was mended and out of hospital. Imagine my disappointment when they switched me to Valium. It was good, but not as good.

Looking back now it's clear to see that that was just lack of experience. Valium can hold its head high in the pharmaceutical hall of fame as far as this traveller is concerned.

Why? Well, it's like this. If you're in a vehicle in the third world which has not been hired by you and you alone, it is almost certain to have twice as many people in it as seats. Then there's the luggage, the animals and other reticule, all of which makes for a thoroughly uncomfortable journey. A couple of 'mummy's little helpers' as Valium is known, and all is well. Valium will send you to sleep if you've a mind to sleep. But as our cousin Tom puts it, you can just 'potter about' on it as well. For example, instead of sitting in a Nissan Urvan in Kenya scowling in misery, you'll be; 'oh'! there's a goat in my lap. Tom had chewed on a few in India and introduced Charlie and I to its non-hospital qualities and uses. The stuff is a handy addition to anyone's backpack.

End of digression

Back to Bolivia where, two hours after popping said pills, my eyes shot open. I had just burped pure sulphur and thrown up down myself. I also had chronic stomach cramps which, added to eggy burps and nausea, can only mean one thing. Illness.

The Amazonian dawn showed that the thick and lush green tree cover had given way to a flat terrain of pampa-like grass. Not a tree in sight. Oh well, here goes. Down to the front to see our resident psycho-pilot, the lunatic driver. '*Disculpe señor, estoy muy malo y necessito salir del autobus,*' I explained in my less than crap Spanish. '*Media hora,*' retorted Ayrton Senna. That was as far as the conversation got in Spanish. 'Look pal, stop the bus NOW! Ahorita.' This last and most urgent, imploring Spanish word did the trick and our rate of deceleration nearly opened the sphincter floodgates. I was already undoing my trousers and had already planned to head for the front of the bus with not a tree or bush in sight. And I made it. Not by much but I didn't 'get any on me', as they say. That was about the only positive I could take from it. I was spraying bum gravy without a hint of a solid in it out of one end like a cat-flap in the Hoover dam, while also barfing my guts up propped up on the front bumper of a Japanese bus in Bolivia. Just as another stomach cramp gripped me, I looked up to see that I had an audience of Bolivian women all sporting the little bowler hats and gold capped teeth they favour in that region, with the obligatory thick A-line skirts, the scourge of every fashion conscious secondary schoolgirl in Britain, to complete the look.

THAT is the image which I was thinking of when Pete enquired as to where we'd been on 'holiday'. Not a word which came to mind as I was propped up on that bumper with half of my life flying out of each orifice.

The point here is that there is a huge gulf of difference between going on holiday and going travelling. You do get ill at times. In this instance it was Giardia, a stomach parasite which gives you what my guidebook graphically described as "sudden, explosive, foul smelling diarrhoea and vomiting". Nice. The original trio – Charlie, Tom and I – had all caught it while walking the Inca trail a few weeks previously in Peru. Ten of us had done that trek together and pretty much everybody had got ill, probably from drinking water taken straight out of Andean streams. Cockney Bastard, who was also on that trek, was one of the five or so who got ill while we were still trekking.

A case in point really. What do you do? You're in the middle of nowhere in Peru at 3500 metres and you get ill. You have to just get on with it really. Yes , you can get your mates to help you if you're not on your own and yes, you can take any medication you think might help. But, in the finish of it, you have to keep going. That's what happened on our trek, and it all ended okay. At the time it makes you wonder what the hell you're doing. You berate yourself for being in the situation instead of at home in front of the fire with a cup of tea. You tell yourself that this is the last time and that you're too old for all this ball ache and misery. Then, two days of incessant rain come to an end and you get to a place selling food. A good hot meal and into your doss bag knowing that you're a couple of clicks away from the glittering prize, the end goal.

Twelve hours of comatose sleep later and the tents and rucksacks are packed and the group's sense of expectation and excitement is infectious. Humour and jocularity make it into the conversation a lot more easily, whereas the day before everybody was mute, looking at their feet, trying to concentrate on the job in hand.

What seemed like a gargantuan near-impossibility the day before, namely walking a couple of kilometres, is completed in no time. And then we're all sat on our gringo arses with slack jaws and not a word being uttered by anyone. We're sitting overlooking the capital of the Inca Empire, Macchu Picchu. Wow.

You will get tired and irritable while on tour. It's unavoidable. At least one person in your group needs to be awake and compus mentus, aware of what is occurring around you, making sure your bags are not all being nicked every time a bus or train stops. But highlights like getting to Macchu Picchu make it all worthwhile.

Up in the Peruvian Andes at 3140 metres and perched precariously on the edge of a couple of cliffs, Macchu Picchu was the hub of a long and illustrious empire. It was discovered relatively recently by American explorer and archaeologist Hiram Bingham in 1911. It really isn't all that surprising that it remained undetected for so long. I mean, who would build a city right up there? It's in the geographical middle of nowhere at the top of a load of mountains. Despite this, someone at some point has said ' we'll build it here'. It's an ancient equivalent of St Petersburg really, in that every civil engineer and architect within a ten mile radius is said to have groaned and winced when the Tsar announced that his new city of the north was to be built on the most improbable piece of marshland imaginable. 'Dissing' a decision of the Tsar was just as bad for your personal longevity as doing the same to an Inca king, but some things you just don't want to hear, do you?

Take another scenario: You're stood in the Prescilli mountains in South Wales on a Monday morning 5000 years ago, having turned up for work after chasing a wild boar around all weekend before finally getting it on the spit and in your stomach. 'Right lads,' grunts the chargehand, 'today we're dragging these five ton bluestone slabs down to the sea so that we can float them on rafts up the River Avon and then drag them to a place called Stonehenge in England.' How disappointing would that be?

The feats of man which are on show around this planet of ours are quite extraordinary.

That pretty much explains why we were all just sat there taking in, and trying to get our heads around what was before us when we got to Macchu Picchu. Yes, we'd all had to dig deep to get there and triumph over illness, misery, trenchfoot, hunger and tiredness, amongst other things, but when you compare that to the hardships of those who put these incredible edifices up, four days hard yakka doesn't seem all that bad. Your choice, four days of walking with stomach cramps, or your whole life working as a slave on the outskirts of Cairo building your pharaoh a tomb to befit his station? Not a difficult decision really, in the great scheme of things. Four days of walking with stomach cramps or a job on the tools building a high altitude capital city a thousand years ago? Again, no umming and ahhring before making an informed decision. The long and short of it is that we've got it pretty easy compared to a lot of our forebears.

No matter at what point in the history of the human race you care to mention, there have been great minds designing incredible feats of engineering. Stonehenge was built by people who hadn't been able to conceive a wheel; but they did drag ton after ton of bluestone from Pembrokeshire in South West Wales to Stonehenge in England, 245 miles away. The pyramids were also erected without the benefit of the wheel, but the architects and mathematicians were so talented that the shafts of these enormous monuments pointed directly at certain stars. The list of flabbergasting achievements is unending and getting longer with each new success and progression.

Sitting there at the 'Puerto del Sol', the sun gate, which is another example of pinpoint alignment, this time with the rising sun, these are the questions and feats which you find yourself mulling over instead of opening your mouth. Things of such grand design and visual impact tend to make you take a bit of time out and have a think. We were there a good long while, dumbstruck by the beauty of it all.

How lucky can you get?

You need three things to be able to go travelling apart from money. These are; 1) that you have to be born, otherwise you can't go in the first place, 2) you have to be lucky in where you get born, and who to, and, 3), you have to form the will to go and discover what's out there. I have my parents to thank for all three of these.

I certainly have my parents to thank for that bit of rumpy pumpy they had between the sheets in about August 1971 by my reckoning. I turned up in May the following year and poked my head out to find myself in Chipping Norton Hospital, in Oxfordshire.

Since then it's all been a bit of a breeze to be honest. I wouldn't consider us to be a wealthy family but it could be a lot worse. We've always had food on the table and a roof over our heads. We've always been a close knit family and we've always all got on. I've had as much formal education as I've wanted (and as much as I could stand), my healthcare has been excellent since before I was born, someone has looked in my mouth every six months, and a nice man even kitted some of my bones out with scaffolding a while back. In a lot of parts of the world a badly broken leg would be a death sentence.

Just as importantly, we don't have to leave our house, let alone our village, to get drinking water, and droughts in Oxfordshire are pretty rare so crop failures are few and far between. None of our neighbouring tribes or countries have invaded us recently. We don't have a despotic, murdering lunatic embezzling the country's wealth and ruling by force (debatable); instead we have democracy. Our civil war was 350 years ago, well before the invention of anti-personnel mines and AK47 assault rifles, so most people have all their limbs and appendages.

A lot of the world's population are not that lucky by a long chalk. It's what the British press call the 'postcode lottery'. Just by virtue of having popped out in Chipping Norton I have benefitted from most of the advantages in life and very few of the pitfalls which befall the human race as a whole every minute of every day of every year. There were a lot of bad things happening in 1972 in a lot of places all over the planet as is, unfortunately, always the case. None of them were happening in Chipping Norton though, except for the traditional scrapping outside the pubs on a Friday night. I could have popped out as a little Vietnamese child during the taking of Quan Tin City. I could have been born in the middle of Guatemala's 36 year civil war. But instead, I got lucky.

What this has meant to me personally is security. If you have that, you have a lot more opportunity to learn, experience more, and develop as a person instead of spending your time battling for survival. I don't own anything of note but I do have a base. I have a base on the bottom end of the Cotswolds where I can leave all my stuff while I'm away. I have parents and other family who I know I can rely on to help me out if I really get thigh deep in the poo, and I have a British passport which will help me out to a certain extent as well.

This security is what I'd say I have my parents to thank for the most. It gives you a base and an element of predictability in life which you can use as a base for everything else. Our parents were also travelling way before we were even thought of and I would estimate that our generation of the family have inherited the travel bug from previous lineage. Our clan have been getting to the outer reaches of the planet for a good long while and we've done our bit to carry that on. Our parents have been about a bit and I reckon that's rubbed off on us. Your parents are probably the biggest influence on you and

I'm pleased to say that ours were a good model to follow in the tracks of. They've done some exciting and interesting things themselves and also started us on the road of discovery. Trot and Chiz, as parents are known , were travelling when it was still hard work; in the times before guidebooks, backpackers hostels and water purification tablets. After meeting at agricultural college Trot, our old dear, went off to Africa to do some nursing and have a look around. Chiz had just buried his mother, leaving him with one living blood relative. He went down to Hull docks and got a job on a boat going to the Far East. His job was to look after a load of sheep going over to Japan and China.

Now, the very fact that you could in those days go down the docks and get a job like that makes the world of the late 1960s a more exciting place than the current antiseptic compensation culture which we currently call the 'developed world'. To get that job now you'd have to have been on about two hundred health and safety courses and have a United Nations Merchant Navy card. Back then, he just had to prove that he could keep the sheep alive and healthy. The old man had a vague plan, which was to meet the old dear in Africa. Apart from that, he was just winging it. Best way to go usually.

Things got more exciting after dropping a load of sheep in Yokohama, Japan. He and the remaining sheep switched boats to an Australian vessel called the 'Eastern Moon' and headed for Tinsin, the port of the city of Peking. Unfortunately, they arrived just in time for the Cultural Revolution and the boat was impounded for six weeks. The crew, our old man included, were only allowed off of the boat once a fortnight to go and report in to the consulate. As a six-footer with a beard, Chiz was quite a novelty for the kids of Tinsin who were used to more vertically challenged and less hirsute people. He vividly remembers being followed down the quay by hundreds of them. The Chinese would come out in their boats and daub

Communist slogans on the side of all the ships. The ones on the 'Eastern Moon' were all left on apart from 'death to the Queen', which would never do on a Commonwealth vessel.

Eventually they were allowed to leave and, wielding his copy of Chairman Mao's 'Little Red Book', he got passage to Durban in South Africa on a French cruise ship out of Macao. He was in third class or 'steerage' as it's less glamorously known; slumming it, in other words. Not to worry, he was getting ever closer to his future wife no matter how close he was to the propellers. He says his enduring image of the whole trip was a gin and tonic. Sgt Pepper's had just come out and he'd got hold of a copy just before the boat sailed for Durban. Gin and tonics are invariably good but being in the middle of the Indian Ocean at sunset listening to 'Lucy In The Sky With Diamonds' watching the whales which were tagging alongside the boat, has got to take some beating.

The two of them had a good time in wilds of Africa as well, by the sounds of it. Sleeping under the Land Rover surrounded by big cats which would like nothing better than to chew on your arse is pretty hair-raising stuff.

Its stories like those which fascinate you as a child and form the basis of your own interest in travel. That's certainly what happened to us and, moreover, we didn't even have to wait until adulthood – which Chiz maintains we have yet to achieve – before our own travel experiences started. This was thanks to some brilliant holidays, both in the UK and around Europe. For Charlie and Tom, our cousin, the fun started aged seven and for me at the age of five, and none of us have ever really looked back.

Planning your trip

Constraints

People – The number of people you're going with is going to be another big deciding factor in what you do on your trip. The unwritten rule while out skiing in the winter is that you ski in a group of no more than six people. Any more than that and you end up trying to decide where to go instead of actually going there. The same goes for travelling. Six is the limit, unless you're in the 'fuck truck', as Oz Experience is known, or on an overland lorry trip. In these cases you're pretty much getting told where to go anyway.

For everyone else, a couple or three is preferable, but half a dozen is the saturation point. If you go on your own it's easy. You go where you want and when you want because you don't have to take anybody else's wishes and desires into account. The more people, the more considerations come into planning your trip, and the harder it is. With that said, it's also important not to set everything in stone. Plans change and circumstances change, so your trip is unlikely to unfold exactly as you envisaged before leaving home. For this reason it's not worth trying to plan everything down to the last second, whether you're going for a month or a year.

Time – You could stay in a country, let alone on a continent, for evermore and never see everything. This is the first thing to consider when going on a trip. Don't get frustrated by not being able to do the lot. You can always go back. It's also very important not to try and fit too much into the time you do have. If you don't watch it you'll spend your time tear-arsing around a country or landmass to try and catch all the highlights and just spend half your time on planes, trains and in automobiles. Much better to take things at a slower pace and fully appreciate what you do fit in, rather than go for the turn up, take a couple of photos, about turn, say 'seen that' and move on to the next 'point of interest'.

This is one reason that guidebooks are very useful; you can sit down and plan what you can hope to fit into a trip before leaving home. You can get a feel for where you're going before getting on the plane. I tend to find that a lengthy drinking session in the pub with your fellow travellers is the way forward. Buy a travel guide and go to the pub. Once installed in the pub, it's important to get down to business as soon as you've got the first pint in. If your friends are anything like mine, you've got about two pints worth of vaguely intelligent conversation and helpful input which will be of benefit to the overall planning of the trip you are about to undertake. Somewhere round about the middle of the third pint, someone will make a childish comment on some unrelated subject, the giggling will start and the whole meeting of (tiny) minds will degenerate into the usual rigmarole. It's all good fun though.

On the subject of guidebooks, it's definitely worth getting one; preferably a Lonely Planet or a Footprint handbook, although any of them will be of great benefit to you. Three things to remember about guidebooks:

1) Buy the one which is latest to come into print. Look inside the front and back covers and somewhere it'll tell you the number of the edition and when it came into print.

2) This brings us smoothly onto the second point, which is that with guidebooks it's not so much a case of which one is most up to date, but more which one is least out of date. By virtue of being a book, your guidebook is never going to be right up to date. The time between the update being written, the book making it to print and into the shops, and you buying it

and going to the region in question will mean that it could be a good year out of date. For this reason, guidebooks are not your best source of information. The best source will always be talking to fellow travellers who will be able to give you the most up to date information on where you are going next. Guidebooks are very handy, but things change. Things improve, things go downhill and new stuff and new thrills get discovered all the time. Guidebooks are very handy for their maps and for most of the information they contain and are perfect for planning the broad outlines of your trip. The fine tuning you'll need to do on the ground.

3) Get your nose out! You're going to see places. You're not going so you can spend months on end with your nose embedded in a guidebook. The amount of people you see reading about the place they are in instead of looking at it is very sad. Make sure you're not that person.

A couple of other things worth considering when you're getting ready to go travelling are:

What to take;

1) You've got a bag, but you don't have to fill it.

You know what they say – take a small bag and you'll fill it; take a bigger bag and you'll still fill it. Don't overdo it on the luggage front. The first time I went backpacking, Tom and Charlie got hold of my rucksack, emptied it on the floor and put back in about a third of what I'd put in. They were right as well. Take the minimum and wash it while you're away. You can also take some travel wash with you and do your own washing. Less clothes also means more room in your bag for knick-knacks which you might want to buy on your roamings.

2) Don't get too carried away with pills. Have all your inoculations and jabs by all means, but don't start carting loads of expensive pharmaceuticals around with you. Malaria is a case in point in this respect. I met lots of people in Africa having problems due to Larium, an expensive anti-malarial

drug which gives a lot of people side effects. Some people have to go home because of the trouble it gives them. You can also only take it for a limited time. I was told about a homeopathic alternative which claims the same 85% success rate as Larium. I got enough for three people for a year for a fiver just as Tom and Charlie were about to spend a hundred and forty five quid each on malaria pills before we went to South America. Check out Helios Homeopathic in Kent, UK instead. Consult your doctor as well, of course.

3) Talking of malaria, don't forget to pack a long-sleeved white round neck T-shirt. If in any doubt as to their worth, see the trip to the jungle section.

4) Last but not least is money. You'll need some of that for sure. Even the lowest budget forays are going to need some. Travel costs money, and money is therefore a major consideration in any project where you may have to go and discover far-flung parts of the planet. Here's a few suggestions preceded by the slight financial tangent below.

Digression No 2 -- money the drug

Money first needs to be considered from its worth to society and the effect it has on the average human. As mentioned, whether you love it or hate it, you have to have some of it. For some people it's an annoying must in all of our lives. I have some money but really just enough to keep ticking over. I'd say I'm in a minority amongst humans. Most of our race are addicted to money and wealth in general. A large majority of our species spend the majority of their time accumulating as much of it as possible. It's what I call the 'Rupert Murdoch factor'. Murdoch is an American octogenarian of Australian origin who is very, very rich. He is one of our planet's top media moguls and has a massive multimedia empire which incorporates everything from newspapers to film studios, passing by publishing houses and satellite TV channels. He is worth a ridiculous amount of money which runs into billions of dollars, pounds or whichever currency you care to name. Just to top, it off he has acquired a very fit new wife who is forty years his junior. It's fair to say that Roops is in a purple patch.

But is he? Yes he's got the wealth, the wife, and all the fixtures and fittings, but what does he do? He tries to make even more money, that's what he does. He accumulates money, buys more companies, launches more satellites and stuff like that. Errors. If I was in his situation, I'd laze the days away enjoying myself and having a look around the glorious planet on which we live. Why doesn't he try a lie in instead of getting up early to try to corner the Chinese satellite TV market? More's the point, why isn't he combining overtime in bed with some horizontal jogging; surely bedroom Olympics with a gorgeous jewel of Asia should take priority over the accumulation of wealth? Not for him. He's got the lot but he still wants more. Gimme, gimme, gimme.

In the finish of it, it all comes down to ego I suppose. Testament to what a sad case Murdoch is is that he'd rather spend his twilight years influencing politicians and imposing his opinions on the world's population than enjoying himself a bit. Crap xenophobic, scaremongering newspapers such as *The Sun* in the UK, and equally goose-stepping TV channels such as Fox News in the US, peddle so much of 'the world according to Roops' that people actually end up believing it. It happens to them all in the end. Just look at Murdoch's former, and now dead arch-rival, Robert Maxwell. He was so convinced of his own importance that he allegedly used to urinate onto the masses below from the top of the NatWest tower in London before getting into his chopper. Choppers everywhere. Same goes for Nestlé executives; how the hell do those people get to sleep at night knowing that they make money by exploiting some of the poorest people on the planet?

The really silly thing about spending your life at the financial altar is that the stuff isn't even worth anything! In days of old you could take a ten pound note into a bank and get the corresponding value in gold. Not anymore. The bits of paper that most of the planet's humans spend the vast majority of their time accumulating are totally worthless.

Apparently, we're the top of the food chain.

End of digression.

a) With our global financial system analysed and thoroughly dissed we need to get back to the fact that you're going to need some money if you want to go travelling. First thing is to earn lots of it. You'll need to get a job and work as many hours as you can. If you're at work earning it, you can't be spending it, so you'll save in double quick time and before you know it you'll be down at the bucket shops buying your plane ticket.

b) The next thing is that it's worth considering the financial clout of the people you're going with. It's a good idea to try and get together the same funds so that you don't end up with a bunch of people who have diverging ideas of what to do and not do because of differing financial circumstances.

c) Always take some cash with you. US dollars cash in small denominations. It always comes in handy, especially in the Third World. While pounds sterling oil the cogs in some parts of the world, a couple of greenbacks light up the eyes of even the most corrupt official. Everybody from Rupert Murdoch to the most far flung resident of outer Mongolia knows what a dollar bill is. Carry a hundred dollars worth and they're bound to come in handy at some point. I've got a regular belt with a zipper concealed in the back of it which is perfect for this. You can buy such safety measures all over the place.

d) Nothing is to stop you from taking a break during your trip. If you're in it for the long haul and are away for a good few months, you could plan to stop in a country, get a work permit and earn some funds to get you back in the black before continuing your trip. This is good for a number of reasons, not least because it's good to stop moving every now and then. Not having to pack up and erect a tent every night is a big relief. Emptying your whole bag and leaving it emptied for a while is a great feeling.

Financially, depending on where you're from, you're even better just getting enough money together to get where you're going and earn abroad, as a lot of Antipodeans and South Africans do in the UK. The important thing, no matter where you end up being based, is not to get bogged down and in a rut. There's a standing joke in Sydney, Australia that the Irish population of the eastern suburbs never actually make it any further out of Sydney than the Kingsford Smith airport. They get off the plane, go into town, meet up with a load of people from home, get a job, and spend their year 'travelling' getting pissed in the Cock and Bull pub in Bondi Junction. Don't let this happen to you. There's more to life than the inside of a pub – honest!

Whether you go for a long term stay in a backpacker's (whereby you'll probably get a discount) or rent a house, enjoy the place where you are but don't forget to put some of your hard earned dosh in the bank! This can be hard to achieve if you end up in a madhouse like 38 Ruthven Street, a residence in Sydney which will be highlighted later on. One thing to remember is that if you are planning to work abroad, check out the work permit situation; if you require one you'll almost certainly have to get it before you leave.

e) Once you have the money and kit you require to go on your trip, try to plan some way of stopping other people nicking it off you while you are on your way round the world. You will as likely as not stick out like a sore thumb while on your travels, and there will be people out there who would like nothing better than to relieve you of all your hard earned money and possessions. Never let your passport out of your sight and buy yourself a money-belt; even better an armpit holster for your cash, documents and passport. Photocopy your passport a few times as well as your travel insurance, as copies always come in useful.

A big stick is a pretty good idea as well. I've carried one about the size of a truncheon ever since what I call the 'Mombasa incident' which you'll read about later on. I've never had to hit anyone with it, thank god, but it is also useful for propping open windows in stuffy hostel rooms!

Most important of all is keeping your wits about you and not ending up in the wrong place at the wrong time. If you can do this, you may manage to not end up lying on your back with some bloke waving a sword in your face. You may also make it home with all your body parts and possessions intact. Guidebooks tend to be pretty good at detailing the dodgier parts of towns, so have a good read up while you're on your way from one to the next. Keep an eye on your mates and get them to keep an eye on you. It's good to have a wingman.

Last but not least on the money front is good comedy moments involving the stuff. The first one which had me chuckling was in Uruguay. As is the case with a lot of countries, Uruguay's currency had a bit of a wobble some years ago. Well, it was more like an economic crash version of a head on collision in a car, actually. As happens in such cases, Uruguay refloated its currency, but they did it with a difference. Instead of wasting lots of money making new banknotes, they just got everybody to get a marker pen and cross out a few of the zeroes on the formerly very high denomination notes! What an inspired money saver. However, what with it being South America and all, it probably later transpired that El Presidente's brother owned the biggest marker pen factory in the southern hemisphere. Corruption is not unknown in those parts, let's face it

Talking of zeroes, Turkey has lost a few in recent years as well. When I was there in 1999 it was zeroes 'r' us, though. I had this forecourt attendant ranting hysterically at me in a petrol station for trying to short change him on a tank of fuel. I was actually totally innocent and had simply counted the wrong number of zeroes on a banknote which were so numerous they nearly covered the whole width of the bill.

Getting there and away

Civil aviation

Of course, if you've the intention of going travelling somewhere as I have a mind to do every once in a while, you first of all have to get there, and, once there, get around. These can all be fraught with danger.

The first major problem is being ripped off before actually getting anywhere. This is due to the cost of anything remotely connected with airports in the UK, especially the cost of getting to them. The 'airbus' as they now call the service from Oxford should be called the 'bend over and let me roger you senseless' or the infinitely more catchy 'think of a number and double it'. What a total rip off. They know that you have to get there and charge what they like for the pleasure of your conveyance. It's never right. There is an alternative though; drive yourself to the airport. The major flaw in this approach is that you can't take your car on holiday with you and the lovely people at the airport charge national-debt-of-Mexico-a-day prices to look after it for you.

The second major problem is a fairly depressing thought. In some ways the fact that the planet is shrinking is a good thing; it is getting ever quicker to get from A to B with the advent of air travel in particular. The equal and opposite effect of this in terms of travel though is that you're never more than a flight and two bus journeys from Carterton in Oxfordshire.

Digression no 3: Carterton, Oxfordshire, UK

It's not the worst place on earth; that accolade goes to Maicao, a dreadful, adjectival shithole of a town on the Venezuelan/Colombian border. Carterton does come pretty close though, and to my mind is the only proof you need that the expression 'you can't polish a turd' is an essential part of everyday English. If you ever get bored of visiting idyllic medieval Cotswold market towns stuffed to the brim with overpriced antique shops selling overpriced antiques to overweight Americans, and of course the obligatory tearooms, you can just nip a few miles down the road and get reacquainted with reality in a truly drab, ordinary place. It's not that there's anything particularly wrong with Carterton, but you'd like to think that if town planners started with a clean sheet (or in this case, some virgin fields) sometime early last century, they could come up with something more stimulating to the eye than what is now there. It's just very, very ordinary. Unfortunately, it is also the nearest town to my folks' house so you sort of have to go there once in a while. Even the name is dull. There are some great place names out there such as The Land of Nod in Yorkshire or Mlada Boleslav in the Czech Republic. Cock's Balding; ooh, how our transit minibus full of childish marquee erectors laughed at that one! And, my all-time favourite place name; Comodoro Rivadavia on Argentina's Atlantic coast, which slips very coolly off the tongue of the locals. But Carterton? Go there if you get time; just the once though.

End of digression.

Sorry about drifting off. Back to airports. The good thing of course is that having been relieved of the contents of your wallet, you do get to go on a plane; and that, as long as you're not Dennis Bergkamp or Charles Gronin's character in the film

'Midnight Run', is pretty exciting. There's something about flying which makes it exciting and glamorous. Look around any airport and most people have a look of expectation, assuming that it's one of the 78 days a year when a French air traffic controllers strike has not brought global civil aviation to a standstill. Flying means holidays and getting togged up in your most 'comfortable' smart casuals. Why is it that people get dressed up poshly to go and sit in a seat for several hours? It's clear to see why someone would want to be wearing a clean pair of under garments if there is even the slightest chance of death by Deep Vein Thrombosis, but why get your best pair of strides all creased up? The other question which has to be asked is, is it compulsory to wear a brand new pair of trainers when flying out of Gatwick to go on a package holiday? I think we should be told.

My first plane ride was in 1977, when I was five, and I thought I was going to die of excitement. So excited was I that I failed to notice that our mother was on the verge of a nervous breakdown. Her fault for trying to go anywhere in an Austin Allegro, I say.

Digression no 4 – British cars of the 1970s

The Austin Allegro is a classic example of the things coming out of Britain when the country was on its knees in the mid-70s. Allegro infers a certain element of speed and sprightliness in piano playing circles and should therefore not be used in the same sentence as this pokey little car. Ours was a white estate version which used more oil than petrol and had brown brushed polyester seats. It was about as aerodynamic as the white cliffs of Dover and had about the same acceleration. The only scant bit of consolation you can take from being an Allegro family is that you're not a Marina family. The Austin

Marina was the worst car ever made. Car designers working for proper companies, which made money in those days, chose to make all the instruments of the vehicle easily visible and accessible to the driver. Not the geniuses who designed the Marina, with everything pointing at the passenger and away from the driver. Cunning or what?

We did have some good times in that Allegro, though. The greatest of these was in Little Clarendon Street in Oxford. The terrible trio – myself, Charlie and Tom – had been left to look after the car while the old dear went to look in an antique shop. Tom needed a pee and, unable to wait any longer, attempted to empty his bilges into an empty 'Lilt' can. Needless to say he missed with the majority of the urine he emitted; about 80% judging by how wet the back seats were. Oh how we laughed!

End of digression.

Back to mother having a nervous breakdown. It was mostly the fault of the Allegro which made it 20 miles towards Gatwick airport before breaking down in Oxford. Her other problem was me and Charlie. Back in the old days, the effects of tartrazine, E102, taurine and sodium benzoate were not as widely known as they are now. Admittedly, the non-functioning car and very unhelpful mechanics were a major hurdle to our mother, but two very hyperactive and badly behaved delinquent offspring high on a cocktail of food additives saying 'are we there yet?' every 300 yards is not going to help matters much either. I think she did very well to get us to the airport at all, but, to her credit, she did. Once there, it was off to Portugal to meet our dad who had been out there on business. We flew on a Boeing 727 belonging to the Portuguese national flag carrier, TAP.

Due to my excitement at going in the air for the first time I didn't have time to think too much about our chances of dying. Good job, really, as they were quite high. TAP are not the best airline on the planet; that's as complimentary as I can be. They're not the worst, but they're not in any danger of winning any awards. Twenty seven years later and me and Charlie have just had the pleasure again. TAP is still a disaster.

Like a lot of asthmatics, I'm allergic to lots of different stuff. One of the less common among them is being allergic to Boeing 727s. A strange allergy really but I don't have a lot of luck with them, and I've only ever been on two. It's a good looking plane but that maiden flight set the benchmark for a tenuous relationship. As our TAP 727 spirited us to Faro in the beautiful Portuguese Algarve, another TAP airliner was taking our luggage somewhere completely different. Right on cue, the first thing I did upon arrival was fall in the swimming pool and was left with nothing dry to wear.

The only other 727 I've ever been on was in Peru in 1998. Tom, Charlie and I were in the north of Peru in a town called Piura. El Niño was in full swing and Peru got it worse than anywhere else. We were hearing nightmare stories from further south of washed out roads and general travel mayhem. We decided to fly to Lima.

Climbing aboard a 727 in 1998, it is unrealistic to expect the vehicle in which you are about to (hopefully) take off to be full of the joys of youth. The 727 is an old plane. This one, however, was a hand me down. I don't mind wearing hand me down clothes, and in fact did so with pride until the age of 16. Second hand clothes aren't expected to, or capable of, maintaining your cruising altitude. The question was, would this second-hand 727 previously operated by NorthWest airlines which was now in the possession of AeroPeru? I got to wondering if, considering that they hadn't bothered to remove the NorthWest livery from the food heating cabinets, had they bothered to get any other minor details right, such as blowing up the tyres?

42

The answer was confirmed by our safe arrival in Lima, although there was a bit of a steward's inquiry along the way. After having been airborne for a while, we suddenly dived for the deck like a Spitfire trying to escape the attentions of a Messcherschmitt 109 in the Second World War. Just when we thought we were going to die, we landed at Chiclayo and picked up some more punters. Tom was white and I had to concur that it was not unreasonable of Tom to expect the pilot to not only inform us of the stopover, but also to take a less vertical trajectory to the tarmac. Unfortunately, this was not be our last experience of the unorthodox style of Peruvian pilots.

Digression no5 – The art of predicting a coup d'état

Just a brief digression in passing, but while we're on the subject of Boeing 727s, any person who loses power in a coup d'état these days only has themselves to blame. This is for the simple reason that anybody who ever stages a coup d'état uses a Boeing 727. Why is unbeknown to me, but 727s do seem to be the regime changer's plane of choice. It is the traditional conveyor of the soldier of fortune, the spiriting device of the 'Dogs of War', as mercenary soldiers are known.

What this means is that if you're some tinpot dictator like the nasty piece of work who put the democratically elected President Limbani in prison in the film 'Wild Geese', all you have to do to maintain your vice-like grip on power is employ a full time Boeing 727 spotter at the capital's airport. If one arrives unannounced it is bound to be full of big burly South African gentlemen. It is not improbable, but neither is it a foregone conclusion that any of them will know Sir Mark Thatcher, but what is as sure-fire a bet as the rising sun is that they will be armed up to their tattooed shoulder blades and looking to get rid of you.

But – the burly Saffers haven't counted on the fact that you, the dictator, have read Will's 727 theory and have long since engaged the services of a 727 expert with 20/20 vision.

All that remains is to blow up the vintage jet airliner and you've saved yourself the rigours of unemployment, death by firing squad and having to move out of your palace – not necessarily in that order – or at best a life in exile. It just goes to show that for despotic maniacs at least, this is a book you can't afford not to read.

End of digression.

Back to civil aviation, and there's nothing worse than a poor imitation. It is important to stress that this isn't a universal or all-embracing sweeping statement. The fake Rolex I bought my old dear in Kuala Lumpur 6 years ago is still going strong, despite several cycles in the washing machine.

Aeroplanes are a different matter, however. Not knowing what time it is because the fake watch your son bought you on the way home from somewhere has packed up, is not life threatening. Crashing into the floor after plummeting 30,000 feet is very life threatening and often happens because a Soviet plane designer couldn't be bothered to copy a Boeing 727 properly. This problem is best demonstrated by the Tupolev 154, aka the Soviet Union's answer to the Boeing 727. I'm not getting on one of them again in a rush. Tupolev have made some very good planes over the years, as well as some right shockers. Look at the 'Concordski', as the Tupolev TU 144 was dubbed. A great example of the Soviets trying to prove that Marxist-Leninism was superior to capitalism by building a bigger and faster version of the Anglo-French Concorde, and getting it airborne three months before its Western rival. After crashing at the Paris airshow, it was used to ferry mail out to the dominions. It just goes to show the contempt with which parts of the Soviet Union were treated, really. If the post office were really serious about getting mail to the outer reaches of Kazakhstan and Kyrgyzstan, they wouldn't have used a plane which crashes every 20 yards.

The 154, in its defence, is a bit better than that. It has made at least one successful return trip. Luckily, it was the one I was on. I had the uninterrupted joy of travelling to Kenya with Aeroflot in 1995. It saved me £100 compared to the next cheapest quote, but cost me and my two companions a lot of brain cells and a very good T-shirt.

The brain cells were mostly surrendered to alcohol in Moscow airport. Vodka, more specifically. A stopover in Sheremetyevo is one of the most God-awful experiences this planet has to offer. Built for the 1980 Moscow Olympic Games by the West Germans, it was designed to give athletes a fitting welcome to the then-Communist nirvana that was the Soviet Union.

For starters, a stopover in Moscow is as long as it is inevitable. All long-haul Aeroflot flights involve a stopover there. A mere eight hours in our case. The problem is that there is nothing to do whatsoever. I was with two friends from university, Charlie and Simon. We were pottering around bored stupid and then walked into the only area of activity in the whole building. There, in a crap airport well on the way to the Urals, is an Irish bar. This one happens to accept Amex traveller's cheques. Lethal.

Fifteen hours later and we're all three suffering terribly. Having done six hours heavy drinking in the Irish bar and then completed the second of our three leg trip to Nairobi, we're on the apron at Cairo airport and the air-con of our Tupolev 154 has ceased functioning. We've all three got about fifteen headaches each after getting vodka'd right out of it in Moscow airport, and the temperature inside the cabin is just breaching the 40 Celsius barrier. I know it's hard to drum up sympathy for piss-head students, but the air-con would have alleviated

45

our suffering somewhat. We were pleading with the stern-faced Khrushchev look-alike stewardesses for water whenever they passed, with very limited success. When they did stop to ask us what we wanted every now and then, they eventually returned with little white plastic cups of a bizarre orange liquid not dissimilar to river silt. This was apparently some sort of orange squash and about as refreshing as a sand dune.

That was when the T-shirt died. Having taken forever to procure another round from the only stewardess who looked more like Brehznev than Khrushchev, she managed to throw one of the cups over Simon while handing it to him, which caused Charlie to burst out laughing. I thought that was a bit harsh until Charlie announced, 'I've just seen the puppy's nose!' The stewardess, leaning over him to reach Simon's foldaway table had revealed one of her breasts to him through her inadequately buttoned blouse and non-existent bra.

The fate of the T-shirt was less amusing. Simon washed it sometime after getting to Kenya, but never to this day has he managed to get the orange stain out of it. Just think what that rubbish does to your insides if you can't get it out of a piece of cotton.

That was the first time in my life that I'd really put a value on my life. Without inferring in any way that I'm of major value to the human race or a linchpin of society, I've decided that my continued existence is worth more than the hundred quid we saved by flying Aerogrot. Simon's girlfriend Ellie arrived a week later on Olympic looking fresh and rested after an incident-free journey. Moreover, we spent most of the hundred quid we each saved in the Irish bar in Moscow.

Just before moving on to the subject of posher airlines, Sheremetyevo airport is worth a further mention due to strange goings-on. My cousin Tom had made the same error as the Kenya expedition; namely, he'd flown somewhere with Aeroflot. He was on his way back from India and was just getting to the more unpleasant stages of amoebic dysentery when his flight arrived in Moscow. Just after finding out that his connecting flight to London had already left without those passengers arriving on the delayed Delhi flight, his backside started showing signs of cat-flap-in-the-Hoover-Dam syndrome; bum gravy on a massive scale. With major intestinal trouble ahead he did the tour of the flight desks to see if he could hitch a lift to Britain. Luck was with him and he got a slot on a BA flight, but had 7 hours to wait in the meantime. He took the entire contents of his medicine cabinet and tried to get some sleep on the unyielding polished granite floor after popping a couple of valium for good measure and pain relief.

He thought he'd lost the plot when he opened his eyes some time later to see the Dalai Lama walking past! He thought he was in some sort of dysentery-induced delirium, but it was in fact the exiled Buddhist monk himself.

Things weren't as bad as they could have been, though. Tom was at the BA desk to get his ticket some hours later when an irate Italian cove jumped the queue and started screaming at the staff that he'd been stuck in Moscow for ten days. My god, ten days in Moscow airport! And there's Steve McQueen thinking he had it hard being incarcerated on Devil's Island in *Papillion*. From personal experience I'd much sooner eat cockroaches and have all my teeth fall out on Devil's Island than spend ten days in Sheremetyevo airport in Moscow. I've never been to Devil's Island but it can't be any worse than that most godforsaken of airports. Give me the French Caribbean penal colonies any day.

Digression no 6 – the art of 'less' civil aviation

Don't be fooled by the title of this latest wandering. It is not meant to be in any way negative. By the age of twelve I'd

47

been on a couple of airlines but had yet to realise how bad things could get. While breakfasting in a VC10 passing Mount Vesuvius however, I started to realise how good aviation could get.

I joined Air Scouts at the age of eleven and we used to get free flights, usually on Royal Air Force pilot training flights known as 'circles and bumps'. The name refers to their circling of the air base before coming in to practice landing again. Occasionally however, you would get to bum a lift to somewhere further afield. As I was scoffing my fry up I was on my way to RAF Akrotiri in Cyprus. It was only a day trip but still a big adventure for a twelve-year-old. I was sat near a chap who turned out to be an air courier for the RAF. He flew around the world delivering documents which, at the time, I thought was an unfeasibly glamorous way to earn a living. His name escapes me, but I do remember him chucking a cup of tea straight into his own crotch which made him produce some very strange facial expressions and noises for a good half hour.

Well bugger me if my luck didn't get better. I went on a two week exchange to the US, more specifically, Virginia. I was fourteen and the whole thing included free flights with the RAF, again on a VC10. The first thing I noticed was the same courier as on the Akrotiri flight sitting in the departure lounge at Brize Norton! Low and behold, half an hour into the flight, some very familiar noises started coming from somewhere behind me and he'd only gone and done it again! Cup of scolding tea, straight in the crown jewels! It was the most painful example of déjà vu I've ever witnessed.

The RAF is fantastic. Not only did it repel the Germans against all odds and allow the whole world to carry on living in non-fascist bliss, but it is also the best airline on the planet. It's free, the food is absolutely delicious, they call you by your Christian name if you're fourteen, and you can choose what time you eat! You really to feel like a king for the duration of the experience. To add to the excitement, I spent most of my time in the cockpit with the four-man crew and the engineer had me synchronising the revs of the plane's four engines. For a fourteen-year-old flying nut it's about as good as it gets. Furthermore, should you be unlucky enough to crash, at least with the RAF the seats face backwards and you've got more chance of not dying.

Flying with the RAF is therefore only 'less civil' aviation in the sense that it's military. It's hard to put in words just how fantastic they are.

End of digression.

Back to civil aviation and more specifically, Peruvian lunatics.

The ravages of El Niño continued to beat up pretty badly on Peru. Trying to get up to Cuzco was going to be a major contract if we attempted it overland.

In the interim, we had a good time in Lima, most of which I spent trying (unsuccessfully) to get in the knickers of a devoutly Catholic stunner. Good job I didn't really as her father was the senior high court judge for the whole of the north of Peru. She was from Trujillo, up north. We – not me and her – stayed in the Hotel Espana near the Plaza de Armas which had a mini zoo on the roof and a very good patisserie/off licence next door. If you're ever in Lima, check out the gold museum and the gorgeous women walking around Miraflores of an evening.

We left Lima as we arrived, by plane. It was taking forever to get up to Cuzco by bus and a lot of them were not getting there at all. 'Less civil' aviation proved the cheapest option and we ended up flying to Cuzco with Groupo Ocho which was the Peruvian air force in disguise. As luck would have it, President Fujimori was just getting into his self-important phase, which often follows a successful start in

49

office and precedes the episode where you're revealed as a corrupt, murdering son of a bitch. That's exactly what happened to Fujimori, who is now back on the continent following the runner he did to Japan, and is planning the most improbable comeback since Liverpool in the 2005 European Cup Final.

At the time though, this son of Japanese immigrants to Peru could do no wrong. He'd got rid of the Marxist guerrillas which had plagued Peru for years and the tourists were flooding back to this beautiful country. He'd also turned the ailing economy around and things were looking good for Peru.

What his growing self-importance meant for us was a Fokker 28. Fu

jimori had decided that he was now so important that he needed a brand new Boeing 737 to get around the world in. The lowly little Fokker was no longer grandiose enough for this 'grand homme' of the Americas. So, the newly redundant Fokker was farmed out to the air force and to this day, is probably still shipping locals and gringos alike up to Cuzco from Lima.

I will never forget that flight as it was the best I've ever been on, and will be difficult to beat between now and when I turn my toes up or 'buy the farm' as the saying goes. From sea level you get catapulted up to 3400 metres, but it's not the gain in height which makes the trip so good. As you approach Cuzco, the pilot is dipping, bobbing, weaving, climbing, accelerating, decelerating and all the other tricks in the book to avoid hitting mountains. Looking out of the window, I would have been shitting myself due to the wing-scratching proximity of the Andes had I not been in such awe of the skills of the pilot and the total exhilaration of being that close to an inanimate object while in a plane. The Andes are about as inanimate as objects can get, so avoiding them is always a good idea. My only regret is being so fixated that I didn't even think to wake the others up. All nine of them were asleep. Then, all of a sudden, after a suitably Peruvian 'chuck it on its side and head for the floor'-style turn, we were on the deck and getting closer to Macchu Picchu by the minute. Charlie was out like a light so we tried to stitch him up. Imagine his surprise if he'd woken up back in Lima, where the plane was heading straight back to. Unfortunately, he woke up when I went back onto the plane to get my water bottle. Stitching your mates and siblings up is good, clean, free fun.

A sense of expectation is not necessarily a good thing if you base it on the airline you're travelling with. Some, such as having faith in Singapore Airlines, are well founded. In my own experience, the best and most alcoholic airline is Japan's JAL. I base my opinion on a single trip I took with them, which is a bit dodgy, but they were great.

I flew to Sydney with them in 1999 and the London to Tokyo leg was very eventful. I was in a window seat with a sixty-something Japanese couple next to me. When it came to ordering food there was a choice of Western or Japanese. I went for Japanese, much to the delight of the lady next to me, who sort of squealed with delight and did a little golf clap. Through a bit of sign language, I managed to get her to show me what needed dipping in what and so on. It was delicious. The only thing which distracted my attention at all from filling my stomach was the deteriorating state of the woman's husband. He was in the aisle seat and was imbibing a whisky and ginger about every ten minutes from the second the rubber left the tarmac. It was obvious to me pretty early on that he was absolutely ring-bolted. He did try to mutter a few things now and then but, judging by his wife's quizzical countenance, he failed to emit a single intelligible word of Japanese. What I found fascinating was that his wife was apparently aware of his drunken state. How could she not be with stewardesses coming from far and wide wielding his preferred tipple? No, what was fascinating was that she didn't show any signs of considering the state her husband had managed to get himself into as anything other than perfectly normal and fully acceptable.

Upon arrival at Narita, he required stabilisers, as just like those on the first pushbike you get at four years of age, but in the form of two stewardesses to hold him up. My god did that fella ever get his money's worth! Good skills.

Mind you, it's not as if I'm pure as the driven snow. Rarely do I ever allow much blood to get in my alcohol stream. Travelling back from Oz on Malaysia Airlines business class a few months earlier, Charlie and I did well. G and Ts aplenty before the engines were even sparked up were accompanied by really tasty beef and chicken satay skewers. They could have poured us out of that plane in Kuala Lumpur.

Another problem with air travel is the flipside of airlines which pleasantly surprise you. Airlines of which you expect a lot, and are then disappointed. BA are okay but their uniforms look like tacky Marks and Spencer red, white and blue acrylic. Moreover, the women they put in them are not a lot to shout about.

They were the first carrier I flew with long-haul on a totally non-smoking flight. It could have been a really bad start to my round the world trip with Charlie (friend not brother), another survivor of the Aeroflot East Africa foray a year previous. We were in this tiny little bar at Heathrow having a pint and, as it had no bog, Charlie had to go elsewhere to point Percy at the porcelain. While within earshot of the tannoy, he heard our names being called. We just made the plane and got in the two front seats with no legroom or view of a TV. Oh well, it could have been worse. And it was.

As a then- smoker, I heard the comforting ping I was waiting for after ten minutes in the air and started rolling a cigarette. That was when a little Thai stewardess told me it was a no-smoking flight! Goodbye fingernails, bonjour tristesse.

BA are paled into insignificance by the worst airline I've ever been on however. Air France. Comfortably. Admittedly, the chances of dying on other airlines are higher, or at least appear so to a person who watches the news. Aeroflot not only have very dangerous orange squash but, more importantly, pilots who allow their sons to have a go at flying the plane. Now, as previously mentioned, planes made in former Communist climes are not of the most sterling construction. We've also established that the Andes are hard and don't move if you fly into them. The same goes for the Urals, or indeed any of our planet's numerous mountain ranges. The fifteen-year-old son of an Aeroflot pilot was the one who proved that the mountains versus aircraft fight always goes to the mountain. Similarly, you can buy 'I've survived Chinese internal airlines' T-shirts. That's because domestic air travel in China is so dangerous you suspect that the regime over there use it as a demographic sluice gate, as a form of airborne population control. They crash a lot.

Those two are airlines you would expect to be pretty ordinary though. France has the fourth biggest economy in the world and should have an airline to match, but it hasn't. Air France is known to many as 'Air Chance' because the chances of you arriving at the same airport as your belongings are about as high as your plane being incinerated in mid-air by the flame coming out of a giant polar bear's arse after it's lit its own fart with a Zippo, having eaten a supertanker full of broad beans or other flatulence-inducing pulses, whilst sitting on an iceberg in hell. In other words, there is not a single recorded incident of this ever happening. Same as there hasn't been a single recorded time when Air Chance baggage handlers have succeeded in matching passenger and luggage. Oh alright, I'm exaggerating a touch, but they are crap.

Tom, Charlie and I flew to South America with them in 1998, or more specifically to Caracas. Tom flew back to

Europe just before Air France announced that they were cutting the salaries of their pilots. They decided to inform their flyers of this three weeks before the biggest sporting event to be staged in France since World War Two, namely the 1998 football World Cup. Cunning or what? As any self-respecting French person does without the slightest encouragement anyway, Air Chance's staff all went on strike. This made mine and Charlie's return to the green and pleasant land of the UK, from Caracas via Paris Charles de Gaulle, a major contract.

Another example is Qantas. Having flown to Sydney via Bangkok on the non-smoking BA flight, mine and Charlie's luck didn't change when we flew with Qantas. I'll concede that it didn't help that we'd been out on the town the night before leaving Cairns to fly to Auckland, but that wasn't all. We were in a Boeing 767 which Charlie threw up in just after take-off. The good thing about throwing up on planes is that it's expected. It's not like going out on the bevvy, ending the evening with a doner kebab, and technicolour yawning all over the back of a minicab in Nottingham. On a plane, you don't get a gentlemen of Asian lineage screaming at you and demanding 50 quid to clean up your vomit. People just assume that you're air-sick.

Ask anybody what they know about Qantas and they'll say, 'it's the only airline never to have crashed.' Well I'm not so sure. When we got to Auckland that morning, we hit the runway so hard and at such an undesirable angle that I assumed that Qantas had just got on the score-sheet in the fantasy crashing league. I stopped a stewardess as she walked past when we were taxiing and asked her why the plane had hit the ground doing an endo. She said, 'Oh don't worry, this is a Boeing 767, it's supposed to land front wheel first!'

'But surely that constitutes a crash doesn't it? 'I retorted. She failed to detect the witty sarcasm in my observation and walked off.

That was a fairly short term bit of being scared. From realising that we were not far off the ground and, at what seemed from the cheap seats, to be a nosedive type angle, we were down and alive. My scariest ever experience on a plane lasted a lot longer. Milling about in a queue to check in for the final leg of my 96-97 trip around the world, I spotted a bloke working the queue with a clipboard. To your average freeloading pikey budget travelling backpacker that means only one thing; free money!

I'd had a hard journey back from Vegas on the Greyhound, with Charlie carrying on around Nevada and California for another three weeks. I was flying LAX to London on BA, back home for the first time in 8 months. I was also flat-arse broke. Not a pot to piss in or a window to throw it out of. Not even enough for a quick last pilgrimage to 'In 'n' Out' burger (see the food chapter) prior to departure, or even a gin and tonic in the bar.

I did what any self-respecting gypo would do and abandoned all my worldly goods to the risk of removal by any pisshead or pipe-hitting scaghead who felt like nicking them in the name of freeloading. I got to the point at once. 'Are you giving away free money?' was my opener. 'I'm looking for people who are prepared to take a different flight and a cash incentive.' The phrase that pays from the formal bloke with the clipboard! Four hundred dollars and get back to London six hours later than I would have anyway? Don't mind if I do.

Of course you have to consider this; if it sounds too good to be true, then it usually is. The flipside of the coin in this case was a flight to JFK where I would get a BA flight to London. So what's wrong with that? An American Airlines DC-10 of 20 years vintage is what's wrong with that. I never want to be that scared or for that long again. This old chunk of shit shook like San Francisco in 1906. I'd rather sit out the rest of my life on the apron of Cairo airport, in a Tupolev 154 with no air-con, a hangover and nothing to drink but Soviet orange squash than ever get in a DC-10 again.

Digression no7 – fear of flying

The combined flights of that round the world trip was the start of my fear of flying. Well it's not fear, more lingering doubt, especially at take off and landing. The Auckland 767 incident was the start of it. It's never stopped me getting on a plane but I'm not the flying nut I used to be. In fact, you have to feel sorry for 'white knucklers' really.

I had to laugh on a London-bound flight out of Belfast in 1993. This little kid of about ten was being chaperoned on the flight. His grandparents had dropped him off in Belfast and his parents were picking him up. He suddenly said very matter-of-factly to the stewardess sitting with him, 'D'you know, when we get to London I think we're going to crash.' Looking up and down the plane, several sets of shoulders went very tight. You could tell the white knuckle club members a mile off. It didn't help matters that he then turned his doom-filled prophecy into a sort of disjointed little song which he did stop singing after much beseeching by his chaperone, who had noticed that it wasn't doing the nerves and sanity of some of the other passengers a lot of good. As a much- diluted sufferer of the same affliction, I chuckled without laughing.

End of digression.

You can go on about planes forever and every flight is a new adventure. I think we'll move onto something else though. There's plenty of other ways of getting around this fair planet of ours.

Trains

Following planes is trains, if you're following in the Steve Martin sequence of things. As with planes, trains are a fascinating way of getting around the planet but also similar in that they can be extremely frustrating. Trains also have a similar degree of fascination and glamour as methods of transport go .This is something that you cannot say of other forms of transport. Animals are too painful to ride to be considered glamorous in this respect, a subject which will be broached later on.

Automotive and pedestrian transport are too every day to qualify. Anything from your two feet to a car to a horse can get you to some great spots, but it's the glamour which gives planes and trains an edge. It's also the distance which you can cover in no time flat.

I'm from a part of Britain which is not particularly close to any of the rail network so my experience of rail travel didn't kick off until a trip to the US in my early teens. More's the point, no British person in their right mind would attempt to use the country's dilapidated and clapped-out rail network to actually get anywhere anytime soon. It's depressing to think that a mere 175 years after Stephenson's Rocket won the right to work the 36 miles of the Liverpool to Manchester railway, the rail network of the country which invented rail transport has been allowed to fall into such a state of disrepair as to attract global ridicule. Rail travel in the UK usually involves large doses of misery and sustained periods of standing up jealously eyeing the small percentage of fellow passengers with their bum on a seat. As if it wasn't bad enough, you get charged a ridiculous amount of money for the 'privilege.'

Planes are okay but there is no permanence to all things airborne. They tend to take off and bugger off pretty quick smart. Watching a jumbo jet take off is very graceful, but after that lingering moment that seems like an age when you're wondering if this huge vehicle is actually going to make it into the air, it does, the undercarriage disappears into its belly, and it's gone in no time.

I used to love being at work at Hampton Court Palace in the summer when Concorde was still taking off from Heathrow twice a day. You just stop. You have to admit defeat. Trying to hear anything being said to you by radio, cellphone or the time honoured method of shouting in someone's ear from close range are all futile. The noise of the old girl is all-invasive and impossible to out-do. Even Motörhead at the Hammersmith Odeon have nothing on Concorde's deafening Rolls Royce-inspired rumble. She used to fly straight over and then hit the gas a couple of miles further on, while putting in a big right hander and roaring off Big Apple-bound at over twice the speed of sound at 60,000 feet. The beauty of the whole event made everybody look up admiringly like alliance troops watching X-wing and Y-wing fighters leaving the planet of Tatooine to attack the ill-fated Death Star in Star Wars. I love the bit where she hits the gas and fishtails the arse end a bit while pulling the big right hand turn. Then, it's over. She's gone. All you're left with is the delicate sound of thunder (blatantly stolen from the Floyd) for half a minute, and you have to wait another few hours before your second fix of the day.

If a plane is further afield, it's no less temporary. The little dot at cruising altitude produces lovely, neat, parallel white vapour trails which you hope, with predictable futility, will last forever. But they don't. Before long they've already deteriorated into fluffy, disjointed lumps and then disappear altogether. No, the only thing permanent about aviation is the asphalt of runways and the airports which inevitably sit on their peripheries.

Trains; now you're talking. You're right there, at ground level, passing things by at a hundred miles an hour, your seat uninhibited by the staticness with which your ever-changing view is saddled. It's like having a conveyor belt of interesting stuff operating outside your window.

The big difference with trains though is that even when there isn't one in sight, or even within earshot, the physical presence of them is still there. I was contemplating this earlier this summer when I should have been concentrating more fully on keeping the motorbike I was riding upright. We were winding our way from Lake Como around Lago Maggiore and ultimately over the Simplon Pass into Switzerland.

It was another fine example of the feats of human engineering. Most nineteenth-century human beings would not even consider going into that far-flung gorge in the middle of nowhere, let alone building a railway line through it. But someone did and the result is a remarkable achievement; the high bridges, multitude of tunnels and cuttings scratched into the side of the cliffs make such scintillating eye candy that you forget about important things like staying alive. As luck would have it, both me and the Kawasaki 750 crotch rocket I was on survived what was a great day in the twisties, unscathed.

I've had as many random train trips proportionally as I've had weird aviation experiences. The first of these was my very first, at the ripe old age of fourteen, on the east coast of the US. It nearly cost me my anal virginity. All I was trying to do was buy a cheeseburger in the buffet car and I was faced with a gay, Anglophile, paedophile till operator who obviously wanted to 'kick my back door in', as the saying goes. I think success on his part would have given me an initially dim view of trains as a method of displacement, but thankfully we remained on different sides of the counter.

As with most things, train travel becomes an infinitely richer experience in the Third World. In my case, this was confirmed during the 1995 foray to East Africa and a train trip rated in the top ten train rides by a BBC series. Three of us got to Nairobi and decided we needed a few days on the beach to get over the rigours and hangovers of flying Aerogrot. That means jumping on the Nairobi to Mombasa narrow gauge railway.

The fun actually started well before the train even showed up with a right old shit-fight to get a ticket from dodgy geezers milling around at the station. Then the whole episode got very colonial with the arrival of a German family. The perfect family turned up: husband, wife and two children, one of each gender. All four were decked out head to toe in khaki colonial attire. The father even had a Pith helmet on! And, wait for it, a swagger stick! A German Windsor Davies lookalike in Nairobi train station; you wouldn't read about it. Well, I suppose you just have actually.

The actual trip, well, what a blast. It's the sort of thing which makes you stop and think, hang on, we refer to ourselves as the 'developed world' and places like Kenya as the 'Third World'. So if that's the case, why were we sat on a train going through Kenya enjoying a three course silver service dinner? That doesn't happen in Britain. The waiters were all resplendent in whiter than white uniforms and the train was on time. In the UK it wouldn't be on time, the staff would probably have their shirt tails hanging out and you certainly can't get a delicious three course meal on a train at our place. So who's 'Third World'?

My favourite bit of the whole trip were the signs up in the sleeper compartments. These stated that you shouldn't be worried should you hear and feel any loud bangs and crashes in the night. It went on to inform you that rhinos have notoriously bad eyesight and can't see past the end of their horns. They occasionally rammed the train! Nice. That doesn't happen at Didcot Parkway but then again, Didcot isn't in the middle of a National Park. Our Kenyan train ride took us straight through Voi National Park. Quite incredible but also a bit of a missed opportunity on the part of the tourist board. Due to pressure from the bus companies, the government had cut the Nairobi-Mombasa service to a daily overnight service. Daytime would have been preferable. When morning came however, the track was lined on the outskirts of Mombasa with little kids shouting 'mzungu', which is Swahili for white man, and waving.

I got a good strong dose of déjà vu on the way back to Cuzco in Peru a few years later after completing our walk to Macchu Picchu. The tracks were lined with kids shouting 'gringo' and throwing water bombs at us. They were deadly shots as well. A Peruvian copper was just asking me if I knew any police at home he could exchange badges and stuff with when a water bomb hit him right in the face.

That was a great trip in both directions just because it was so eventful. On the out trip, it was the sense of expectation at going to Macchu Picchu. It was going up the train ladder outside Cuzco which allows the train to go up a very steep hill by way of a number of zigzags. Last but not least was the delicious hot 'choclo con queso' (corn on the cob with cheese) which hawkers were selling on the train. This proved to be a very addictive combination.

On the way back it was more a sense of relief that we were all still in the land of the living combined with trying to avoid the efforts of the water terrorists on the side of the tracks.

Of course if you're talking glamorous trains, the Orient Express has to enter the conversation at some point. My old man has the dubious honour of having been hauled off of it by the Bulgarian Secret Service, and not a lot of people can say that! Very James Bond. Not satisfied with having got caught up in the Cultural Revolution in China, this was his next brush with Communism. They took umbrage at the fact that he'd arrived in Bulgaria by car and was going home by train. I suppose they figured he'd sold it or something. Once he'd explained that it was being driven back by a friend they let him carry on along his way home.

The UK does have its fair share of railway highlights, it has to be said. You just have to be very patient and have very thick skin to get about the place. I've never done the Carlisle to Settle run, but it's going to have to be done at some point. It looks stunning on TV and things which look good on TV usually look better when you're there on the ground. This is certainly true of the Firth of Forth rail bridge which is one of the most beautiful structures in the world. Totally over-engineered it may be, but it is a semi-permanent monument to the human imagination. Definitely on my list of wonders of the modern world.

I used to sit on the Law, an extinct volcano in Dundee, reading and looking over the Tay estuary as the trains pottered across the bridge from time to time. In a vain attempt to offset the effects of cigarette smoking and burn a few calories before an afternoon eating and drinking in the pub, I used to walk up there every Sunday. You can have a rest at the top and enjoy a variety of activities. If it's turned out nice, look north and contemplate the glory days of the black and tangerines of Dundee United, whose football stadium, Tannadice, sits side by side with arch rivals Dundee FC's hugely inferior Dens Park. Or admire the rugged, beautiful landscape of Scotland on both sides of the Tay. I arrived one Sunday just in time for a blizzard. Not the best place to be for one of those. There was a huge BBC production unit up there. It turns out that the Scottish comic legend Billy Connolly had been up there reciting McGonagall's poem 'The Tay Bridge Disaster', about the fate of the short-lived first Tay rail bridge, which collapsed in 1879, killing more than 70 people. Bad weather, bad disaster, and bad poet. McGonagall is widely accepted to be the worst poet in history.

I loved Scotland and after four years had a degree, a lot of good memories and an interest in Eastern Europe. The last of these would set me off on another voyage a few years later.

Train travel, like anything, can be full of the melancholy of unfulfilled expectations. I had it bad in Bolivia. It's such a shame that these things don't always go as well as you would wish, especially when it's for reasons of petty politics between countries or between bus and train companies, as was the case in Kenya.

In Bolivia, the problem was the strained relations between Bolivia and Chile. The former had become a landlocked country following the late nineteenth century Pacific War, following which the vanquished Bolivia ceded territory and all its coastline to the Chilean victors.

My mind to go to Chile by train was made up in the silver mining town of Potosi. I'd seen that the Uyuni (Boliv) to Calama (Ch) line was on the BBC series about the great train trips of the world, but had not seen the actual programme. It was something that had to be done. Just when my mind was pretty much made up anyway, two emails sealed it.

Transcripts which made my mind up:

From: boykelly@yahoo.com
Hope all is well. I'm down in Santiago having just come up from further south.

Going to see Oasis tonight and have bought some big balloons to let off in the crowd. Be here now! hope you can make the gig.

If not, see you soon Charlie x

From: tomvod@hotmail.com

Will, I've just walked out of Burger King having eaten a Big King XL meal.

Nicole and I have been in Bahia Inglesa for 10 days and have now come down to Santiago and hooked up with Charlie. Are you heading this way?

Take it easy

T x

If there was any doubt about my next destination, there wasn't after getting those two notes from the other members of the original trio. I got a bus to Uyuni and planned to take the train to Calama. That's what happened but not as quickly as I would have liked. That's quite often the way though; you just have to grin and bear it.

I bought a ticket and was told to be at the station for midnight, which I was. Six hours later after a night of abject, cold misery on the hard floor of the station, the train turned up. It would have been less annoying if it hadn't been parked up fifty yards away. Even worse was that all the locals were in the know and didn't start turning up to get onto it until just before it left, while all the gringos had endured the night in the station. How they must have chuckled at our foolishness!

Like haemorrhoids, it got worse, but, unlike 'arse grapes', not before getting better. The train finally left and made very good time as it embarked on its trip to the seaside. From a start of about 3,300 metres on the Altiplano of Bolivia, our train was eating up the miles; the 382 miles to sea level at Antofagasta would go by in no time. Yeah, right. Dream on.

Our train hit the brick wall otherwise known as the Chilean border after a couple of morale-restoring, fast-moving, miles-eating-up hours. We were there an absolute age. It wasn't so much the sitting in a wooden shed all day which got on my nerves as the fact that I knew that we were going to miss an opportunity to see some incredible views as the daylight hours passed, painfully slowly, one after the other. The train was going to drop to sea level from nearly four kilometres up in a couple of hundred miles. Due to a bit of petty wrangling amongst uncomfortable neighbours, we would do the trip at night and see nothing.

Digression no 8 – Customs officers of the world part 1

Due to an unfortunate series of events, related only by the fact that they all happened on the same continent, by the time I got to the Chilean border my rucksack wasn't feeling very well. Its zip had been replaced by a cunning system of laces which took an age to do up every time access to the aforementioned clothes carrier was required.

A giant leap forward in backpacking was achieved with the arrival on the scene in the 90s of the 'frontloader' rucksack to challenge the previously uncontested dominance of the 'toploader.' It was now official; rucksacks were going the same way as washing machines had in the 70s and VCRs had in the 80s. Now, in the 90s, it was the turn of the rucksack. Revolution is not too stronger word.

Everything that you ever need in a rucksack is in the bottom, it's just one of life's sorrier facts. So the very fact that you could now get something out of the bottom of your bag in under half an hour was indeed a revolution; the budget travel equivalent of being on the road to Damascus.

Only until the zip breaks, though. Then your life becomes a battle to fit anything into your day apart from wrestling with your rucksack. It's as hard as discovering masturbation at the age of ten and trying to squeeze something into your day other than tugging yourself inside out. Of course, the easy option would have been to buy another rucksack, but that would have cost money and was therefore crossed off the options list.

So there's this Chilean Customs bloke who we'd finally been sent to after being in the big wooden shed all day. 'Open the bag' he says and then looks on with a mix of curiosity and hostility as the unknotting of the laces starts. With that done I flipped back the lid of my bag with great ceremony to the sight of… my clothes.

As the Customs bloke was starting to get on my tits I must say, but as a mate of my dad's says in less than perfect Latin, *nil illegitimi carborundum*. Or in less Latin parlance, 'don't let the bastards grind you down.' So I didn't let him. What he did next, however, took me to the brink of letting fly and giving him some advice which would, I've no doubt, have resulted in him or one of his associates 'marigolding' me like a vet dragging baler twine out of a cow's arse. 'Marigolding' is the verb pertaining to the insertion of a rubber gloved hand up a fellow human's arse by a Customs Officer. If I'd given him a load of mouth I'm sure it would have been unlubricated as well.

What he did was not enough. He half flipped over the top T-shirt in my rucksack, said 'okay', made a closing gesture and walked off. Bastard. I hadn't really thought about what I expected of him from an effort point of view until that moment. I expected him to go through my bag with a fine toothcomb. I expected him to ask me questions about where I'd been and was going, to try and steal something or suggest that I should give him a 'present'. I don't know what, but he should have done something; anything more than nothing. More than flicking the edge of one T-shirt over. I wanted his effort to at least partly reflect the effort I'd already contributed, as well as that which I was going to have to put in, to return my bag to a state in which I could carry my worldly possessions around in. Bastard.

I stood there and did nothing. The bag remained open and I waited for him to come back and search it properly. He walked back past me making a lace-tying sign. That's the worst of it. He knew full well the amount of effort which had gone into opening the bag for his viewing enjoyment. He'd stood there, almost tapping his fingers, waiting to be able to search it. I was very unimpressed with what followed, as you've probably worked out for yourself. Bastard.

End of digression.

Back on the train, we did indeed see nothing. I spent a few hours contemplating how badly the day had gone and looking at my reflection in the window, reflecting off the light inside and the darkness outside. Two good things were approaching though. One I knew about and that was that I was getting closer to my brother and cousin and a reunion of predictably large proportions. The other I didn't know about for sure. I'd heard rumours but thought it was some huge joke. It would be a few hours until I could confirm from personal experience that strange things do happen on buses in Chile.

I live in France for a lot of the year, which is a good state to be in from a getting around point of view. The trouble with the French, though is that they expect their train network to be quiet, spacious and clean. They expect the trains to be on time, cheap, and for them to have a seat for every passenger. Ridiculous! 'A quoi pensez vous?' as we say in the south Cotswolds. Any British person will be glad to point out to you that this is an unrealistic pipe dream and that train travel is not viable both financially or emotionally. It is in the UK anyway. In France, as with most developed (and quite a lot of developing) countries, people are used to the train network being efficient. The real problem in France is that, on the rare occasions when it doesn't run like clockwork, people lose their tempers very quickly. I was recently in Gare du Nord, Paris, and just about to ask an SNCF railways employee a question, when this evil little cow with badly-dyed hair nipped in front of me. After putting up with her abusing him for twenty seconds because her train to Lille was thirty minutes late leaving, I interjected and told her that she had the manners of a goat. As she looked at me dumbfounded, I also suggested that a move to the UK would, considering her levels of hysteria at a thirty minute delay, be unwise. She'd die of a nervous breakdown within a week or three train rides, whichever was sooner. The SNCF guard looked at me like I'd saved his life.

Things that need ticking off on the 'to do by train' list remain numerous. I've been to quite a few places where I've regretted not going by train, such as over Arthur's Pass in New Zealand. The Indian-Pacific and Ghan services in Australia are going to get the benefit of my custom at some point as well. The list goes on but the Trans-Siberian is a must as well. If it's good enough for North Korean lunatic dictators with big porn collections and a penchant for fine cognac, it's good enough for me.

Time to get off the tracks and on the road, I reckon.

On the road

To say that our family have a tenuous relationship with road-going vehicles is by no means an exaggeration. We've all had our fair share of bumps and scrapes, and a lot worse unfortunately.

Vehicles may be noisy, polluting and dangerous but they're also very, very convenient. 'Give me convenience or give me death,' in the immortal words of the Dead Kennedys. The simple fact of the matter is that most people will take the easy option most of the time. Fair enough, you have to take your hat off to the human race for inventing easy options, but we are, in a lot of respects, lazy buggers. Pure and simple.

Conceded, while it is an easier option than carrying something by hand, you would not put a wheelbarrow in the easy options section. It does make your life easier but it is essentially a practical tool, a workhorse. Hats off to the Chinese for that back-saving gem. This can also be said of motor vehicles. They also carry things and are used in a professional capacity, and again, you can't fault people for using them in this way.

Vehicles now though, are being used in a way which almost completely negates the necessity for walking. Legs to a lot of people these days are for getting around the house (although Stannah stairlifts are fast taking over on the steep bits) but no longer for getting around the village, countryside or city. We have cars, motorbikes, SUVs, people carriers, gopeds, mopeds, tuktuks, rickshaws, tubes, metros, subways, escalators, elevators, travelators, taxis, minicabs, buses and minibuses, all of which take us from one place to another without us having to do anything. Be it buildings, cities, counties, countries or continents, man has invented stuff to get us up, down, round, under or over just about anything. This type of grand scale displacement is not without its pitfalls and I think it's fair to say that our clan have experienced a good load of these in lots of different places.

Of all of us, no contest, Tom's parents had it the worst. They died in a car accident when he was nine months old, in 1971. It affected everyone terribly at the time and has done ever since, really. Our gran, my mother and my aunty are all ace at worrying. They could worry for the UK at the Olympics should it ever become an Olympic sport.

You can't rightly blame them though, I suppose. Luckily for our generation, Charlie was a year old, Tom nine months and me just about still a billion of the old man's little tadpoles in a swimming race to get to the old dear's ovaries. With them too young and me all but non-existent, we were not as affected as we would have been had we been older. Tom has been left without real parents, but now has at least three surrogate sets. It's a terrible shame that things like that happen, but it's all part of the merry dance that life is.

Nobody else has had a huge amount of luck either. Trot, our mum, is a total psycho-pilot in a car and has paid the price every once in a while. The bloke who endured the ordeal of examining her driving skills said at the end of her test (after removing his fingernails from the dashboard), 'well you've passed Miss Flower, but please remember that you're not a racing driver!' The trouble is that she didn't listen. A couple of years later she was hurtling down a single track country lane and wallop. To be sure, the combine harvester should have had a warning vehicle in front of it, but she was going too fast, simple as that. She ended up in the ditch with her front teeth knocked out. Not the last thing her driving would terminate.

Her marriage got off to a bad start when, on honeymoon in Scotland, she tailgated a brewery wagon. They'd gone in the only new car the old man had ever owned up until then, a white Mini. She dinged it into the piss truck and there started their ongoing ability to have lengthy heated disagreements, something which has been an ongoing feature of their marriage.

Following her front teeth and the white Mini, the next thing terminated by the old dear's driving was our dreadful little Austin Allegro, whose life was ended by a combination of two things. Firstly, she used to cram it full of as many antiques as most other dealers at auction would put in a long wheelbase Ford Transit Luton. Unfortunately for the poor old Allegro's suspension and general well-being, it was fitted with a roof rack which was also loaded up to the hilt. She used to come round the last corner into the village loaded half way to the heavens with antiques which swayed about like the Anthill Mob making a human pyramid to catch the pigeon in *Wacky Races*. Whereas the old man used to bury his head in his hands, I was more expectant. I used to keep mine fixed on the car, fully expecting Muttley to stick his head out of a Welsh dresser swaying perilously in the breeze like cork on a Portuguese lorry, and start sniggering wheezily into his hand.

Secondly, she used to drive the Allegro (or 'all-aggro' as it was known), load or otherwise, as if it was a performance sports car. In fact, it wasn't. It did have a fair amount of intelligence though and, realising that things weren't going to get any better, it died on its arse. Can't say I blame it.

The replacement for the underpowered, under-engineered, un-aerodynamic, un-everything was HKP 686 V. That was the registration of a full blooded 2000 cc Ford Cortina estate with double overhead cams or something. Not that that meant anything to me then or now, but it did matter. 'Look at the difference,' she'd relish in telling us as she dropped it into third and we swerved out of the slipstream of yet another car obeying the speed limit, 'I'd have been behind him all day in the Allegro.'

She took us to Bristol ice rink once and we ended up sliding across a grass verge outside Leigh Delamere services on the M4 motorway. Incredibly frightening, and quite embarrassing to have three of your friends looking at you wondering what the crack is as the car doughnutted out of control in the middle of its second spin.

Digression no 9 – customs officers of the world pt 2

'You lot get the bags out and I'll go and check in' were our orders from the old man as the Cortina fishtailed its way into Portsmouth ferry terminal with the old dear at the helm. She'd been driving it at 100 miles per hour down the M27 which she'd probably have done even if we weren't late, which we were.

It was futile. As we came back for the second round of bags, we saw the ferry reversing out of its moorings. We were going on a skiing holiday and we'd missed the boat. Boats, planes, trains or any vehicle you've missed are very hypnotic, don't you think? Usually, yes, and you get those few minutes of calm staring at the vehicle or vessel you want to be on after hours of hectic rushing, but not when your mother points out that your family car is on fire.

'There's smoke coming out of the bonnet of the car!' she shrieked. She was right as well, there was. Unfortunately, the smoke was joined a couple of seconds later by flames which started lapping around the side of the bonnet. I now considered the car to be officially on fire. Like all people wanting to remain alive, I walked away from it. That went for all but two people. Our mum went towards the car, opened the door, and started rummaging through the glove box for her sunglasses. The old man emerged from the terminal to see the scene and decided to drag the old dear out of the car and to safety. 'But I really liked those sunglasses,' she said when he enquired as to why she was being so stupid.

The other person tired of living was a port employee who approached the car with a fire extinguisher. The old man had already had a disagreement with the port manager. He'd not realised that the ferry had sailed and suggested that we leave the car there, on fire in front of the terminal building, and concentrate on getting on the ferry. The manager said that that would not be a satisfactory state of affairs, to which our dad said he wasn't overly interested in the manager's opinions.

Fire extinguisher bloke presented a different problem though. 'Spray that thing at my car and I'll kill you.' Not the most diplomatic start to a conversation with a complete stranger you'll ever hear, but that was our old man's opening line. Now that the car was on fire, he figured it might as well remain on fire. That was because he had a fully comprehensive insurance policy and wanted a new car and not a repaired one which had previously been on fire. Fire extinguisher bloke was still showing all the signs of a man attempting to use a fire extinguisher, despite a large, frightening, bearded six-footer having explained that his termination would be the result.

Luckily for his longevity, he was thick and couldn't work it. He must have been thick because, as any student returning from a night of alcohol abuse will readily confirm, fire extinguishers are as easy to operate as traffic cones are to nick and kebabs are to drop. The upshot of his inability to operate the extinguisher was that the car was a write-off. We caught the next ferry and went to see *Back to the Future* in the meantime, apart from mumster, who cut and blow-dried her own hair in the bogs at the ferry terminal. Our next visit to Portsmouth was to be even less pleasant.

You'd have thought that the old boy would have learnt his lesson on the Bulgarian/Yugoslav border, but no. A cunning plan was hatched on the ferry which went as follows: your car's blown up, bad (actually, the only disappointing thing was that it didn't blow up, which I was looking forward to) but; upon leaving work in France a couple of years previous, you've bought your much-travelled company car from the firm for a pittance, good. Even better, that car is in a friend of yours' barn in France. Combine that with the fact that the bloke who owns the barn is the one picking you up from the ferry anyway, and you're cooking with gas! It was all perfect. We got to Normandy and put the car in for new tyres to replace the flat ones, a new battery and general de-dusting while we went for a great week's skiing. Pick the car up a week later and back of the net! You've got yourself a new car and a way of getting back to the UK. Spot on.

You'd make the same mistake as all of us Joneses if you thought it was going to be that simple. The hitch came in the form of Portsmouth Customs. The car we'd recouped in Normandy happened to be the same car which was embroiled in the Bulgarian border incident a few years previous. It was 9706 RG 22; a left hooking, French registered, silver top of the range Renault 20 diesel; the most comfortable car I've ever sat in.

'I'm going to have to take your fucking car to pieces unless you can give me some answers, Mr Jones,' the public servant informed my tax-paying, law-abiding father. 'Why are you being so unpleasant to my husband?' the old dear asked, at which point she was ejected from the proceedings and came back out to join us in the left hooker. Customs bloke didn't take 9706 RG 22 to pieces, or inspect the old man's innards with a gloved hand, but he did interrogate him for a good while longer, after which we wound our way back to West Oxfordshire. We didn't blame him for wanting to know why we'd gone to France as foot passengers and come back in a foreign registered car, but he could've asked these questions in a more diplomatic way. I suppose that's just not in the nature of customs officers, though.

Secretly, I also wanted to know how he could aim the word 'fuck' at our dad without getting a really good hiding, which was always the result when I did it.

End of digression, but not of 9706 RG 22's part in our family's automotive history.

That Renault 20 was a truly great vehicle. I would have thought it would be dangerous to make cars that comfortable for the simple fact that the deep filled seats would encourage passengers and drivers alike to fall asleep. It was a great car, and if we liked it, the old man was in love with it. He had spent a lot of time in it over the last few years, mostly on the roads of continental Europe, driving around inspecting the pig breeding units he was responsible for. He'd done 300,000 odd kilometres in it by the time it got to the UK.

As luck would have it, it was in the Renault 20 that the old dear decided to have her next accident. I blame Charlie for going to New Zealand.

He was the first to break for the border and go on a long trip to a different continent. We went to drop him off at Heathrow and the old dear was crying for England from the word go. She insisted on driving home even though I suspected that she couldn't see through the tears. My worst suspicions were confirmed on the M 25 when, still gurning profusely, she stuffed the Renault 20 straight up the arse of the stationary car in front of us. There's a lot of those on the M 25, stationary cars that is. To her credit, I can't recall her having a crash since then.

The Renault 20 had one more crash after that, at which point its life came to an end. Charlie had been in New Zealand six months, and a mere three days after he got back, the Renault 20 lay, mortally wounded, at the bottom of a lamp post in Saxel Close, Aston, Oxfordshire. Charlie had clipped the back of another car and done a couple of pirouettes before mounting the kerb. That put paid to the front axle and then the lamppost which he knocked over took the rest of the Renault 20 out for good. Andy Adams, who was the passenger, thought he'd died and was in heaven. In actual fact he was alive and in a Renault which had just crashed with two bags of sawdust in the boot. They had gone everywhere upon impact, hence Andy's presumed arrival in the afterlife. Fortunately he was mistaken but, bless him, he did drop down dead while loading a concrete mixer at work fifteen years later at a mere forty years of age, poor sod.

At the ripe old age of eighteen, Charlie was already the veteran of one vehicular near-catastrophe. Whilst in New Zealand, he had rolled down a steep hill on a three-wheeled motorbike of the type which is now long since banned because people crashed them a lot. He was very lucky – it could easily have mashed or killed him.

The Renault 20 wasn't the last of the old man's cars which Charlie was to consign to the great scrapyard in the sky. E 486 GJM, the third of them, was nothing like the Renault 20, but did share a similar history, and fate. E 486 GJM was a white Japanese pickup which, like the Renault 20, had been driven around for nearly 300,000 trouble-free miles by the old man. It cashed in its chips on a blind corner of a single track road with Charlie at the controls. As is often the case, Charlie was at the controls but not using them very well, and he ploughed the old tour bus straight into the front of a delivery van. It was a right and big shame because the other thing that the white Ute had in common with the Renault 20 was that the old man loved them both. He'd spent a lot of time in both vehicles and had become best friends with them. In fact, he had become such a successful part-time tax avoider that he clocked up a load of miles on the pickup. When he was farming pigs, he used to get some of them slaughtered and sell them for cash, butchered and ready to go in the freezer. Friday was delivery day and he used to potter all over the Cotswolds every Friday, filling his friends' freezers with porcine delights. I thought that pickup was an uncomfortable chunk of shit, but you couldn't deny its reliability.

In fairness to Charlie, he didn't do it again until October 2003. This latest incident was definitely the highlight of his car rearranging career. It was the car crash equivalent of Nadia Comaneci's dismount from the beam at the Montreal Olympics. Coming home from seeing some friends, he was on yet another single track road and failed to learn from the mistakes of car wrecks past. Failing to take a kinked bend, he hit the high earth kerb and performed a 'Greg Louganis 1988'. The American diver, famous for cracking his head on the board while diving in the Seoul Olympics, recovered to perform a triple somersault with pike. So did Charlie, but in a 1994 Austin Maestro. To be exact, he did two front flips and a side roll and landed Comaneci-like in a field upside down, and had to crawl out of the boot door as none of the others were in service. Luckily, he was wearing a seatbelt. I couldn't believe his luck at getting out of the crash having seen the car afterwards, and also the fact that he chose that night to wear a seatbelt for the first time in living memory.

Last but not least is mishap number two which happened very shortly after number one. In fact number one happened because of number two. You'll all say that's not possible because four dimensional space continuums have yet to be invented, but bear with me. When the Renault 20 got the good news, Charlie was on his way to our pig farm. He was taking some mates to have a thrash round the edge of the farm in the bright yellow ex-British Telecom van. By that time it was sort of mine, but really still belonged to the old man. It had been his 'company car' until he bought the new pickup. It was then retired to the farm and I used to use it for thrashing around the edge of our outdoor pig unit. Unlike Charlie, I could do this without hitting badger setts in the long grass and ripping half the front axle off. Two rolls later and another vehicle had bitten the dust.

I didn't know he was going to the farm that day, or on the day he nearly made it to the farm, I should say. The Telecom van brings to a grand total of four the number of our dad's cars which have died prematurely as a direct consequence of having Charlie behind the steering wheel. Luckily, due to a combination of financial destitution, bad taste and high mileage, all of the vehicles he terminated were approaching the end of their usefulness; some of them had passed it by a considerable distance. In the case of Austin Maestros, they're past their sell by date before they come out of the factory.

Fair play to the boy though, he does damage his own cars as well. He had a bright orange Hillman Avenger which went like hell. Unfortunately, it was so full of crap that it was dangerous. This was made vividly clear one day in Maidenhead town centre when Charlie realised that the brake pedal didn't work as we fast approached the back end of someone's car. He panicked like hell before swerving into a huge pile of sand conveniently dumped by some building workers. They were all laughing like hell and I was wondering what had happened to the brakes. It transpired that amongst the crap on the floor was a full can of Coke which had got stuck behind the brake pedal! He got stopped a couple of weeks later by the police and the copper got his partner out of the police car to come and see how much crap was in the this beat up old Hillman. He told Charlie to get it cleaned out because it was dangerous; little did he know that he couldn't have been more right considering the sand incident. As it turned out, Charlie's best mate saved him the trouble by pumping cow slurry into the car as a practical joke. Another car bites the dust!

Nobody in our family writes off their own cars, which is a good arrangement. The old dear writes off communal vehicles, Charlie anything he can get his hands on and the old man prangs the old dear's French thing. I remember it because it was on my birthday last year. He'd been at Stow rugby club for a committee meeting and swerved to miss a deer which ran across the road. Having reversed into a Cotswold dry stone wall – see inanimate objects in chapters passim – he then found out that he was not insured to drive the newly un-functioning Citroën and had to shell out £750 for a new one! Poor sod.

Tom has continued the tradition by writing off a friend's Fiat X 1-9 many moons ago, but is fairly blameless apart from that.

It has to be said that I'm not totally devoid of guilt myself. I've never had a car accident on a public highway. That's not much consolation to the Ford Transit of UK Marina Supplies Limited, though. They do some work at our show every year and hail from Portsmouth on the south coast of England. I was driving around in a JCB digger one day when I got the back actor caught in the sliding door of their transit. I was trucking on through in fourth gear and didn't even notice the initial impact on the front wing of the other vehicle. Then the rear bucket got caught in the side door and I had a loss of power which I tried to solve by stamping on the accelerator. When that didn't work, I looked over my shoulder and immediately decided that the loss of power may have been connected to the fact that I had dragged a Ford Transit van forty odd yards down the way from its original parking spot. It took them three weeks to fix it! Proper job.

Even in this respect, Charlie still outdoes me. We have a variety of plant machinery at the show we both work at every summer. My brother spends a lot of his time in a little two-tonne telescopic machine called a 'buggiscopic'. Over the years he's had a couple of good 'comings together', shall we say. This year he drove straight into the bonnet of a Jaguar – only one of them cheap new ones though, his best effort was three years ago when he pretty much knocked the whole back end off of this woman's VW Golf. She was quite pissed off, but not as much as she was the next year. When Charlie approached her newly repaired Golf in the same machine, she eyed him with a mixture of suspicion, hatred and anxiety. She needn't have feared for her Golf though – he missed it by a good six inches as he swung into a corner with the rear wheel steer. He did manage to run over her make-up bag though; she'd left it on the floor, silly woman. She looked at him in the same resigned way as Wile E Coyote looks at the camera when he's about to suffer a very painful misfortune.

Considering the amount of 'incidents' suffered by my immediate family without even leaving Britain's shores, you'd have thought that we might have given it up as a bad job and found another way of getting around the world. But we're not nearly that clever. The only thing more stupid than crashing yourself is getting in a car with a load of strangers and a driver whose talents, or lack of, behind the wheel you have no idea of prior to take off.

Digression No 10 – Will's theory on the connection between wedding procession behaviour and a nation's approach to driving

Living in France is great. Driving there is not. The scenery is, just by the fact that it's in France, invariably stunning. The French really are very lucky to live in such a beautiful part of the world. The problem is that you don't get too much chance to enjoy it because going out on the roads here is a constant battle for survival. The French use vehicles more as guided missiles than as a useful means of getting from A to B. More's the point, so many of them die going from A to B that a car can't really be counted as a 'useful' way of embarking on the aforementioned journey. Long shot would be a better way of putting it. Due to the French population's inability to remove the macho element from their brains before getting in a vehicle, they die in droves every year. So bad is the problem that while the UK and France have similar populations, you are a lot more likely to die on the roads of France. This is despite the fact that they have less cars and almost twice as many kilometres of roads. It's not only the fact that they're well behind with the installation of speed cameras, but also that, until last year, the police were making little more than token attempts to curb both speed and drink-driving. The overriding problem though is the national psyche and the way it converts into poor road behaviour.

You can't blame the drivers and only the drivers, though. One reason for this is the aforementioned government inaction on the endemic drink-driving and speeding from which France suffers. The second reason is the signposts. What is that all about? France is a civilised and prosperous country. How the hell can a country which has become so wealthy and prosperous as France has, managed to when no one knows where they're going? The signposting is so rubbish that businesses must lose a combined total of about seven million man hours a year from delivery drivers and truckers being lost all over the place. Their signposting is diabolical. It's either non-existent or disappears and reappears at inconsistent intervals as you make your way through a town or city. This is not only annoying but very dangerous. Everybody, French folk and foreigners alike are so busy trying to spot a signpost that wallop! Another tailgating or broadsiding is the only possible consequence of so few eyes actually being on the road ahead.

Last but not least is the ability of French road builders to turn even the simplest road junction into the most complicated mind-boggling rubbish you've ever attempted to get a vehicle round. Combine their complexity with the fact that the locals are all coming in at warp speed, and every junction becomes a graveyard filler.

Where does the wedding procession fit into all this? In Port Saïd, Egypt. That was where I first developed the wedding procession theory. Sitting there in Egypt contemplating life in general, a wedding procession approached. You've never seen the likes of it.

Now, I don't know where folk go to get married in Egypt, and I don't know where they go for the reception afterwards. What is beyond question is that the intervening journey is very exciting. The first thing of note is that you hear the motorcade a long time before you see it. Horns and the screeching of tyres greet your ears as the front-runners fishtail round the final bend and dive dramatically into view. As more and more vehicles pile round the corner your bottom jaw falls ever closer to the floor.

The same procession in the UK would be a sedate apparition of Ford Mondeos all sticking strictly to the road traffic regulations. Every wedding has a joker though, and in the UK that is the one maverick who dares to give a quick toot on the horn going down the high street. Only a quick half second, though. Any greater expression of a party atmosphere while in control of a vehicle would be vulgar in the extreme.

Back to Port Saïd, a different approach is taken. Having barely negotiated the corner, the wedding revellers fly up the street and into the square in which I'm sitting having an iced coffee. Horns blaring, lights flashing and passengers hanging out of windows, doors and sunroofs, the cars start doing handbrake turns all over the place. The combination of this and the wheel-spinning of others turns the whole square into an

Egyptian vehicular re-enactment of Cliff Richard performing his not entirely good song 'Some People' on *Top of the Pops*. You remember, back in the 80s when the BBC employed an over-enthusiastic dry ice machine operator who filled the stage with so much smoke that the poor old 'Peter Pan of Pop' (aka Cliff) completely disappeared and had to stop singing? Oh well, at least some good came of it. Pretty much the same thing occurred that afternoon in Port Saïd, except that the smoke was a bit bluer, having been produced by shredding an entire week of Indian rubber production.

The basis of the wedding procession theory is therefore that the more lunatic the behaviour of the drivers in a wedding procession of any given country, the more ordinary the driving behaviour of the country's drivers as a whole, and the higher your chances of dying in that country. This theory is upheld by the fact that France lies somewhere between the volatile Egypt and the sedate UK on the scale of lunacy. The French give it large on the horn lights and leaning out of the window bits, but tend to stop short of the doughnuts and other stunts.

End of digression.

I've ridden into the centres of both Istanbul and Cairo on a motorbike and survived. I was quite pleased about that because at no point during the final run in to the centre of either those two fair cities did I ever hold even the slightest hope of survival. I spent the whole time watching my flanks and imagining some poor junior mandarin in the British Embassy practicing his sympathy lines before ringing the parents up to ask them where they wanted the body bag sent to. They have a canny ability to turn a two-lane road into eight lanes of horn-blowing mayhem. Istanbul was bad, but Cairo was proper carnage.

Muslims seem to put a lot of faith in God when they're driving, which could be part of the problem.

I don't want to attract the attentions of the literary censorship departments of any Middle Eastern Islamic theocracies, but as an agnostic, I would rather my Muslim taxi drivers forgot the 'Insha'Allah' approach and instead tried to guarantee our survival by observing the Highway Code. 'If it is God's will' is the literal translation, but God's not the one with his hands on the steering wheel or his foot floored on the accelerator.

So where does that leave the Italians? No idea. Never witnessed a wedding in Italy, a country I'd never been to until three years ago. You would have to assume though, from first impressions, that they'd be more at the Egyptian end of the scale than the British end. Sitting on the bypass around Turin in summer 2001 with a Lancia so far up my arse he must have been able to tell that I'd had chicken for lunch, I was shaking with fear and trying to work out why I'd taken the scenic route.

If you're mulling over which airport to go to from Val d'Isère in the winter, it's not a hard decision. That's because there's only one way out of town. Downhill. The road up the mountain is a ski run and therefore closed. In the summer though, the snow melts and leaves you with a stunning drive up Alp and down dale. A couple or three mountains and ninety minutes later, you're going over the Italian border and shortly after, in Turin airport. In the winter it takes you four hours and involves traffic jams, motorways and tunnels under the Alps. In the summer it involves a pair of sunnies, Foo Fighters full tilt on the stereo, and a great windy mountain drive.

It was one of the most enjoyable drives I'd ever done until the Turin bypass. It then turned into a living nightmare during which I learnt that Italians are total psycho-pilots. Italians in cars adhere to a theory you often see used here in neighbouring France. It's the theory that if you follow the car in front at a close distance, should that car become involved in an accident, it won't get a lot of chance to slow down before you hit it up

84

the backside. By this rationale, if everybody tailgates the car in front, everybody'll be fine. Sounds fantastic doesn't it? The only trouble is that loads of people die in countries where it is followed because it doesn't work.

The quality of the driver is of paramount importance on public transport, as well, in what concerns road-going transport. The only difference between a car and a bus is the number of people who die.

Most people will be able to relate to this. You walk up the steps of a bus in foreign climes and there's the driver, craning his neck sideways and looking nonchalantly down at you climbing the steps, usually chewing on a toothpick, trying to gauge you to see just how badly he'll have to drive to scare the living daylights out of you. Scaring you is something these people usually achieve. As you have already read, I've had some bad brushes with bus transport in Bolivia, but that misery was largely due to the intestinal problems I was suffering at the time. True, the danger factor did exist, but was due mostly to the lie of the land, and the fact that some dipstick had built a road on a cliff. The driver, apart from having decided to head out in the first place, was pretty good. That goes for pretty much the whole of the South American experience. The only bad bus driver on the whole trip was in Colombia. No, South America is definitely a continent where any person with even the slightest sign of mentalist tendencies is carted off to pilot training. The same most certainly does not apply to Africa, and it's incredible how quickly your luck can change as well.

The good thing about trains is that the rules are hard to break. You're on a set of tracks which remove the ability of even the most psychotic fruit loop to do anything too mad. This is not true of buses which are capable of some extraordinary stunts in the hands of the wrong person. All this becomes more abundantly clear when you do the same trip on two different forms of transport. As previously recounted, three of us did the

Nairobi to Mombasa run by train, and it was a great experience. The same trip by bus is hell on earth. You pinch yourself every once in a while to try and escape the all-enveloping horror and stress of it, but it's very much a reality which you'd do anything to escape. Having a word with the driver is not an option as he's not concentrating enough as it is without you distracting him. Sitting there and praying for survival is the only option.

The problem is threefold. The road is not wide enough for heavy traffic to go both ways and remain on the road. That's the first problem. To get to a satisfactory level of fear you have to combine this with the second part of the problem. This is that buses and oil tankers are the most common vehicles on the Nairobi to Mombasa run, with buses going both ways and oil tankers taking oil inland from the Indian Ocean ports. The whole experience is a big game of chicken. Bus versus bus or bus versus tanker, it makes little difference. The drivers drive straight at each other until it's too late and you shut your eyes and wait for the impact and breaking bones, followed by certain death. You are conscious of a swerving motion as your teeth grind together and the vehicles somehow miss each other. It is extremely frightening, and more so at night. Being stupid and unable to learn from my mistakes, I endured that trip three times in three weeks, twice northbound and once south.

At night it was even worse. Out of sheer tiredness, I dozed off at some point during one night. I woke up to see a Shell advert inches from the bus window. The only thing was that it wasn't a billboard, it was the side of an oil tanker we were overtaking. Our bus kept bumping into it! I hope the bus company got all my shit off their seat. No, actually, I don't.

The third part of the problem adds to the fear and makes the articulated tankers a lot more frightening. The road is so potholed as to make vehicles bounce all over the shop, as well as swerve, whenever traffic allows, to miss them. Southbound tankers are invariably empty and bounce all over the place looking like they're going to jackknife at any moment. We're not talking little things which the council come and shove a bit of spare tarmac in here, we're talking the sort of pothole you could hide a 72 Cadillac Eldorado in. When your bus hits one, you're quite often thrown up in the air a couple of feet only to come back down and bust your coccyx on the armrest. Proper, uninterrupted, industrial-strength misery.

Sorry if it sounds like I've got a universally dim view of bus travel. That's not the case at all. In the train section, the trip from Bolivia into Chile got as far as Calama. From there down to Santiago it was bliss. Strange things do indeed happen on buses in Chile, but pretty much all of them are good. On you get fearing the worst and expecting the smell of coriander to hit you any second. South America is full of women carrying bunches of coriander, until you get to Chile. The bus out of Antofagasta was brand new and looked the part of a modern bus with all mod cons. More surprisingly, it was. Once installed and off and running on the 1300 kilometres down to Santiago, the hostess (for there is one) brings you some food. Nothing award winning admittedly, but food all the same. Would you rather a comfortable seat, some legroom and a bit of not too bad grub, or a night on the Mombasa express? No contest.

So there you are, just getting ready to settle in and watch the film (another mod con) and the hostess is back out distributing stuff. This time it looks like a bingo card, but what I couldn't work out was what it was really for. Well, it turned out that it looked like a bingo card because it was. As the saying goes, if it looks like an elephant, the chances are it is. Same goes for bingo cards.

Before you can work out how to say 'what is this thing you've given me which looks like a bingo card?' in Spanish, someone is barking numbers and you're trying to keep up.

Digression no 11 – Bingo

That bus trip in Chile was the fourth occasion that bingo had come into my life. The second was in Dundee which, when I went to university there, boasted the largest bingo hall in Europe.

The first was on holiday in Scarborough, Yorkshire, when we were kids. South Bay in Scarborough is the world capital of beach cricket. After a hard day's putting willow on tennis ball, we used to be given a bit of money to go and spend in the amusement arcades. We could never understand why all these old women with pink-rinsed hair would sit at their brightly coloured desks when there were exciting arcade games such as Pit Stop, Pacman, Scramble, Bomb Jack and Defender to play. They would sit there flicking little covers over the numbers they got, while laughing jovially at the jokes the caller came out with every now and then. 'Two little ducks,' he would call. 'Quack Quack' all the grave dodgers would answer before the ensuing five seconds of tittering laughter. How sad, we thought as we stuck our ten pence bits into the car racing games.

By far, my best bingo experience was number three. 'D'you want to go to Butlin's in Minehead for three days between Christmas and New Year with me, Andy and Rick?' Charlie had asked me. I was up in Dundee and nearly at the end of Autumn term. 'Yes' is the only reply any self-respecting Brit can give to such an unorthodox question. Butlin's, for those of you who aren't aware of some of the more bizarre elements of British society, is a chain of holiday camps, and not very good ones at that. They're very outdated in a 1950s kind of way and are in places like Minehead and Skegness; towns by the seaside but nothing like Rio. Going there in the summer is a brave decision, but in December? Serious error.

The thing was that it sounded like such an unfeasibly stupid thing to do that it was impossible to say no, so I didn't.

The outing started badly. The 125 miles from our place to Minehead was undertaken in my Skoda, a proper Communist vehicle of Czech construction. Apart from having its engine in the boot, the Skoda had about as much in common with a Porsche 911 as Minehead has with Rio. The car was fine and got us there, albeit slowly. The problem was Andy, who was riding shotgun. For some reason, this occasional drinker had brought a bottle of sherry with him for the journey. By the time we got to Minehead it was empty and he was drunk. Upon arrival, while I was leaning out of one window talking to a 'red coat' Butlin's employee, Andy was leaning out of the other vomiting out the bottle of sherry, along with all the other contents of his digestive system. The only other things I remember about that weekend are: 1) Andy taking a dump between two cars in the car park about three minutes later, 2) Andy having a knee wobbler against a phone box outside an Irish bar a few hours later after having made a miraculous recovery from the sherry incident, 3) The bingo.

The four of us sat down to play bingo with the experts. Some of these people are capable of managing about ten lines of bingo at a time. I was laughing so hard at the time that I couldn't even manage one.

The sort of laughter I'm on about is the most debilitating type. It happens to everyone at least once. Even the most miserable son of a bitch gets caught out by uncontrollable laughter once in their lifetime. Bingo was the catalyst this time. The four of us were sitting in a line, concentrating like hell, trying to keep up. We all just started giggling as we fell behind, and then laughing, and then crying. You know, when you're laughing so hard that you think all your ribs are going to break, you can't breathe and you can't see because your eyes are so full of tears. Butlin's is great.

End of digression.

Back in Chile, I soon discovered that bingo is even harder in Spanish. It didn't really matter though. It was such a surreal experience playing bingo on a bus. I was a stranger in a strange land, wielding a biro and crossing the boxes. After not too long some bloke exclaimed and was declared the winner. He was given some description of fruit basket, and, much to my continued mirth, a polite round of applause from us, his fellow bingoites. With that, life returned to normal. A film went on and bus travel returned to more established norms, after having been off on its bingo-induced tangent for a while. It's little memories of the bizarre and beautiful like that which make travelling worthwhile.

Downsizing a bit from buses, minibuses warrant serious consideration because they get a lot of people around this planet. Whether it's 'matatus' in Africa, 'porpuesos' in South America, or any of the multitude of names they take on around the world, they are a big player in the global transport network. The trouble is that a lot of them are pretty awful to get anywhere in. It tends to work like this: the poorer the country, the worse the roads are, the more people they squeeze into the minibus and the worse the condition of the vehicle. The vans are usually a Nissan Urvan or the corresponding Toyota or Mitsubishi, and they've always had a very, very hard life.

As discussed in chapter one, these vans are a cheap way of getting around but the flipside is that they always contain at least double the amount of people that they would if they were ferrying people around the developed world. Add to this the fact that there are often plenty of chickens and other animals on board, as well as everyone's luggage. Furthermore, they don't change the tyres when there are less than six millimetres of tread on them; racing slicks are a very common sight.

So, to sum up, you've got an old vehicle which has double the gross weight recommended in the maker's manual being driven on roads which may as well be a ploughed field, on tyres which are down to the canvas and cross-ply. Not the safest vehicle you'll ever get into. The frustrating result is that they frequently stop, not only to pick up passengers, but also to change punctured tyres, snapped prop shafts and God knows what else.

My most nervous day in this minibus transport was in Northern Kenya when we were travelling near Eldoret, a dusty sort of town whose claim to fame is the filming of a *Mad Max* film. Charlie and I had somehow been allocated the fabled spot in any Kenyan matatu, the front seat. This is a sought after spot in the vehicle, not because you have a sadistic desire to be the first out of the windscreen in the event of a crash, but because there's only an overpopulation of 33%. In the rest of the vehicle it's usually at least 50%. In less complicated terms, it meant that we had four people in three seats. The driver had his seat, Charlie and some bloke had the passenger seat, and lucky old me made up the front four sitting on the engine cover. I didn't start getting nervous until we stopped for the first time with the engine overheating. We all got out of the front and he lifted my seat up to fill the radiator with water. The process was repeated about half an hour later and then we started what turned out to be about a fifty odd mile descent down a fairly steep hill. By the way, 'drive' was thrashing the crap out of the lower gears and never venturing into third. I assumed his brake pads were about as non-existent as Zola Budd's running spikes at the 84 Olympics. With the engine squealing out high revs and overheating, who would want to be the bloke sitting on top of the engine cowling? I wouldn't, but I was. I wasn't looking forward to the worst case scenario which would have been a doctor in a grubby Third World hospital pulling bits of the rocker cover and head gasket out of my arse after they'd flown straight out of the top of the disintegrating engine with such a force as to also make progress through the engine cover.

Before moving on to other subjects, just a quick discussion about tractors, which are another much-used method of transport. I spent most of my time in the beautiful if troubled city of Jerusalem trying fruitlessly to get into the pants of a beautiful lady from South Korea. I was staying on the roof of a hostel in the Arab quarter. It's a good cheap way to get accommodation if you've got a good doss bag. I was armed with the trusty Norwegian Ajungilak (with left hand zip) and had many a good night on that roof. I love my sleeping bag and you couldn't get another person inside its figure hugging contours if you tried. Not that it mattered because the Korean wasn't having any of it anyway.

Jerusalem is a fascinating city. You can feel the tension in the place and there are quite a lot of weirdos there, but apart from that, I really liked it. The tractors are brilliant though, as are their drivers. The tractors themselves are cheeky little green articulated efforts each of which have a trailer to carry stuff around in. Their size reflects the streets of Jerusalem; they're not very big and not very wide either. This is what is fascinating about Jerusalem and its tractors. It's Venice but completely different. There are no canals, but they have equally large goods conveyance problems. All the gates into Jerusalem are tiny so what does the humanity in and around the town do? It adapts of course. It's the one thing humans have mastered beyond all else. You build a town on a marsh – error – and adapt your maritime transport accordingly. Different situation, same principle. You build a fortified town with small gates. Errors. But humans are able to recover from initially high levels of foolishness.

In the case of Jerusalem, the recovery comes in the form of the little green tractors. They're great bits of kit which have been designed, it would seem, specifically for the purpose of getting around the maze of narrow streets which is old town Jerusalem. They are as vital to the lifeblood of Jerusalem as boats are to that of Venice. Everything going inside the city walls is either carried or goes in the trailers which faithfully follow the little green tractors to which they are hitched.

With that said, you have to take into account the rubbish in, rubbish out factor. You can't just parachute any given person into the driver's seat and expect everything to run like clockwork. Jerusalem tractor drivers are surely the best in the world. They'd definitely all get a job on the corn cart in England. It's hard to explain just how good they are. They fly up the stairs of the walled city without easing off the throttle, despite the ramps for the tractors being no wider than the tyres. They fly round right angled corners, from one seven foot wide alley into the next with pinpoint accuracy; you couldn't get a cigarette paper between the side of the trailer and the wall. But none of them ever hit anything. Their reversing skills are even harder to believe. These guys are seriously talented.

Jerusalem is a great place to visit, despite all the weirdos. The worst of them are the Christian fundamentalists who turn up by the bus load to carry the cross down the Via Dolorosa. This is the road which Jesus is supposed to have walked down on his way to his crucifixion, dragging his cross. Nowadays, it's all about tourism, but the bloodletting, martyrdom and pain of it all are still very much a part of it. The whole fiasco starts outside the walled city. As the need for defensive walls suggest, Jerusalem has been laid siege to several times over the centuries. These days though, the siege is constant and made up of buses, which surround the religious hub that is Jerusalem in an almost uninterrupted cordon. Most of the coaches have signs emblazoned across the front which read 'Baton Rouge evangelists in the holy land in 2000', 'New York state Episcopalians celebrating 2000 years of our lord Jesus Christ' or 'Reverend Bobby Pringle Jr's millennium Baptist pilgrimage'

These vehicles all spew forth large people, many of them American, who are in the Holy Land to see where it all happened and where everyone got persecuted/ resurrected/ stoned/ beheaded, and other unpleasant or unbelievable things. The average number of heart bypasses per coach is probably about 120ish (for a regular 52 seater coach) and the average weight is probably about the same in kilos.

Once inside the walls and hot on the trail of the Via Dolorosa, these people become a nauseating sight. It's sad enough seeing a group of people walking down a street re-enacting someone's suffering. A lot of them get very emotional and overcome with religious fervour whilst encouraging the lucky sod who's currently in the Jesus, cross wielding role. Cringe factor 40+. This factor goes off the scale when you realise that they're using a lightweight, scaled down version of the cross! Sad bastards. I spent a number of hours trying to come to terms with the crass bollocks which was unfolding in front of me. It's nauseatingly good entertainment.

Digression No 12 – Americans

While we're on the subject of Americans, it's worth discussing their value to this planet whilst in the Jerusalem neck of the woods. The reason I say this is because of an incident which occurred at the Dead Sea, during that very same trip, which is one of my favourite ever American 'moments'.

There I was lying in, or rather on, the Dead Sea. You can't really get in it. It's a very weird feeling because although you're buoyant, you're a lot more buoyant than you're used to being in water, and it takes some getting used to. You feel like your centre of gravity is about twenty feet above your head.

The other thing which takes some getting used to is actually being able to count your haemorrhoids without physically seeing them. It's immediately apparent where every bit of broken skin on your body is as soon as you get into the Dead Sea. It doesn't hurt but you're aware of it. Because the Dead Sea is below sea level, it contains a lot more minerals than other expanses of water, such as five times as much bromide, for example. If you whirl your hand around in the water it's like stirring a straw in your Ribena, and not dissimilar in colour from blackcurrant juice either.

Between trying to stay upright on the water and the dulcet stinging coming from every mosquito bite, scratch and cut on my body, as well as the bum grapes, I failed to spot a bus rocking up at the official swimming area I was at. The first I knew was when Americans started pouring out of the changing rooms and into the swimming area. Most of them were rotund and oldish, but all harmless enough. Then, bursting out of the changing rooms came Jabba the Hutt's sister. She was huge, was wearing loud frilly swimming attire and was making a completely unnecessary amount of noise complete with over-acted histrionics. The sort of loud, fat annoying cow who can't do a single thing in life without making a big fuss.

Having waddled down to the water she sort of fell in and started laughing. 'Oh my gawd,' she declared in a sort of scream- cum-shouted New York accent, 'back home I just sink!'

I had to laugh with her. It was the delivery of the whole thing which was inspired. I'm sure that it's a great advantage to have skin four inches thick and no shame at times. It was a priceless moment which I've never forgotten and never will.

I've been to the States on a number of occasions and had a great time every time. It's a big, beautiful country with some very friendly and very hospitable people populating it. It is also the most self-centred, inward looking country on our planet.

Whatever the reason, be it its geographical location, history or whatever, it is a constant source of wonderment to the rest of us earthlings how little Americans know about the rest of the planet, and how little they want to know about the rest of the planet. Never before in human history has there been such an economic powerhouse of a country or empire which has been as insular as the United States is today. We've had empires in the form of Ancient Greece, Egypt, the Roman Empire, the British Empire, Napoleon's France, the Mongols, the Ottomans, the Spanish; the list is endless. But all of these civilisations and empires were expansionist and curious to discover and conquer new parts of the world. We've also had the insularity in medieval Japan or modern-day North Korea, but we've never had the two together. America is the confluence of the two and probably the first to date. It's incredible to outsiders to find out just how little the average American knows about the world and how little desire a lot of them have to go and see any of it. Admittedly, they have a very big country which you could travel for a lifetime without ever seeing it all, but their lack of curiosity is still puzzling.

Curiosity and global inquisitiveness are not compulsory though, and a lack of them is not a crime. It's also a generalisation to say that they're not well travelled as a nation; although they have one of the lowest rates of passport possession in the world, Americans are out there travelling and seeing the sights. Usually the expensive way, but they are out there.

Two of them walked into the restaurant my brother and I were in one afternoon in Baños in Southern Ecuador. He was a young version of John Goodman with a big 'housewives' favourite' SLR camera round his neck, a flowery shirt, and very thick pink legs sticking out of the bottom of a pair of shorts the size of a windsock. She was very petite and wearing highish heels and some very dainty lacy sort of stuff, not the

96

first thing you'd put in the bag to go to Ecuador. I'd been on the point of shoving a fork full of 'churrasco' ,the hearty local mixed grill, into my mouth when this spectacle appeared, but my fork stalled at the entrance to my mouth. 'Oh my, you two have just *got* to be American,' she said, waving her hands around at about shoulder height without moving the rest of her arms, to put emphasis on the *got*. She was very excited to meet what she thought were some of her countryfolk. 'We're from Seattle, Washington,' her man helpfully added. 'You guys?'

Charlie and I had already had a couple of looks at each other to make sure all that appeared to be happening, was. 'England,' we said in unison, 'in the UK,' I added while thinking how do they ever do the missionary without her getting crushed to death?

The big question that needs answering is: Why do Americans always give the name of the state they're from as well as the city? Okay, if it's Shitsville, Wyoming and no one's likely to have heard of it, fair enough. But why do they say LA, California, Houston, Texas or Miami, Florida? Anyone know, because I'd like to?

The great thing about America and Americans is that they're very good at what they do. The other Charlie (my mate) and I were sitting in Vegas contemplating this over a bottle of Fijian gin (see booze) which we were washing down mixed with a 7-eleven 64oz super slurp of Sprite. We were in the youth hostel at the top of the strip which was full of other people doing it on the cheap. There was this group we got talking to, one of whom was a girl of twenty-odd who'd just come from Asia. She said she thought Las Vegas was disgusting, which immediately gained Charlie's attention. Charlie rightly thinks that Elvis and anything to do with him is cool, Vegas included, so he asked her what she meant. She explained that she'd been in Asia and how it was 'chilled out'.

Yawn. She'd been to all these Buddhist temples, met the monks and started going on about serenity and inner fulfilment.

I could see that Charlie wasn't going to put up with that kind of bollocks for long. That's one of the perils of travelling the planet; you meet some great people, see some incredible stuff and have a great time. You also meet some insufferably sanctimonious bores like her who usually say 'like' about every third word and want to be really 'with it' ethnically and at one with the world. Fully 'right on' in other words. You can spot them a mile off because they're all beads, ethnic fishing pants and other baggy, ill-fitting stuff. Cross-legged sitting, deeply intense people who frown a lot when they talk about the subject they're currently hooked on and assume you want to hear all about.

Buddhist temples; love 'em, and there's no doubt that they do provide a good spot for quiet contemplation as well as some lovely sights and sounds. Vegas is none of those things. Vegas is a fast, noisy and neon-lit hotbed of immorality and gambling, and it's great!

'What are you doing here then? Why don't you just fuck off somewhere else, if you don't like Vegas?' was how Charlie finally delivered the question which had been brewing a while. His abrupt and rude style of questioning did everyone there the service of shutting the lassie up for a few seconds after which she said that she thought the States would be the same all over and that she was going to go back home and earn some money before heading back to Asia. Good. Bugger off. I hope she's learnt to take herself a bit less seriously in the decade or so since.

False is the last thing that you can accuse Vegas, or in fact the States in general, of being. What you see is very much what you get. Okay, in the physical sense, Vegas is very false. Fake volcanoes, pyramids, medieval castles, Venetian canals and so on. But Vegas at no point tries to disguise the fact that it is what it looks like. A city in the middle of nowhere built for fun and enjoyment. It's pretty much a one street town, but what a street! Yes it is tacky, but what's wrong with that? Elvis impersonators, wedding chapels and volcanoes which erupt on the hour every hour have an essential role to play in society. So what if the place is full to brimming with prostitutes, Mafia and lap dancers? The whole place is great fun and it's important to have places to go and have fun.

It's because of that open, honest, what you see is what you get sort approach that I like the States full stop. I've always been very warmly welcomed and had a great time wherever I've been there. You're quite often aware that it can also be a pretty dangerous place at times, but where isn't these days? A friend of Charlie's parents took us into downtown LA to catch a Greyhound and locked the doors of the car we were in. He said he hadn't been downtown for seven years! Couldn't say that I blamed him once we got there.

Food will be discussed later on, but the service which comes with it on the other side of the pond is out of this world. How the hell they all cope when they come to Europe is anyone's guess. There, they expect good service and are prepared to pay for it. They usually get it as well because tipping is performance related. Give good service and you get a good tip. Don't and you don't. Simple. As with their table service, a lot of things in the States are bigger, better, faster and done with a smile, and you have to take your hat off to them for that.

The main challenge for the new leaders of the free world over the coming decades is to overcome not being able to see beyond their own borders. There are a lot of things which Americans don't know. Go over there and you'd think that terrorism was invented on 9/11/2001. They may be surprised to learn that Brits have been getting maimed since the late 60s by terrorists who have been let into America for fundraising events throughout that period. Americans have a very romantic view of Ireland and its freedom fighters wandering about in tweed suits with a shotgun crooked over their elbow. Well that's not the reality. The reality is bombs, flesh lying in the street, and death.

Terrorist attacks have been happening all over the world for centuries, but now that it's happened at their place, on the United States mainland, suddenly something has to be done about it. They've gone about it in a very heavy handed and unsubtle way as well, which is very unfortunate.

The world has had a hell of a lot to thank the Americans for over the last century, but you can't help feeling that the respect that they've earned during that time has all but vanished in the eyes of a majority of earthlings over the very short number of years since 2001. That exodus of respect is all down to one president and his big business cronies. A man who was installed in the White house by Fox News, who got re-elected by using lies and scaremongering, despite being the worst thing to happen to this planet and its inhabitants for a generation.

That all got a bit serious for a minute, didn't it?

End of digression.

The other thing to watch out for in Jerusalem is closing time. *The Life of Brian*, comfortably the best film ever made, very neatly included the perils of closing time in a great scene with Graham Chapman. I nipped into a coffee house with full trading still going on in the early evening. When I came out, nothing. The whole place was packed up. Shops which had previously had their wares stacked up out in the streets were now locked up and every street looked the same. How the hell do they put it all away so quickly? With all the streets looking pretty much identical I was as lost as Brian, and it took me ages to get my bearings and find my way back to the hostel.

With the tractors of Jerusalem now discussed, the next chapter will explore the infinitely more dangerous area of transport – two or less wheels.

Transport, the sequel – two wheels or less

Three, that's the magic number, according to De La Soul. Probably the most dangerous number of wheels to have on a vehicle as well, as my brother had found out in New Zealand whilst rolling down a hill on a three wheeled ATV motorbike. Two, from a safety point of view, is a pretty poor number as well. I once asked my dad if he'd ever ridden motorbikes. 'Yes,' he replied, 'but I gave it up after leaving half of my arse on the roundabouts of Yorkshire.' It may well be hereditary. Considering that my grandad on my mum's side had a motorbike crash bad enough to tear his father's raincoat completely to shreds, maybe I'm the confluence of two lineages of pisspoor motorcycle riders. I've crashed every motorcycle I've ever owned apart from my current one. The way I avoid crashing that is by living in the French Alps and leaving the bike at my cousin Tom's in Bristol in the UK.

The other problem apart from lack of personal riding talent is the Scandinavian motor industry. To be 'Volvoed' is a verb in current English usage, if you talk to motorcyclists. For those who've never had the experience, it involves being knocked off a motorcycle. Whenever this happens, it's almost always by a very heftily built estate car – station wagon – of Scandinavian origin. It's likely to have an inattentive accountant or whimsical mother-of-four behind the wheel. The couple of dogs in the boot and a few kids in the back restrict any chance the driver may have of seeing anything out of the back window and it is apparently traditional not to use the wing mirrors of these vehicles. As to looking out of the front, judging by the number of people they manage to hit, this would also appear to be optional. When they hit you they hurt, due to being made out of steel girders, and quite often kill or maim you.

That is the real crux of the problem; motorcycles are a hell of a lot of fun, but the chances of being killed on one are pretty high, really. Shame, that. It's worth the risk though. Ever since seeing a bloke riding a BMW down the beach on Zanzibar in 95 I'd been thinking,' I need to do that.' And I have done, repeatedly.

Charlie thought I'd stopped to take a photo, and who could have blamed me if I had? We'd just got off of the ferry from Wellington and were biking around the stunningly beautiful Queen Charlotte Sound on the top coast of the South Island of New Zealand. But I hadn't stopped to take a photo. I was in fact lying in a ditch next to the Suzuki GS1000E I'd just crashed. That was my first motorbike crash and what a rush!

Clever people don't go out and buy an 18 year old, 1000 cc Suzuki a mere two months after passing their motorbike test. Why? Because when you're getting used to the scheme of things you buy yourself a bike which is easy to ride and you can't get too over-excited on. But, as we've already established, I'm not clever. Old motorcycles with their big engines and thin tyres are heavy, hard to stop and, if you have no experience, hard to ride. It took me a trip to the ditches of New Zealand to realise this, following which I was so full of adrenalin I thought I was going to burst. Despite the fact that a GS 1000 weighs about the same as three modern bikes of the same size, I was on such a rush that I picked that bike up as if it was a toothpick. Funny stuff, adrenalin. Luckily, and no thanks to my intelligence deficit, I was unharmed save for dented pride, and the bike was fine, save for a dented tank and scratched clutch plate.

If only that had been the end of it. Sliding down a road on my arse at about 50 miles per hour in Slovakia a couple or three years later, I was overtaken by my Honda Transalp. Until a few seconds previously, I had been riding it. Now I was being out-slid by it. How disappointing.

That's always been the story with me and motorbikes. I should probably have thrown in the towel by now, but biking is just too much fun. With me on the seat, my latest crotch rocket, an ageing GT750 from the Kawasaki stable, had a great summer (it happened the next summer as well) riding all the mountain passes of the European Alps. It's very addictive and hard to give up. On a nice day in the twisties you forget the times when you've been sat there, soaked down to your credit cards and depressed to a level you can't even attain by listening to Leonard Cohen records all day. A day on a motorbike on a nice twisty road in bright sunshine is as much fun as you can have with your clothes on.

Take the Shipka Pass in Bulgaria. That, I'm pretty sure, was my best day's motorcycling ever. The Honda Transalp had survived the hardships and slides further up Eastern Europe, albeit with a few war wounds, and we were now heading for the Middle East. With its billiard table flat, twisty and meandering EU-financed road, the Shipka Pass is a Mecca for two-wheeled petrolheads. I was knackered and ready for a break when I got to the top of the pass, having hooned it all the way up from the city of Gabrovo, but I would have stopped anyway. The views are fantastic and the huge 'monument of freedom' is really something to behold, as are the cannons up there. It's just a sort of sit down, chill out and take in the view sort of a place, like White Horse Hill in England. Somewhere to have a contemplative think.

Big is not necessarily best though. Another great day out on two wheels was had riding from Chiang Mai in Northern Thailand up to the very beautiful Buddhist temple of Doi

Suthep, some fifteen miles away. We thrashed it up there on a couple of C 90 Honda step-through mopeds which are probably the most bullet-proof form of transport on the planet.

Digression no 13 – The Japanese

You have to hand it to the Japanese, they really do know how to build stuff. The post-war Japanese motorcycle industry is everything to engineering efficiency that the Morris Marina isn't. Japanese motorcycles – and cars for that matter – just keep going and going and going.

Waiting for a ferry to take us back to the North Island of New Zealand, Charlie and I were talking to a couple on a BMW when a loud rumble started. With that, Harley Davidsons started streaming round the corner and we thought, shit; motorbike gang. It was a load of 'Highway 61' blokes out of Rotorua. 'What are you two doing riding fuckin' riceburners?' was the first sound emitted by the big, really hard looking bloke at the front. We naturally assumed that we were going to die. Gangs are big news in New Zealand and regularly kill members of rival gangs. That's okay, and as far as I'm concerned; they can all kill each other to their hearts content. They're also known for their dislike of Japanese motorcycles, or 'riceburners' as they are derogatorily known. If you're in a bike gang in New Zealand you're on a Harley or something European. As we weren't, and also pommies, I assumed that the Highway 61 guys were going to make some sort of attempt on our lives. I was wrong, but that said, it was clear that they weren't very keen on us.

What these people don't realise is that they're wrong; not that I was going to tell them, but if you want a bike which doesn't have enough braking capacity, buy a Harley. If you want a bike which'll break down every now and then, buy a

Ducati. If you want a well- balanced, reliable and fairly cheap motorbike, buy anything Japanese. Charlie and I had conveyed these views to the last person before the Highway 61 guys to show disrespect to our 'riceburners'. He was an inbred pisshead in the middle of nowhere with a three-legged dog called 'Pizza Hut'. Surreal.

Okay, so tourism Japanese-style warrants the ridicule it invariably attracts. They are nice as people go and very good at getting hammered on planes. But they also do things considered fairly bizarre by others and Robbie Williams must have been having Japanese thoughts when entitling one of his albums 'Life Through A Lens'. They are keen on the odd photo or five thousand, it has to be said. My favourite Japanese moment apart from a great JAL flight was in Queenstown, NZ, the adrenalin capital of the southern hemisphere, where I saw ten members of the same Japanese family, from four different generations all wearing matching shell suits. Fashion police, intercept that group of ten!

Their motorbikes are great though. Half the planet has a C90 or equivalent moped as their family car and they're well practiced at getting two adults and three kids onto one. The bigger, more powerful versions are damn fine as well; in short, don't diss Jap bikes.

End of digression.

A motorcycle is a great way to get around the planet, but any vehicle can become a fair sized millstone as well, especially when arriving at international borders. What do you do if some official just says 'no?. You are stuck at a brick wall and all your plans for going any further are scuppered by a single word from some bloke you've never met in your life. This happened to me after what had been a great day on the road and one of those chance encounters which is what makes wandering around the world worthwhile.

I'd been on the road for about two months and had already met former President Ion Maurer of Romania and other such luminaries as a bloke called Nando Veheranda, who used to be a goalkeeper for the Italian series 'A' football team Fiorentina, and was now wandering around on a big BMW 1100 with his lovely wife Laura.

I had arrived in the Gaza Strip and was heading for Egypt. My latest chance encounter happened because I noticed that petrol was slightly cheaper than it had been in Israel so thought I'd stop and fill up. I got talking to the bloke who owned the petrol station, who also happened to be the local mayor. The Arabs are unfeasibly friendly people and he was no exception. He persuaded me that I was thirsty and got his employee to bring me a drink. With that, the local police chief arrived for a chat with his best friend, and the three of us ended up chatting for an hour and a half in the shade of the forecourt roof. During that time the mayor had got his chap to bring us all some lunch and we had a really good feed and enlightening conversation. If someone rings a friend up and says, 'What did you do for lunch today'? how many people ever reply, 'I had some local fayre in a petrol station in the Gaza Strip'. Not a lot. I thanked my lunch companions and bade them 'adieu'.

Digression no 14 – customs officers of the world pt 3

'Adieu' nearly became 'au revoir' a few miles later. I nearly had to do a U-turn. Having had such a great day, I should have known something would go wrong. It hadn't been a great day from a scenery point of view; Gaza is a dusty and broken sort of place where the buildings all look unkempt and the sense of oppression is strong. From a human interaction standpoint it had been great. Some people just can't do enough for you with that petrol station being a prime example I'll never forget.

The rest of the day was taken up with a high concentration of frontier buffoons.

The first was upon exiting Gaza. Having gone through the Palestinian checkpoint, I was effectively back in Israel. There is an Israeli checkpoint to go through as well before you regain Israel proper. The guard saw the Union flag on the Transalp and went green. The fear on his face was very much in evidence and before my visor was even up said 'where have you been?', with some alarm. Knowing full well where I'd come from he added 'Don't you know there's a road all the way round the outside of the Gaza strip?' 'No' was my truthful reply. Considering the great people I'd met while there, I was pleased not to have been shepherded around the peripheral road by Israeli soldiers with probably not the most objective view of that strip of territory.

The second random was a mere mile or so down the road. She was a hefty, hard-nosed, fat-arsed Israeli border guard at the frontier with Egypt. She brought my passport back covered in Hebrew stamps, despite the fact that I'd told her I didn't want any in it to avoid what's known as 'stamp stigma'. Less tolerant Muslim countries such as Iran and Saudi won't let you in if you've been to Israel. I went off at her for a moment, furious with what she'd done. She spoke perfect English and had done it deliberately, but what can you do?

The third muppet of the day turned the Transalp into an instant millstone. He looked at my 'carnet de passage', the international registration document, and said, 'No, back to Israel,' and walked off at pace. Having waited a fruitless hour during which his staff had refused to even look at my perfectly valid documents, the man seriously restricting my chances of getting into Egypt returned. With a bit of acting and sign language from yours truly, he became enlightened as to the document's validity and I was into the land of the Pharaohs, complete with Transalp. High concentrations of dipshit border guards like that day are very bad for your heart. Three in one afternoon are just too much.

End of digression.

Motorbikes are truly great vehicles even if they are also very dangerous. The really good thing is that you can't get stuck in traffic on one. Traffic filtering is one of the most satisfying activities this earth has to offer. You're flying along whilst all the losers with no imagination who have selected a car as their carriage are sat there going nowhere. Tough titties I say; serves them right for not having the imagination to buy a motorbike.

Boredom is a factor on motorbikes the same as it is in cars. I was riding through Turkey a few years ago on the Honda Transalp and had spent about six hours riding past nothing but cotton fields. After a few hours I was verging on bored. The problem is that your head is enclosed and you can't even listen to the radio.

The good thing about being in Turkey is that it's impossible to run out of petrol. Even if you've somehow forgotten you're already on reserve and your motorbike's engine starts choking of fuel starvation, you're never any more than a hundred metres from a petrol station so you can just pull in the clutch and coast in. Turkey has more petrol stations than mosques, and that's going some.

On the boredom front, in Australia I left the same Honda Transalp in Sydney and went around the place in our beaten up old Mazda. The Stuart Highway on a motorbike would be dull as bat shit, I would estimate. More's the point, me and that Transalp had spent so much time in each other's company by that point that we were fed up of the sight of each other. I went off in the Mazda with Foxy and the Transalp enjoyed a couple of months with a twenty stone plumber from Southall in the saddle. Surely endured?

Digression no 15 – being bored in cars

Regressing back to four wheels for this digression, just a few quick cures for boredom in cars. Car-style vehicles are pretty easy to get bored in compared to the two-wheel variety. That's because in big countries you go in a straight line for hours or even days on end in cruise control. In fun-size countries like the UK it's because you're in a traffic jam. But, you have a variety of options should you get bored on a bus, in a car or in some description of minibus.

You can of course use the grin and bear it technique and just be bored. I used to use this technique when driving my Skoda to Dundee from Oxfordshire. The stereo was bust so I used to wear my headphones and listen to tunes while smoking non-stop roll-your-own cigarettes from door to door. Imagine my surprise one day while sitting Glasgow-bound on the M74 when, on looking out of the driver's side window I noticed a blue Shearings holiday coach overtaking me slowly but surely. As with all Shearings coaches, it was both turquoise and full of really old people off on holiday. Three of the old biddies on this one were looking down at me in the scud missile. Nothing wrong with that except that at that point I had my finger knuckle deep up my right nostril picking a winner.

With the bogey selected and extracted, I for some reason held it up to show them with a look of pride on my face. That made the three blue-rinsed grave dodgers watching grimace a bit. Then, all of a sudden, looking them straight in the eye, I ate it. That made the wrinklies avert their gaze with looks of total disgust on their faces. I was laughing so hard I nearly crashed! Very good sport indeed that is.

Other than accepting the boredom, a variety of other options exist. The first of these is pharmaceutical. As discussed previously, a bit of Valium sorts you right out if you should find yourself in some far-flung spot with no legroom and nothing to do or look at. Sleep is a good fall back in any situation.

The other options are for those who can't actually go to sleep because they are controlling the vehicle in which they are being bored. Taking Valium while at the helm of a car or other vehicle could be considered a touch reckless. So, what else is on offer? Games, that's what. Car games. I'm not talking 'I-Spy', which is incredibly boring by the time you reach six years old. I'm talking good car games.

Game one is a game for two or more persons. It's the strip game. Last time I played this was in my brother's Hillman Avenger on the way back from Scarborough where we'd been on the bevvy for a few days. The rules are very simple; all the people in the car take all the clothes off their top half and you open all the windows. The first one to submit to the cold and concede is the loser. If no one yields, the first to die of hypothermia is the loser. Then, with everyone frozen to death, you all wind up the windows, put every single item of clothing you have with you on, and turn the heater on full blast. The first to pass out, faint or submit is the loser. Great game.

Games two and three are both one person games. It's reassuring to know that I'm not the only crackpot in the world. I was reading an Iain Banks book a few years ago and both of these were in it. I couldn't believe anybody else does rubbish like this. Number two is the number plate game, where you have to make up words out of the letters on the number plate of the car or lorry (or Shearing's holiday coach) in front of you. Number three is the trying to change lanes without hitting any of the cat's eyes in the road surface. Very tricky. Both of these are quality ways of passing the time.

As to two-wheel games, obviously game number one is incompatible with outdoor vehicles such as motorbikes. Game two is playable but game three is too easy.

Game four is again suitable for all forms of transport but especially motorbikes in big countries. If you find a straight bit of road, see how long you can shut your eyes for at sixty miles per hour before you bottle it and open them. Charlie managed about thirty seconds on his Kawasaki in New Zealand. I was much more scared.

Last but not least is not so much a game as a laugh. Car stickers are sometimes so inspired and witty that it lifts you out of your boredom for a while. My personal favourites are 'Caution, bits may fall off' on a classic VW camper in the UK, and two offerings from Australia: 'Mutant food? Yuck no!!' was one of them which is not only funny, but was on a Volvo Estate. Volvo drivers with a sense of humour? Whatever next. The other was 'Just because I'm paranoid doesn't mean that they're not all against me'. Brilliant.

End of digression.

Having two wheels doesn't of course mean that you have an engine. Some people do without and actually choose to go cycling. Wild. I do count myself amongst the cycling fraternity but only under certain circumstances.

The first of these is that it is not too far to destination. I met a couple next to a paddock of llamas in Bolivia who were not adhering to this all important criteria. It's not every day you meet an albino Englishman wearing an Ajax Amsterdam footy shirt, let alone in the heights of Bolivia. He was with his Dutch wife and they were cycling to Alaska. Hang on you might think, Alaska's in north-west North America and they're not even half way up…! My sentiments exactly. They'd left Ushuaia on the Tierra del Fuego (down the bottom) and had so far got to Bolivia. Mad so they are. I love pottering around on a push-bike but I've never considered them to be an intercontinental mode of transport. I could probably be persuaded to ride one over the Bosphorous Bridge in Istanbul just to say that I'd completed an intercontinental bike ride, but that'd be it.

Second; no hills. Very important as well. I don't object to slight inclines and even the odd gear change, but anything too steep and I'm blowing like a windsock. I went out one afternoon six years ago to gently saunter up to the top of the Col de l'Iseran just outside Val d'Isère on my bike. It damn near killed me and I turned round well under half way from the top. Never again.

Third; it is preferable that there be a pub or some other form of drinking establishment at the end of any bike ride. The main advantage of pedal power is that you can have a few beverages without feeling too guilty about riding home. Further to this, thinking of a route to your destination which incorporates a couple of other 'watering holes' along the way is not without merit. I'm currently enjoying pottering about on my grandad's vintage Raleigh 'sit up and beg' push bike, wandering the single track lanes of the Cotswolds. The farmers are harvesting the last of the linseed crop and the air is full of the smell of blackberries and elderberries which pack the hedgerows and camouflage the dry stone walls. It makes you want to stop and start making jam and fruit compote on the spot. Woah, that rhymes. The Indian summer of 06 has made it all the more enjoyable. A lovely old pushbike which keeps you very fit and gives me fond and vivid memories of its recently departed owner, good views, good pubs to stop at and loads of time to get nowhere in particular. What's more, it gets your legs into really good shape before heading out for the ski season.

Fourth; no taking it seriously. Why do cyclists wear such silly clothes? It's as if it were a competition to see who can look the most stupid. It's the hats which really do it though. I suppose the Lycra does have some aerodynamic advantages but those stupid little hats with the upturned peaks they wear are just too much. Jimmy Somerville central. Camp as Christmas.

Five; don't be a tosser. The only thing about cycling sadder than those god-awful hats is the snobbery. Cyclists say hello to people pursuing the same sport heading in the other direction on a road, but if they see someone just out for a ride in a pair of jeans and a T-shirt, they blank them. You have to be wearing the silly clothes to get the hello. Get over it you sad bastards. You're no better than that other equally sad species, the Harley Davidson rider, who are the motorised equivalent of the Lycra crew. They only say hello to other fat middle-aged men with ponytails and leather waistcoats, and blank riders of anything other than a 'hog'. You also have to have a leather waistcoat on. It's another form of apartheid. Tragic behaviour.

The Dutch are undoubtedly the people to go and see on the subject of bicycles; they're all at it and their country is perfectly suited to this method of displacement. Just to make things even better, a lot of them are six-foot tall blond-haired fitties in flowing skirts!

One other thing; cycling, like a lot of things in life, is not just a bed of roses, especially if you're stupid like me. Being a child at heart I still love skidding despite the fact that I'm now thirty-four years old. Immaturity combined with cycling the other day to send me straight over the handlebars of a push-bike in France. Just goes to show you that you should always read the label, or in the case of push-bikes, always check that brake levers are set up on French pushies on the same sides of the handlebars as they are on British ones. They weren't and I've got the scars to prove it having pulled the front brake on full and sailed over the front.

In the same way as having two wheels doesn't necessarily mean you've got an engine, having an engine doesn't

114

necessarily mean that you have any wheels. This will be discussed further in the maritime chapter to follow. Before heading onto the blue water, just a quick word about white water and how it led to one of the greatest experiences of my life.

Digression No 16 – the greatest day of my life part 1

Despite being in the French Alps, Val d'Isère is only a couple of miles from Italy. A resort down the road called La Rosière is linked to the resort of La Thuile in Italy and four of us ended up there a few years ago. From La Thuile it's a bus ride to Courmayeur where a friend of ours was running a hotel for the winter. A good night out on the town ensued and myself, Mehrtens, Jules and Tony the permanent punter turned up at the lifts in La Thuile the next day very much worse for wear. Grappa and Red Bull; lethal mix. Things started to go wrong at the lift pass office. The top lifts were shut because of the wind. No high lift means no link with France. No link with France means no way of getting back to Val in time to do my evening radio slot and the sack. The others just started laughing. Jules and Mehrtens, both hotel managers, were off work until the following afternoon and Tony, who had retired twelve years previously at the ripe old age of thirty-two, very helpfully suggested that we go back to Bar Roma in Courmayeur and get back on it.

Much more helpful than the idiots I was with was the girl in the lift pass office. If it had been France she would have shrugged her shoulders and not tried to help. But, this was Italy, and she told me to have a word with Luca, the chap who ran the piste security team. After discovering our plight, he told us to go up the first gondola where we'd be met by a bloke called Gianluca. Right enough, there he was with three of his mates and four skidoos. We loaded ourselves and our skis onto the back of the skidoos and off went our chauffeurs. I mean they really went off at absolute breakneck speed. Bearing in mind that it was a full blizzard, blowing a hoolie and you couldn't see twenty yards, I was as scared as a bloke on Turin's ring road.

It really was the experience of a lifetime and at one stage the bloke Mehrtens was riding with turned his snowmobile over on its side, much to the amusement of the rest of us. As we helped to right it, a little gap in the weather allowed us to see that we were right on the edge of a pretty high cliff. Once back up and running, we skidooed for another five minutes or so, at which point we came upon a bloke standing in the middle of nowhere with his skis on and two dogs by his side. 'Bonjour,' he said, as if he stood around in blizzards all the time, 'I'm here to guide you back to La Rosière.'

Well, we bade farewell to our chauffeurs after passing round Jules' hipflask and off we went. We arrived at a chairlift and the guide went into the hut to turn it on. He sat on the lift and whistled, at which command the dogs jumped on the bench either side of him in perfect unison. It was like Crufts in a blizzard. From the top of the lift we skied down into resort and that was it. The whole thing had taken well under an hour and cost us 23 Euros each!

It was an incredible once in a lifetime experience none of us will ever forget. It was definitely once in a lifetime as well because the next year we did the same trip, had the same problem and had to go through the Mont Blanc tunnel and get a 270 Euro taxi back to the car in La Rosière from Chamonix. Ouch!

Maritime

The tyres are the things on your car that make contact with the
road,
The tyres are the things on your car that make contact with the
road,
The tyres are the things on your car that make contact with the
road,
The car is the thing on the road that takes you back to your
abode.

There we were sitting in the middle of the Bay of Biscay,
listening to the brilliant 'Contact', a song by Phish. Well, we
weren't actually in the Atlantic, but the boat we were sailing
was. 'We' were myself, my eighteen-year-old cousin Mikey,
his mum Cals and his stepdad Ron. The boat was a beautiful
yacht called 'Dream Chaser'. It was a Farr 50 and we were
going along at a good 12 knots. Mikey and I were on watch and
listening to a few tunes while reading our books. Ron and Cals
were sleeping between watches.

In fact I wasn't reading my book at all. It was the 18th of
October 2003, and I couldn't concentrate on my book because
England had played South Africa in the crunch match of Pool
'C' in the Rugby World Cup that day and I didn't know the
result.

'Over there!' said Mikey all of a sudden, jolting me from
my oval ball reverie. 'There's definitely something over there.'
I didn't doubt him for a second. This is someone who had
completed a circumnavigation of the planet in a sailboat by the
age of ten. Mikey had already forgotten more about sailing
than I'll ever know. Sure enough, there they were, a hundred

yards distant to starboard. A pod of about twenty pilot whales. I forgot all about the World Cup for a few minutes at least, and enjoyed the grace with which they travelled through the water. Pilot whales always remind me of Heinkel 111 bombers. They have the same blunt, unaerodynamic nose as the bombers used by the Luftwaffe sixty years ago, and more recently by British heavy-metal outfit Mötörhead on the cover of the brilliant 'Bomber' album. As we were getting along pretty well in a favourable wind, the pilots fell behind pretty quickly, but it wasn't to be our last contact with marine wildlife on the journey.

We were three days out of Hamble in the UK and heading for Gran Canaria, in the Spanish Canary Islands. Cals and Ron had bought the Farr 50 brand new in Sweden that May and then sailed it to Hamble on the south coast of England where they based themselves for the summer. Mikey joined them for the trip to Gran Canaria and I was along to make the numbers up so that there would be two watches of two people.

I was having a great time. I'd never really sailed before a trip to Greece in May 2003 where I was taught to sail a Lazer (a little sailboat made in England) by an affable Australian instructor called Marcus. It was great to do something which puts you on the edge again; I'd done a lot of skiing in recent years and it was all getting a bit too easy. Sailing made it all feel a bit dangerous again, which was great. The first time I ended up on my back in the middle of the sail having capsized just of the coast of Kos, I couldn't stop laughing, but in a wide-eyed, shocked sort of way. It all happened so quickly I couldn't believe it. I also couldn't believe what completely exhilarating fun sailing was.

Now it was a different matter. A Lazer is not a fifty foot yacht with a sixty foot mast and I was completely out of my depth; just doing as I was told, when I was told to do it. The sitting down, reading, listening to good tunes and rolling along on the waves of the Atlantic I was getting used to without too much trouble. It really was an exhilarating trip.

Not many people ever sail around the world. Of those who do, you could count on one hand the number who've done it with three children. That's exactly what Ron and Cals did. They set off from home in the USA and circumnavigated the planet in a Sundeer '64 with three children aged seven, ten and thirteen. What an incredible feat and what a wealth of experience it had given them. I could help out and do things asked of me, but I couldn't pre-empt a request or think for myself in any part of the boat outside of the galley, where I got pretty handy at making tea in rolling seas.

The highlight for me was on the sixth night when Mikey and me had been back on watch about an hour. It was ten at night and we were just about to knuckle down to a hard night of sitting on our arses. Mikey, very rarely one to raise his voice simply said; 'They're all over the place, we're surrounded.' And yet again, as was the case with the first sighting of the pilot whales, the turtles, dolphins and other wildlife we'd seen over the past few days, he was right. Porpoises, dozens of them, and they were having a ball.

A lot of marine life consider sailboats to be playgrounds in the ocean. Cargo ships tend to be too fast for them but sailboats often travel at a speed which allows them to play in the bow waves. This is exactly what they did to us. They would swim alongside and then cut across the bow wave of Dream Chaser, like cyclists dropping into the back of a relay team in a velodrome, missing the bow by a whisker's breadth .There were so many of them that's it's a job to know how they avoided colliding. What added to the spectacle was that it was a lovely, starlit night of proportions I hadn't seen since lying on my back on a roof in Cooper Pedy, Australia. The intensity of the moon and stars lit the whole scene up beautifully. To add to the night's entertainment there was also a lot of phosphorescence in the water. Mikey had been on the bow for about five minutes and then came back to the helm and told me to go and sit there a while. I sat there looking straight between my dangling legs at the porpoises playing in the bow wave. One of them had a shot at the title and came flying across the bow just as a blob of phosphorescence, very reminiscent of the lumps of ectoplasm in the film *Ghostbusters* arrived. The blob exploded into a thousand smaller pieces on the forehead of the porpoise as it diced with death across the front of the boat. It was so beautiful, like a sort of underwater starburst shell, that I just shouted 'whoa' at the top of my voice. I will never forget it and often wonder if it was as bigger rush for that porpoise as it was for me.

It's not all plain sailing though you know, this sailing lark. The following night we were in deep trouble. We were eating supper at eight o'clock-ish and had two ships on the radar. Mikey got in touch on the radio to ask what the intentions of the nearest one were. What he didn't know was that the reply came from the other boat which was another three miles away and turning away from us. The other was a cargo boat which was running parallel with us in the other direction. Or so we thought, because we could only see his starboard navigation light. It was in fact coming straight at us, and its navigation lights were faulty.

The next few minutes were very scary and involved a bit of evasive action on our part. The cargo was doing about 25 knots and was a good hundred yards long. It would have turned us into toothpicks had it T-boned us. Thanks to Ron and Mikey, we missed it by about forty yards. It was right there, huge and threatening, looming large and very much the centre of all our attentions. Ron pointed us straight into its wake and the front third of Dream Chaser was disappearing every time she dipped into another trough between the bow wake waves of the cargo vessel. I assumed we were going to die but remained calm in the same way as I tend to when crashing a motorbike. As soon as the ship had passed us, Mikey was on the blower to ask them what the hell they thought they were playing at. He got not a single response. My first maritime near miss was not the first for the other three, however.

I'd once asked my best mate from school's dad, who was a pilot in the RAF, what the closest near miss he'd ever had was. 'Forty feet,' was his answer; 'approximately,' he added with a wry smile. He was in an ageing Shackleton over the North Sea when a Nimrod passed in front of the cockpit. In the same way, although we'd just had very close encounter with a very large object, made of steel and travelling a lot faster than us, it was not the closest that Ron, Cals and Mikey had ever come to being killed at sea. During their circumnavigation, they were becalmed in the Pacific. They were missed by a Korean trawler by less than the forty or so yards that we had come from that cargo ship that night in the Atlantic. The one thing we had in our favour was that we had some wind. That night in the Pacific, they just had to sit there and see if the trawler was going to miss them; at least we had been able to turn into the wind and therefore the wake of the cargo ship as well. If the wake had broadsided us it may well have been a different story.

As if nearly dying wasn't enough of a buzz, I had my first experience of racing boats in the autumn of 2005. I don't mind admitting that I am totally hooked on sailing and had to get another fix this summer. After another foray down to Greece to cane a Lazer around and eat some lobsters in May, I ended up having another maritime Autumn, this time on the Côte d'Azur, paid for by a couple of months working in London. I eased into it gently with a couple of very un-maritime, very lazy weeks lying on the beach with my girlfriend.

Then it was straight in at the deep end. In this case the deep end took the form of a fortnight of classic sailboat racing

121

which was one of the biggest rushes I've ever had. Pretty damn frightening at times as well, though, but I supposed that's half the reason it's such a rush.

I got the job by just walking the dock of the old port in Cannes and was invited to go out racing on a beautiful eighty five foot ketch called Nordwind. She'd been built in 1938 in Bremen for the Fastnet race the following year which she not only won, but did so in such impressive style that her record stood for over twenty years.

We went out for the first morning's racing in Cannes and the wind started to get up nicely as our class' start time approached. We'd done a few practice tacks during the morning to make sure we all knew what we were on with and the skipper, James, was now barking out the countdown to the start. I was on staysail sheets as I heard the committee boat fire the one minute to go gun and then James shout 'one minute'. I'd been so busy until then that I hadn't noticed all the other boats in our class converging on the same spot from different angles.

The idea of racing sailboats is to cross the line the very second the start gun goes off. Although the start line is several hundred yards long, a lot of the boats use similar tactics and therefore all want to start at a certain point on the start line to get the best of the wind. That afternoon in Cannes, that mutual point happened to be right where we were going to be in just under a minute's time. My lack of experience combined with three boats all over seventy tons in weight converging on the same spot made my arse pucker right up and my vocabulary get quite Tourettes-esque. To add to the fear of impending death, the skippers are all shouting like hell at each other. Oh yes, they're actually close enough to have an argument! James was at the helm and shouting, 'I will not yield,' or something similarly polite but firm, at the captain of *Hallowe'en*, who cut us up (according to the rules) like a Spanish snowboarder in December.

Apart from the thinking you're going to die at the startline aspect, race sailing is great fun. No, in fact, even the thinking you're going to die bit is all part of the buzz. After the week in Cannes we took part in the feeder race down to St Tropez for another regatta and another week of glorious racing and fun. The wind was strong and gusting at up to 47 knots. At one point I was trying to get a stuck sail tie of the mezzen mast sail near the stern and the boom flew out over the water. Luckily, having done a lot of marquee work, it didn't faze me too much and I had one arm over the boom with the other one trying to undo the tie so that they could pull the sail up. Good job really; no matter how comfortable you feel hanging off stuff it's going to unnerve you a bit when the skipper looks over his shoulder in the cockpit and says, 'For god's sake somebody keep hold of him.' I felt like a vital member of the crew until he added, 'If he falls in the piss (the sea), we'll have to go and pick him up.' It's the rules,' he further pointed out, just so I knew that, were it not for the rules, he would much sooner have maintained our lead and let me drown, than tack to pick me out of the piss. The whole race all the way to St Tropez was incredible with the starboard rail pretty much constantly in the sea, the boat crashing into the moody water and us all soaked and knackered by the time we went over the finish line in third. Not a bad day out all in all.

The night wasn't bad either. We'd had some big ones in Cannes and that didn't stop once we got to St Tropez. The sailing fraternity know which end of a glass has got a hole in it, that's for sure! Another great week of sailing and partying was brought to an end by a picturesque and sun-drenched prize giving ceremony at the fortified citadel overlooking the old port. The view over the Med, the laid back jazz combo and the enormous buffet all made for a great afternoon and a fitting end to what had been a great couple of weeks racing.

Of course, being on a sailboat doesn't necessarily mean that you have to hit the high seas. You can get some good sailing in on the rivers of the world. I'd wanted to go and investigate Luxor and the Valley of the Kings. The Transalp got a week's holiday in Cairo because someone told me that if I tried to ride down to Luxor I'd get shot at on the road! So train it was then. After touring the archaeological sites of Luxor for a few days, I followed the advice of some folk and carried on south to Aswan.

Some rivers are so unfeasibly large that you can get a good long run in before having to tack or gybe. Big rivers don't come much bigger than the Nile, the only major waterway in the world which flows north. One of my favourite trips ever was a three day trip from Aswan downstream towards Luxor in a felucca. Felucca are very basic boats and use the same sort of sail arrangement as a dhow. Ours was about thirty foot long and I got some good advice from other travellers in going about Aswan and finding Captain Fazi. We went to visit a couple of temples on the way down and also ran down some of the highest sand dunes outside of New Zealand, which was a right giggle. Nights were spent on the deck of the boat sleeping under the stars which was lovely. There were five of us on the trip so there was plenty of room. We didn't even have to sail the boat. You could chill out and watch the hustle and bustle of a day in the life of the river, which is fascinating. A river like the Nile is the hub of a whole country. It's like a human being with one artery. Everything runs off of it, and everything depends and relies on it. That's been the case in Egypt since time began. It's the same in South America where the Amazon is the hub of about half the continent. Watching life go on on these rivers is unending entertainment. The only major disaster on the felucca trip was a very pleasant Slovakian chap called

Jurij, one of the other four passengers. More about that in the alcohols of the world section.

Boats of any description are fantastic. Sailboats are now top of the heap for me but whether big, small, wind or engine powered , no matter. They're all good news. We got some firsthand experience from a very early age due to regular stints of living in France. Cross Channel ferries; great fun if you're a kid. For a start it means you're going to another country, or going home to see your family.

Second, the olds usually chuck you a couple of coins to go and play some video games for a while. Third, it's like a wedding in a Peter Kay comedy sketch. The Bolton comedian, talking about things you always at wedding, starts sliding across the stage on his knees, in hilarious imitation of kids you see doing exactly that at weddings the world over. In the same vein, passenger ferries always seem to have a group of kids running nowhere in particular, just running, here, there and everywhere for a large part of the night if it's a night crossing, and all day nonstop if it's a day crossing. They're usually complete strangers who've never met before or since, and run around panting and laughing, narrowly avoiding 'grown ups' on their umpteenth circuit of the cabin corridors.

Twenty five years ago, those kids were us. One crossing on the long 36-hour boat from Spain to Plymouth in 1981, I reckon I did more miles running around that boat than El Gherrouj does in a year on the athletics Grand Prix circuit.

Good times, bad times applies as much to maritime travel as anything else though, and we did have some nightmares as well. With the old man away on business, Trot decided to take us back to England to see the family on the spur of the moment for New Year 1981. The only ferry not booked up was from Roscoff to Plymouth so off we went in the asthmatic old Allegro (see 'Shit Cars' section).

I was scared of night crossings at the age of eight. I didn't mind the ferry sinking and me dying as long as I could see. The captain decided to let off all the sirens at midnight to welcome in the New Year without telling anyone in advance. All my worst fears came true on the first honk of the sirens and I was scared rigid with fear. As soon as it had been established that the ferry was not sinking, Trot went off in pursuit of the captain. She found him and he got a lot of high volume advice from our extremely irate mother about how he should be using his alarm system as exactly that and not as an audio addition to the New Year festivities. He was very scared of Trot and I can't say I blamed him. She was on one.

Ferry trips rarely pass off without some form of anthropological oddity, occurrence or misfortune. Tom had already had a pretty bad day when me and he got on a Dover to Calais ferry in 1989. It was January and the grandparents had bought us the very generous, if fairly bizarre, Christmas present of a weekend in Paris. We were supposed to get across the water on a hovercraft but it was too choppy. This by definition meant it was going to be an interesting crossing, as rough seas invariably mean shallow stomachs. Poor old Tom had just had the front of one of his Converse All-Stars (his pride and joy and the trainers anyone who was anyone were wearing that year) ripped off by an escalator. It was the whole of the white vinyl bit on the toe ends; state of the art high fashion in those days. He was gutted.

To compound matters, the ferry left the harbour in a hell of a storm. We went to go out of the door shortly after the boat started rolling all over the place. As the door opened, some nauseous bird threw up all the way down the bottom half of Tom's jeans. I tried not to laugh, and succeeded for about as long as I had when he had the front of his trainer ripped off; a full quarter of a second. Then I was off and howling; unstoppable mirth, much to Tom's discontent. Poor sod, but I

126

just couldn't help it; it all happened so quickly. The things that happen on ferries.

That goes for cargo ferries as well as passenger ones. 'Have that you bastard!' Evans said. To call Evans competitive is by no stretch of the imagination an exaggeration. You could be staying in the seediest dive in the world and he'd bet you on which cockroach would make it to the other end of the room first. I was contemplating the aggressiveness of his chess technique as I took my trousers off, while watching a couple of seals messing around on a lump of iceberg. It was about ten in the morning and we were both drunk.

As I'm sure you've already guessed, we were playing strip chess on the top deck of a freight boat in the fjords of Southern Chile, and the rules were that you'd lose an item of clothing for every piece taken. We'd arrived at that point by a variety of means. Evans, being better at chess than me, was wearing a bit more clothing, but being better than me doesn't make him Nigel Short, let alone Kasparov. He was probably a T-shirt and a pair of strides ahead but I knew full well that he didn't have any long-johns with him, so the lead was slender.

Concentrating on my next move, I failed to notice the approach of a lady and the sourness of her countenance. She confronted Evans. 'Where's my husband?' she quizzed the grand master from Leeds. 'No idea,' retorted Evans. 'Same here,' says me. We weren't lying. Her husband had left the gaming table in the canteen the night before and had not been seen since. We'd been playing 'pyramid', a drinking game which can get the uninitiated drunk so quickly that by the time you realise you can't walk, it's too late. He was in a hell of a state and had attempted a tactical retreat at about 4.30 am. The good news was that he was eventually found sleeping in a heap somewhere as opposed to falling overboard.

The NAVIMAG is quite a strange carry on. First and foremost it's a freight boat, taking lorries and the like from

Puerto Montt to Puerto Natales, 2300 kilometres to the south. Second, it just so happens that it takes a winding route through some of the most stunning coastal scenery on the planet, and the extra cabins are filled up with gringos making their merry way down to the south of Chile. I'd hooked up with Evans and his travel companions Foxy and Cockings for the trip. We'd all originally met in Ecuador on a footy pitch, and had seen each other here and there every now and then ever since. We've also been friends ever since.

Up on the top deck of the NAVIMAG a couple of days later and luckily, due to the weather and proximity of icebergs, we'd made the rules feet friendly. Extreme strip chess where socks don't count. If we'd included socks, we'd both have been barefoot and have had frostbite as well as hypothermia. Why were we playing strip chess? No idea. We were coming out the back of a big night of drinking games and had probably failed to notice that it was daylight. With no clear winners after a five hour game of the global domination board game 'Risk' and then countless games of Pyramid, Evans and myself were pushing through the pain barrier. We had had a break for breakfast. You can't play extreme strip chess, especially at a latitude that southerly, without a full stomach. Apart from that, we were still technically in the latter stages of an all-night bender. I'm not sure that we reached a result in the chess. What I do know is that the bloke who nearly died of liver failure playing us at Pyramid was banned from associating with us by his sour-faced wife for the rest of the journey down to Puerto Natales. What a great trip it was too. Chile is the most incredible country, from its weird shape to its kind (if formal) people, to its beautiful scenery and National Parks. It really is a place I can't wait to get back to. From Puerto Natales we went on a trip to Torres del Paine national park, home to my favourite mountain on the planet.

Digression no 17 – good mountains

Coming in a very close but just outside the top three in the Fantasy Mountains League is the Rocher de Bellevarde in Val d'Isère, France. It gets a mention though for the simple fact that I get to look at it every morning on my way to work. Not the worst view whilst walking, what with its beautiful crags up top, our radio station transmitter perched on top, and the 1992 Olympic downhill course meandering down the front of the hill. Some mornings, when town is in the upper limits of a sea of clouds and the sun is shining above, you can see the Rocher de Bellevarde and its soulmate the Rocher de Charvet right next door through the cloud and I've always thought that must be what heaven is like.

In third place, the lovely Mount Kenya which merits further discussion later on as the first really high thing I climbed up and a good, solid, mountain-looking mountain.

A very close second, nearly as close as Alan Wells and Mike MacFarlane in the Commonwealth Games' 100 yard dash, is the Grande Casse in Tignes. What a beautiful lump of weather-beaten, triangular rock. First however, and my favourite mountain on the planet, is Cuernos del Paines, the mountain which looks like a tin opener in Torres del Paine National Park in Chile. Not a big posh tin opener like you'd buy out of Habitat but the tiny little sharp buggers that Armies the world over use. It's an incredible shape and an incredible National Park full stop.

It was a good day out that, both from a fiscal and a scenic point of view. We crammed the four of us into the tiniest little hire car I've ever seen. It was a sort of white rollerskate, and having your knees up round your ears didn't help. It was like being back in a Kenyan matatu but without the chickens and luggage.

I say from a fiscal point of view as well because after touring the park we were at a piss stop when Evans got competitive. He reckoned that I couldn't run to the top of this hill and back down in half an hour, which as the honed athlete I am, I did. Someone took a great photo of Evans with his head in his hands as I trotted back down the last few yards. Luckily, he'd put his money where his considerable mouth was and bet me a one hundred US dollars that I wouldn't do it in half an hour, so I was also better off. However, we'd all been on the road a good few months and funds were scarce, so we decided that Evans, despite being a muppet, should get the chance to win the hundred back.

I'd rather have the memory of his winning the hundred back than the money itself. Having moved on a country, Cockings decided that Evans had to get up on a table in Henry J Bean's in Buenos Aires and do ten twirls with his pants around his ankles. This he started to do, much to the amazement of the woman occupying the table he chose to stand on, and to the annoyance of the bouncer who rugby tackled him off the table onto the floor and dragged him unceremoniously out of the door about halfway through his routine. Foxy, Cockings and me were doubled over laughing and therefore identified as accomplices to the crime. 'Sale' isn't just the name of a rugby club in the English Premiership or a chance to buy some cheap clothes on Boxing Day; it's also means 'get out' in Spanish. We did.

End of digression.

Sailboats are the mutt's nuts of the maritime world, there's no doubt about that. We've also dwelled on the merits of travelling the oceans by ferry, which is also pretty cool if in a different, more hands off sort of way. Also not bad are inland waterways; getting around countries using the natural watercourses and much less natural, but no less useful, canal

130

network. I've only ever done this once but came away with a lot of great memories and a very favourable impression of travel by motor launch.

The great thing about being unemployed is that you can go out drinking at lunchtime. My brother Charlie and I were doing just that. In fact we were getting pretty pissed. The topic under discussion during this daylight drinking extravaganza was Tiny's wedding to some bird whose name escapes me.

Tiny wasn't. It was a nickname which must have been given to him as one of those reverse nicknames, because he was massive. A man-mountain. Charlie had been to college with him the previous year and we'd both been invited to his and his intended's wedding reception just outside Henley-on-Thames. The discussion had got specifically down to how we were going to get there as we were both carless at the time.

I don't know if I got my inspiration from the Thames-side pub we were sitting in at the time, the Swan at Radcot Bridge, but I said 'why don't we go on Grandpa's boat?' Five minutes later we'd made the call, got a favourable response and started our preparations. The main problem was that the wedding reception was on Saturday evening and it was Thursday afternoon when we had the idea; and we were drunk.

Meet *Jorvik* (Norse for York), Grandpa's twenty-three foot long motor launch, which was moored in Lechlade-on-Thames in Gloucestershire, where the grandparents lived at the time. From up there near the source of the Thames, at 6am on a Friday morning, started an epic journey. We had a great time. It was late spring, The Lightnings Seeds were riding high in the charts with 'The Life of Riley' and the weather was great. Loaded up with food, booze, gas, fuel and a large stereo, we headed downstream into the early morning fog.

The first thing to come out of the fog was Brandy, a fat and stupid Springer Spaniel we were acquainted with, who was trotting up the bank looking worriedly over his shoulder an hour and a bit downstream from Lechlade. Being nearly at Radcot Bridge, where the boat trip plan was hatched, we were passing the Hichens' farm on the north bank of the river. Next to break out of the fog, a couple of minutes after Brandy was Lionel Hichens, son number two, complete with shotgun crooked over arm, which explained the worried look on Brandy's face. It's quite surreal seeing a bloke standing six feet five inches come marauding out of a fog bank at that time of day. Had we seen his 'fucking idiotic imbecile of a dog, 'because I'm going to shoot the bastard,' was his first question-cum-qualified statement, to which we pointed him in the right direction. After thanking us and trudging off he turned back around and asked us what we were doing boating down the Thames at just gone seven in the morning. Good question. Only the Jones boys; it could only be the Jones boys.

Well I think I speak for us both when I say that it was one of the best holidays we've ever had. What a giggle. Eighty four miles it was to Henley by river and we made it in time for the wedding reception. We even stopped early on the first night at Sandford, just the other side of Oxford because they were doing nighttime repairs on the lock there. It was a good spot, though. We found a pub called the Fox which was in a time warp. It was all linoleum floors and Formica tables with a dartboard, but nothing modern like a fruit machine, pool table or jukebox. Considering that we had forgotten to stop at an autobank, had no credit card and were in pre-cashback 1989, it's lucky that the prices were in a time warp as well. We both got spangled on the thirteen quid and change we had between us.

The next day went well as did Tiny's wedding reception. After that there was the small matter of getting home. It was going to take longer than getting down there because we'd be going upstream of course. Being the Jones boys, or 'the Freak Brothers' as we're known in some circles, it took us four times as long to get home as it had done to get there. The downstream leg of the trip was good but we did have time constraints. Now on the upstream leg we could relax a bit and take our time. Being unemployed and prone to surrendering to the draws of the good life, we did just that.

The good thing about being out on the river is that nothing seems to be worth rushing for. For a start the pace is sedate anyway because there are speed limits to respect, and this slow progress tends to rub off on you. You can pull up and have a swim, cook breakfast and make endless cups of tea as you're going along, fling a bit of bread at the ducks and swans, or crack your first tinny at ten in the morning while pottering up the river. We did all of these. The Lightning Seeds being on the playlist of every radio station was just good timing because 'The Life of Riley' just seemed to sum up what we were doing on that trip. It really was The Life of Riley.

Boats are easy to drive. This was proved by the fact that we got to Henley and back without crashing. Considering that Charlie has crashed pretty much every vehicle known to man except for grandpa's motor launch is proof enough for me. The steering is a bit delayed on a boat but once you're used to that it's a doddle. In those days you were allowed to drink bevvies on the river as well. We got through a good number of slabs of cider and beer during the week it took us to get back, as well as a few long lunches. It's a bit naughty getting drunk while out in a vehicle but the sun was out and the ghettoblaster was banging out the hits; a combination of which just makes you want to flip the lid of a tinny. It's not as if we were getting paraletically drunk at the controls either. Consistent supping is an adequate way of putting it.

Mind you, it did get beyond that at times. When we eventually hit Oxford our progress slowed to a virtual standstill. After making very little progress one morning, we decided it would be a good idea to go to the Head of the River, a riverside pub as you come into Oxford from a downstream direction, for lunch. Steak and kidney pie was washed down with at least a gallon of bevvies each so as we rolled out of the beer garden at sixish, any thoughts of using the boat again that day had long since disappeared. Instead, we went for a bit of a tactical sleep on the boat and then went out on a pub crawl followed by a night of clubbing.

Needless to say we both woke up the next morning feeling like dog shit. Not the really fresh glistening stuff which gives all the signs of coming out the back of a healthy animal, either. More the white sun-dried stuff you used to see in the seventies. Why doesn't dog shit turn white in the sun any more anyway? With no provisions on the *Good Ship Venus*, we stumbled off to the supermarket and came back armed with the makings of a fry up, hot caffeine facilities in the form of tea bags, sugar and milk, and a couple of slabs of booze we bought by accident, or maybe habit? Running out of food is not in any way desirable, but would also not have put the whole expedition in jeopardy. Running out of disco juice on the other hand would have involved us getting some blood in our alcohol streams and that could have spelled serious trouble.

So there we were in the middle of Oxford, and things were looking up. Cumberland sausages, black pudding, loads of other fried things and PG Tips were taking care of the hangovers and we were underway again and heading upriver before eleven. I took the helm and after quarter of an hour or so rounded another bend in the river to see the Perch sitting there in front of me, three hundred yards distant. I don't write perch with a capital 'p' by accident. The Perch at Binsey; for the uninitiated, a great pub on the banks of the river Thames which you'd do well to visit at some point. For those in the know, a must stop situation. Charlie was sitting on a bench reading a magazine so I told him to come and have a look at what I'd found. 'Lunch' was his concise response to the view although I never really asked him whether it was a question or an order. Mind you, he didn't have to twist my arm. We moored up and took a good long while over the first pint, but after that hurdle they started flying down. Another day's river-boating had come to a premature end. Oh well. We fell out of the Perch at God-only-knows o'clock and went to bed.

After that, the pace picked up a bit, and I do mean a bit. The pace didn't reach Malcolm Campbell on Coniston Water sort of heights, but we did manage more than the five hundred yards a day pace we 'achieved' in Oxford. The rest of the return leg was just as much fun with us winding our way merrily through rural Oxfordshire on *Jorvik*. A couple more stops here and there, the longest of which was an over-nighter at the Swan at Radcot and then we were back. In fact Radcot lock was the only time we came even close to an incident on the whole trip. I nearly fell in the lock, but considering how many cans of piss we'd drunk each, we were fully expecting some sort of calamity long before then, considering that Radcot was three locks from the end of a journey which had covered about a hundred and seventy miles as well as fifty-two locks.

Back to the very maritime autumn of 2003 and bigger boats with engines. After a pleasant week and a half scoffing seafood on Gran Canaria at the end of our eight day sailing voyage on the Farr 50 *Dream Chaser*, I bade Ron, Cals and Mikey goodbye and headed back to the UK. I watched England squeeze past Wales in the quarter finals of the Rugby World Cup before heading off to Croatia via Venice.

Venice is a great place. For me it's not just the buildings which are impressive but also the way the whole place works. Venice is of course one of the most beautiful cities on the planet, be it architecturally, culturally or anything-ly. Call me a philistine if you like but, despite all the grandiose buildings, art and culture, it was the maritime way in which business is done in the place which fascinated me most. The way that that fair city has adapted to doing everything on water is mightily impressive. This was highlighted for me in three ways:

1)   In Venice, you don't just turn up and start building; there's the small matter of water. What do they do? Rock up with a barge on which sits a 360° excavator and start banging posts into the bottom of the canal. Come back an hour later and they've got the whole frontage shuttered up and the water pumped out, and the work is ready to begin. Brilliant. This grabbed my attention because it was going on right outside my lodgings. They were in the nascent stages of rebuilding a worn-out section of canal side pavement.

2)   So you've drained all the water. Next, where do you get the reinforce bar and concrete from? Enter the smaller members of the Venice fleet, the lifeblood of the city, the small delivery boats with a hydraulic lifting crane (or HIAB as we call them in in the UK). These boats deliver everything and anything to anywhere you can get by water in the city. From there on in its Piaggio three-wheeler pick-up all the way. It's another example of how humans adapt in adversity to a very impressive degree. I suppose it's just a fleet of floating lorries really, but the way Venice is supplied is of huge interest to the casual observer and especially to the first time visitor.

3)   Water taxis; how skilled are their drivers? One second you're cruising straight at the train station pontoon, and the next second you're pulled up next to it and hopping off of the taxi to go and get your train. I must say that despite being impressed, I would come to learn in the next two weeks that Venetian water taxi drivers still had a lot to learn, and that Croatian ferry captains were the big boys on the block when it came to doing stunts in boats.

PS - Venice rocks. Go there.

The maritime Autumn of 2003 changed countries again after a short train journey from Venice down to Ancona. From there it was back in the drink and a ferry across the Adriatic to the beautiful, interesting and Dalmatian former part of Yugoslavia that is Croatia. It all started so well. A couple of bottles of wine in the smoky, convivial atmosphere of the ferry bar before a Brit who lived in Italy offered me the spare bunk in his cabin. A good night's sleep replaced what I thought was going to be a hard night on a hard floor, pitting me and the handmade Norwegian sleeping bag with left hand zipper against the dark forces of insomnia in yet another strange and alien place. Instead, I woke up with the help of the ship's crew knocking on the door just before dawn. I was up and dressed and ready for what the day may bring.

Not wanting to put a dampener on things but I've seen enough films on the Second World War starring Burton, Sutherland, Peck, Heston, Eastwood, Wayne et al to know that all is not what it seems at dawn. Attacks happen at dawn. Our boat had docked at the pretty bleak looking port of Zadar, with the town itself a good four miles distant.

Digression No 18 – Customs Officers of the world part 4 (with a footnote from Ian Astbury)

Passengers were all called into the self-service canteen for a passport check from immigration. Great, good idea, was the first thought that came to mind. Better here than outside where it was looking not inconsiderably bollock-hardeningly cold. Then you spot 'It'; the customs officer of questionable gender, who you decide is a woman despite the stubble and shoulders like a Gary Glitter costume. What gives the gender away is the peroxide hair, wrenched backwards from the fringe into a bun at the back. She's sitting down because she knows she's still going to tower over the majority of people, so she can keep her air of authority and still rest her large but muscular behind.

Croatia produces some incredibly powerful women as well as some incredibly beautiful ones. Some are even both beautiful and powerful.

This one was only in the powerful category. Not fat, just powerful. Another example is Janica Kostelic, the Olympic and World Champion skier. She walked past our radio station window in Val d'Isère once. I thought it was an eclipse. What a woman. Legs like trees, and Californian redwoods at that, not some poxy, wispy little two year old birch tree.

Anyway, I've sighted this big Customs-style unit, and had her identified as a trouble maker from twenty yards. No surprise, I get to the front of the queue and say 'hello' with a bit of a smile. A glare is her response and after a couple of seconds of twanging, a 'what is this?' What she was twanging was a thin elastic and metal silver band which runs through the middle of my passport and down the spine. This band is very handy for holding Yellow Fever certificates, photocopies of driving licenses and passports and other essential bits of paper reticule in the middle of your passport. It'd been there for about seven years during which time even the most officious, workish border guards had not given it a second look. 'You have to take out,' she said at which point I obeyed.

I would have laughed at that point had I not been scared of her, because all her colleagues nodded like lapdogs, or brown-nosing MPs at Prime Minister's questions, despite the fact that some of them were obviously senior to her. They'd obviously had a good pasting off from her. She proceeded to ask me where every single visa in my passport was for, during which I watched all the other passengers and the bus which they travelled in drive off towards town.

I eventually alighted the ferry, post interrogation, to find rain and a little fat man in customs uniform and a huge hat – one of those stiff peaked military caps of a size reminiscent of the Soviet Union which are still favoured by North Korea and former Communist countries. Only the seeming absence of a neck and massive folds of fat stopped his head falling off from sheer top-heaviness. 'Bus?' I enquired hopefully; a question at which he just wafted an arm while searching for a word. 'Gone,' he eventually correctly conjugated. It was still raining. I thought nothing of the battered old skip lorry doing a U-turn outside.

No- neck then whistled with such force that he probably affected the outcome of a 'one man and his dog' heat in the heart of Wales. The skip lorry ground to a halt. Fat lad opened the door and skip bloke turned down his radio headlines from full volume to just below. The two Croats had a very brief discussion as to where the lorry was going, at which point I was invited on board! Result. I thanked Customs bloke, got in and shut the door, before saying hello to the smiling skip lorry driver. Then, we were off, at a speed which increased rapidly to well over what you would expect of a very old skip lorry. Between the noisy acceleration the headlines ended, and I could have sworn I heard a flanger-assisted electric guitar. Then, to confirm my suspicions, drums and another guitar exploded into life. Before you know it, the sweet tones of Ian Astbury came to the party and I'm flying into downtown Zadar, Croatia, with my feet on the dashboard of an ageing skip lorry, playing air guitar and singing 'She Sells Sanctuary' by The Cult! That doesn't happen every day. Hasn't happened again since anyway.

End of digression.

Croatia was the culmination of the maritime Autumn of 2003, and boy have they got it down to a T. Croatia is right up there with Chile and Uzbekistan in the strange-shaped countries league and has a lot of beautiful Dalmatian coast to its name as a result. It also has some 700 islands off of its coast as well. Result? Ferries, thousands of them. Much like Greece,

Croatia has little choice but to put loads of ferries on. It's either that, never see any of the island folk, build a lot of suspension bridges or drive up and down the coast. The last of these is the least desirable as all Croatians have been to the Italian school of stunt driving and are complete lunatics.

Getting a ferry down the coast is a much better, more relaxing and safer way of getting around the place. Of course, while roads are an option for coastal displacements, ferries are essential for getting out to the islands. The really impressive thing is that the driving techniques learnt from the Italians are also applied to maritime travel. It's quite a buzz going into a natural deep water harbour at flank speed thinking that the ferry you're on is about to make serious inroads onto dry land and up the high street of a medieval Croatian island town. My favourite buzz was upon arrival at the island of Korçula. Two hundred yards from the quay and Captain bloke is showing no signs of trying to slow the 9000 tonne roll-on,roll-off ferry down. I was not the only passenger glancing nervously up at the bridge for signs of someone pulling a big lever or other slowing down-related thing. And then, one 'drive it like you've stolen it' handbrake turn later, and he's only gone and parked the thing perfectly parallel to the quay. I doubt if ferries have handbrakes but he must have wrenched something. Very impressive.

Croatia is not just about the sea though. I may have given the impression that it's nothing but great coastline and islands, but not at all. Croatia will reappear later because it does have a hell of a lot to offer with its geographical diversity and great people.

The 2006 maritime experience has involved firstly, a week on a beautiful boat built in 1903 called *Kelpie* at Cowes week, and secondly, the Cape Verde archipelago and a lot of puke. The locals of the Cape Verde islands are pretty shallow gutted when it comes to travelling from island to island, and there's always a lot of puking going on, even in the lightest of swells. This makes travelling deck class pretty dangerous. The otherwise usually pretty enjoyable experience of sleeping in the ropes gets pretty dicey. Dicey as in diced carrots. Oh well, it's all part and parcel of being in the cheap seats, I suppose.

Last but not least in the 'afloat' section was a very surreal incident in the beautiful Gorges del l'Ardèche in southern France. My brother had been there the year previous and I went there on his advice. Very beautiful it is too and pottering down the river in a canoe was a good break from the motorbike.

Sail-power is not the only eco friendly way of getting around in a boat and in the Gorges de l'Ardèche it was shoulder power. Downstream, of course. I did a two day trip and stopped the night in a campsite where I got pretty muddled up on red wine with a load of Belgian lads and this French bloke and a Russian wife he'd obviously got off the Internet. I was following down behind the Belgians the next day when I noticed a nudist colony sign on the side of the river. With that, the last of the Belgians capsizes in a mini set of rapids and loses his paddle. As I came down the rapids I tried to back-paddle into the whirlpool into which the Belgian bloke's paddle had veered, but combine the previous night's festivities with my lack of canoeing talent and the force of the water and I failed, ending up down in the calm water twenty yards further on with the Belgians.

Help was at hand though. It came out of nowhere in the form of a wrinkly old bloke of about sixty five with straggly hair and a beard. He appeared from behind a rock and waded out into the river to get the paddle. He didn't have a stitch on, save for a pair of sandals, and his penis was flopping around like the trunk of an elephant leading the herd across Africa. I'd probably be a nudist if I had a knob that big. Bloody show off.

He brought the paddle down to where we were and stared at us without saying a word through a diving mask with lenses so thick that they probably started life as the bottom of 1930s Coca-Cola bottles. On then, after a nod to acknowledge our thanks, he walked off up the river with his bellend making a bit of a bow wave as it dragged upstream through the river. Bizarre.

As transport goes, that brings us to the end of vehicles powered by jet engines and the internal combustion engine. We've also had a look at the more natural power of the wind as a means of getting around. The next bit of getting around to painfully recount is transport by animal, and if you thought that our family had a fairly tenuous relationship with vehicles, the same can be said to at least as great an extent with animals. In this instance our old dear is the uncontested Queen of Misfortune. Not only that but she tends to combine a series of misfortunes to roll them into a massive disaster.

A case in point is the incident in which she lost her front teeth when she was twenty-one. Losing your front teeth is painful. I know; I knocked mine out on Paignton seafront by kissing some concrete at about 3 am, pissed right up, in 1992. The old dear did hers on a steering wheel but had the added advantage of a father who was a dentist. A bit of pain, but easily fixed and who's to tell the difference, especially as our grandad was the best dentist ever.

Not content with having no front teeth through a combination of excessive speed, ditches and combine harvester avoidance, she topped that the day after. Leaning over a fence to feed her pet donkey Zebedee, the bloody thing decided to go for a change of menu. It bit her top lip off, and nearly her nose as well. A lot of injuries make you wince when recounted to you, but to have that happen to you on a part of the body which is so visible is horrendous. It's safe to assume, I would have thought, that the old dear went from being a stunner on the Saturday morning to being pretty second-hand by Sunday

142

evening. The only good things to come out of the whole thing was the skill of the surgeons who looked after her injury, and the death of that bastard of a donkey.

I've never really considered our old dear to have any description of injury on her face. It's always looked totally normal to me. Plastic surgeons in the 60s had had so much practice with the huge number of burns victims from the Second World War, that they were able to fix her up really well. Her new top lip was made of flexible skin taken from the roof of her mouth. The donkey, well, he got the good news. Bloody right too.

Animals can be fairly difficult to get on with. I first found this out, in the equine sense, when on a pony trekking camp in Wales with the 2nd Brize Norton Air Scouts. It was a great camp and we had a great time, all things considered. I was assigned Bob, a brown pony, for the week. I could tell from the minute I first laid eyes on Bob that he was a bad bastard. That's probably a bit strong actually, but he had an attention deficit problem and a very thick mischievous streak. That first morning he looked at me with that 'come and ride my bus if you think you're not scared enough' countenance you get from public transport drivers in the Third World. Bob would be trotting along perfectly happily a lot of the time and then just stop, just like that, with no regard for what you told him to do or what the other ponies were up to. His ears would prick a bit as he surveyed the lie of the land, and then he'd run into a bush. Strange sort of an animal really. He'd only do it a couple of times a day and you were powerless to stop him but it just left me wondering why? Why run into a bush and just stand there? If only they could speak and explain such actions. Bob was good with planes though, as were all the ponies. On our first day out, two RAF Tornado fighter jets flew down the valley we were in about forty feet off the ground. All you could see were Air Scouts everywhere ducking for cover and falling off ponies. We had been warned that this might happen but nothing prepares you for the sudden rush of noise and speed. The ponies didn't bat an eyelid.

The next pony to look at me in a thought-betraying way had an expression on his face which said, 'surely you're not going to get on poor old me; you're six feet and thirteen stone and I'm on the brink of death anyway.' He was Colombian and looked like death warmed up. Imagine how surprised I was to find that he would gallop, flat out, without the slightest encouragement. We were in San Agustín in Colombia which is a town and an area of great archaeological significance. It's so spread out that walking it is unrealistic. Instead we got some horses and ended up with three contenders for the glue factory. Or so we thought. Tom got lucky in Ecuador a month later when we went riding in the 'Valley of Longevity.' He'd got a right goer there but this time got a nag which proved to be a medium pacer. Charlie got a right pig in a poke which wasn't at all keen. I got the equine equivalent of Thrust 2.

My brother has the most piercing whistle I've ever heard. It's very distinctive as well. In Colombia he used it to try and coax his old nag into going faster, or, in fact, anywhere. It didn't have the slightest effect on the animal or its speed, which remained at a painstakingly slow walk. My pony answered the call to speed with a lot more gusto. Having already mistaken a couple of gentle brushes of a stirrup on his flanks for a command to get as close to a new land speed record as possible, a loud, high-pitch whistle from a couple of yards away had him up to warp speed in seconds. I spent the first two hundred yards trying to remain in the saddle and calling my brother every name under the sun. By the time I had managed to get back into a vaguely upright riding position we were catching up with an ageing Toyota Land Cruiser. On the roof was an American chap with a big professional shoulder-held video camera, which he was pointing at me and psycho-pony. He was whooping and going 'yeah' which only encouraged my equine vehicle to dig deep and try to go faster. Not good news. Trying to stop the confounded animal by reining it in had no effect on our speed at all and by this time we were only five yards behind the 4 x 4. It was a dirt track and my sinuses were taking a lot of dust on board. With stopping not an option, I decided that we were going to have to overtake the Toyota and gave Red Rum a tap in the flanks. Not many horses overtake cars. That's an assumption, but probably quite a safe one. This one pulled out of the 4 x 4's slipstream and had actually got level before throwing in the towel and slowing up. I hasten to add that I had nothing to do with the decision to slow down and had long since conceded that the direction and velocity in which we would go around that bit of southern Colombia together would be dictated by the animal on which I was sitting.

If donkeys had fingers they would stick the Vs up at you pretty much constantly. They quite simply do not give a shit about anything. They're camels without the humps and syphilis. Bad bastards with a bad attitude and a very negative outlook on life. Sour grapes I hear you all cry in unison. Reading this you've all got to thinking; 'ah, well I can see the problem here. His mum's had her top lip bitten off by the one bad apple in the barrel and he's taking it out on the entire donkey population of the planet.' Not true. My mum's had a chunk taken out of her calf by a Border Collie. I still like dogs. I've been bitten by several dogs; I still like dogs. Donkeys. When have you ever met a nice donkey?

Merída, Venezuela—what a lovely place. By far the most chilled out town in a country of constantly simmering tension. This university town, perched up at 1640 metres is at the northern extremity of the Andes and also, amongst other things, home to the longest cable car in the world. Its other important claim to fame is that it is home to one of the world's biggest ice cream parlours which boasts over five hundred flavours. We had a great few days in Merida before going on a two day trip up into the Sierra Nevada National Park. The first part of the trip was completed in Jeeps before spending the night in the village of Los Nevados, a good way up in the middle of nowhere. What a great place. We stayed in some description of B&B with hammock beds. There was a festival on which was huge considering the population of the village and its far-flung, isolated location. There was lots of dancing, drinking, music and market stalls and a good time was had by all.

The next part of the excursion was undertaken on a collection of very obstreperous looking donkeys. We must have looked a pretty sight as we headed out of town, especially Andy, a tall Melbournian who was on the trip. At well over six feet, he made his donkey look very top-heavy once aboard. He hung around with me near the back after we quickly realised that our transport had done the trip a thousand times and would do it at their own pace no matter the incentives or otherwise. Tom had backed a winner, having been assigned a donkey which aspired to being a racehorse. His was off into the distance.

I had a sore arse after about 25 yards but had a great day on that bastard of an animal. Needless to say, the scenery was incredible and that National Park is teeming with wildlife. Not only that, but being on a donkey means that you don't have to carry anything; perfect for your average lazy bugger. The third advantage was a source of distraction almost as great as the scenery. It came in the form of a rotund little restaurateur from Kitzbühel in Austria.

As mentioned, those of us with either a realistic outlook on life, or a deep knowledge of donkeys' psychological make-up – or both – had long since given up trying to control our pigheaded carriages. Not the bloke from Kitzbühel though. His donkey had as little aspiration for the lead as those which Andy and I were riding. The difference being that we just sat there and accepted it, whereas the Austrian bloke did his damndest to catch up with Tom's and the other expedition frontrunners.

Tom's was the undisputed Peter Elliott of the field. Remember the chap who used to lead from the front in the 800 metres all the time only to be overtaken by Steve Cram on the final bend? Tom, while the hot favourite, was always within sight. That was enough incentive for the Austrian who had a bad case of Germanic over-competitiveness. It's the only time I've ever felt sorry for a donkey. He thrashed, tweaked, hit, pinched, kicked and cajoled that poor animal all day long, wanting nothing more than to overtake the field and pip Tom to the finish post. What a sad case. You can bet your last tenner on the fact that those donkeys have arrived in the same order every single time they've done the same jaunt, before and after our boney arses sat on them. Needless to say, he didn't get any joy out of the animal, which didn't once show the slightest sign of speeding up due to the Austrian ass-thrasher's efforts. Oh well, at least it provided us others with some entertainment.

Donkeys don't make up the entirety of the list of animals that you can but shouldn't attempt get around on. They could well not be the most unpleasant either. It's a real toss-up between donkeys and camels. The difference is that you meet quite a lot of donkeys who appear pleasant enough, who have a nice agreeable countenance. It's always a front and they all turn out nasty, but there you go. Camels are all horrible. They look at you with a superior, arrogant sneer and treat you like shit. Also, they smell and they've all got the clap. It's true! I'll admit that I'm biased and not exactly trying to pass off as Chairman of the Northern Hemisphere Pro-Camel Association, but camels, every single one on the planet, have syphilis. I really hope it itches as well.

Furthermore, having been to the biggest camel market in the world just outside Cairo, I can confirm to you that camels smell as well. Not as much as sea lions though.

Digression No 19 -- the aroma of sea lions

Jesus Christ on a bike do sea lions ever smell. They also cough, slaver, spit, sneeze, fart, burp, wallow around being fat and constantly fight each other. They're a sort of hybrid of Jabba the Hutt out of Star Wars and Chet, the unpleasant brother in the film *Woman In Red*, after Kelly LeBrock has cast her spell on him.

The only colony of them I've ever seen was in Mar del Plata in Argentina in 1998, shortly before one of the most spectacular asthma attacks I've ever had. I blame the ensuing breathing problems on the pong of those huge great big dirty smelly ocean- goers.

Mind you, they could have put their pong to good use this week. At the time of writing, George 'Dubya' Bush has been in Mar del Plata for an Americas Summit. His fellow heads of state could have done worse than to drag him down to the port and chuck him into the middle of the sea lions down there and watch while their pong and slaver slowly asphyxiated him to a miserable lingering and painful death.

Just a thought. End of digression.

Let's face it, there's no point in being kind. Camels are just a pack of bastards. Even if they do get narrowly edged out by sea lions in the fantasy animal bad aroma league, they're still the most obstinate bastards going amongst the planet's animals. What's more, they're boring to ride. I've never had the honour of sitting on a camel. Elephants are a good ride but I've always assumed that riding a camel is an activity you may

148

as well avoid at all costs. I'm sure I'll get round to it at some point though.

The other problem with this form of transport, apart from the fact that your vehicle is an obstreperous clap-riddled son of a bitch, is that if you find yourself on a camel, you're either on a racetrack in one of the Emirates or in the middle of a desert. The former is very unlikely and the latter is boring. I know this because a friend of mine told us about it during a cricket match once. He and his then girlfriend were camel trekking in Turkmenistan and he ended up being so bored that he had a game of five against one whilst in the saddle. Being in the middle of a desert is not like being on the M74; there are no cars or cat's eyes so games two and three of the 'Things To Do When You're Bored In A Car' are not possible. You're also outdoors and on your own so game one is not an option either. Therefore our anonymous friend, with his options seriously limited, decided to 'rough up the suspect'. Not only were they in the middle of nowhere but all the camels were about half a mile apart so he didn't even have anyone to talk to. As the raconteur suggested at the time, rod walloping is a strange activity to pursue while piloting a camel and is probably illegal in a lot of countries, but what else do you do? Sing a song, talk to yourself, sing to the camel or observe the approaching terrain. Or, have a wank. The wanker in question will remain nameless as he now holds a job of some import on the London social circuit.

Camels? you're better off walking. Or, you can find yourself a better animal to sit on. May I be so bold as to suggest the very viable alternative of elephants?

The main problem with this is that the chances of you being sat on a camel, thinking 'bollocks to this, I'll find a less obstreperous animal to sit on', jumping off and finding an elephant there waiting, are pretty slim. Camels and elephants don't tend to frequent the same bits of the planet. With that said, don't allow a crap voyage on one animal to dissuade you from trying different ones. Elephants are great to potter around on, easy going and mild of character.

Shanks' pony, an expression and piece of English slang I've never known the origins of. At the moment I can't be arsed to look it up as I'm drunk and watching the sun setting on Mount Athos in Greece before going to get another glass of wine out of the fridge, but I should really get round to looking it up.

What I do know is what it means, what it can entail, and the effects it can have on the human body. Shanks' pony means walking, an activity which I've pursued at varying speeds and levels of depression and wetness, in a lot of different regions on our planet. It's also the only method of displacement yet to be discussed in this here book but before we get to walking itself, let's get the variations on the theme out of the way.

1)
Running-- the fastest amongst the variations on walking, running is actually a valid activity because it's gets you to the pub in time for last orders. It has other uses as well such as catching a bus which would otherwise leave without you. Running can also stop you from getting killed, which is very useful. A dawn brush I had with some muggers in Cuzco, Peru highlighted this almost perfectly. I'd been out on the town all night with everybody who had done the walk to Macchu Picchu together. As already recounted, we'd had a pretty hard time of it over the four days of the trek and decided that we deserved a big night out on the town to celebrate the end of what was ultimately a successful outing. Weaving my way home at daybreak after finishing the night off in the brilliant 'Mama Africa' nightclub, I didn't really have my wits about me due to being pissed. Luckily, the lads who tried to mug me

were so incredibly unsubtle that even the pissed-up gringo that was me could still deduce what they were up to.

They drove past me in a small car and then all piled out of it a hundred metres or so further up the road. Then, after guiltily eyeing me walking up the street, all five of them pretended to be very interested in the contents of a shoe shop window.

I suppose it's possible that Imelda Marcos went shoe shopping at a quarter to five in the morning; I mean, you'd have to start early every day to accumulate two thousand pairs of shoes, which is what the former Filipino dictator's wife accumulated according to legend. But five dodgy Peruvians? I think not. So, I walked up within twenty five metres of them and stopped. Not knowing the Spanish for mugging, I informed them that I was one metre eighty-five tall and had a pair of steel toe capped boots on. I also told them that if they did attempt to mug me, at least two of them were going to get the good news and that I didn't have anything of value on me anyway. All of this was true except for the last bit. I had my passport on me which I valued a lot more than the few US Dollars and Peruvian Soles I had not blown that night.

While they were mulling all of this over, I turned round and casually walked off taking the first street at right angles I could, which luckily was only ten metres back downhill. As soon as I got round the corner, I pegged it. That's English slang for doing a runner, getting out of there as quick as possible. I'd already been the victim of one really bad mugging in Africa and really wasn't very keen on it happening again. Luckily this time it was in Peru. Six feet tall is pretty unheard of in Peru and with a shock of peroxide blond hair and a pair of steelies on, I probably wasn't the least frightening target they could have chosen. The best news for me was that it worked. They never even rounded the street corner and obviously decided that they'd go and mug someone who wasn't a deranged pissed-up gringo. So you see, running is just as useful for prolonging your life as it is for sporting activities.

2)

Jogging – my parents are still letter writers which I really like. It's all one way traffic I'm afraid as I've stopped sending them in the other direction, but it's great to get them. I used to write all the time but now that email has taken over, I've got lazy which is really bad. Emails are just not the same for some reason and every time an envelope turns up for me in the radio station in the Alps, I know I'm in for a few laughs.

My dad has a great habit when writing which is to collect newspaper clippings he thinks I'll find interesting and putting his comments on the bottom as to why he's included them. A couple of years ago he sent me one entitled 'Jogging – your shortcut to an early grave'. The old man had written across the top of the article; THERE YOU GO, I TOLD YOU SO! in big bold capitals.

The next time I spoke to him I pointed out that refraining from jogging was not a guarantee of eternal life and that he would probably do well to cut out the twenty full-strength, black tobacco, unfiltered French cigarettes he smoked a day back then. Knocking the fried breakfasts on the head might not do him any harm either, I pointed out.

But the old man did have a point. Jogging, another variant of walking, is a crock of shit, a completely pointless waste of time. For me the two worst types are the Londoners and the oldies. It's said that a half-hour run in Hyde Park in London is the equivalent of smoking twenty cigarettes a day. Presumably, people are doing it to improve their health. But not only does it not do so, it does the opposite. Add to this the fact that it takes up loads of time and that it pisses it down a lot in London and I reckon you're on a right loser.

Old people, just stop it. While I'm sure that there are some who are up to it such as the numerous octogenarians who run marathons, most old people who go jogging look like they're on the brink of death or at best, an ambulance ride and cardiac massage. Mind you, so do a lot of the younger ones. I'm all in favour of keep fit and physical exercise, but just go and do something else. Jogging is a ridiculous invention.

3)

Power walking – at least jogging doesn't look particularly stupid. Whereas joggers tend to be mostly normal people who are simply a touch misguided, the same cannot be said of 'power walkers', a strange breed who practice the weirdest offshoot of the whole walking world. Thankfully, my only live experience of this activity was on the Greek island of Kos a couple of years ago. I'd gone out for an early morning swim to get over the ardures of the night's clubbing which we'd just got back from. I wasn't really swimming but just lolloping about in the shallows and enjoying the early morning sun.

Then I started to hear some strange noises. Being pretty chilled out and quite knackered, I didn't bother opening my eyes until the noises, which were becoming progressively louder, got quite close. Imagine my surprise when I opened my eyes to see a couple of dozen Germans 'power walking' down the beach towards me with some short, squat and pushy woman barking orders at them.

They were from the German resort further round the bay and all looked very silly. I have to admit that despite this they were making very impressive inroads into the distance between me and them. Being a lazy lard-arse busy doing nothing, I knew that the shrinking of the distance between me and them had nothing to do with me. With that established, I decided that their stupid walking technique must work. Although they were wiggling their hips like Travolta's dance-mad Tony Minero, and pumping their arms up to eye level in a very military way, I had to admit that they were making impressive progress. But, in the final analysis, they did look stupid. The despotic barking which they had to endure in a coarse guttural language and the ridiculous Python-esque gait they had all adopted, combined to produce what I can only assume would be one the most miserable ways to see in a new day ever devised. I have the same amount of desire to see a power walker again, let alone a German one, as I do to get a job taste testing dog shit.

Despite the downsides of silly walking, the fact that it works is confirmed by the Olympic Games. Just have a look at the times that those athletes put in to walk fifty kilometres and you have to take your hat off to them. Mind you, you've also got to feel sorry for some of them as well. When saying that I'm thinking especially of the joker who got red carded with about four hundred metres to go in the fifty km walk in Athens. Walking has a yellow and red card system just like football, except that you don't get them for two footed tackles. In walking you get them for not having either foot on the floor. The rules dictate that you have to have one foot on the ground at all times because if not, you're considered to be running. That bloke at the Olympics in Athens got shown the red for a second offence while well in contention for a medal. The anguished look on his face as he gradually came to a grinding halt with tears in his eyes was one of the more touching moments of the games. He's probably taken up jogging now.

Right, with the variations on the theme out of the way, we can get down to discussing the activity in question, walking. That is the normal bona fide slow unwiggling version.

Trains, planes and automobiles are all good and well for getting around the place, but if you want to get right down to the nitty gritty of our planet and into the darker, more distant, less visited spots, you have to get involved. Walking is not only very good for you but also the only true access-all-areas method of transport around. In the fifty-odd thousand years between us coming down from the trees and the present day, mankind has still to invent another method of getting to all parts of everywhere other than the original one. We've invented roads which you can use to get here and there, as you can on train lines, underground tunnels and airborne vehicles. But, you can't get *everywhere* on them like you can on your own two feet.

Of course there are a lot of places which are accessible by other methods as well as walking. As already recounted at length, ten of us endured a pretty hard slog in 1998 to get to the lost city of the Inca Empire, Macchu Picchu. The four day walk is not the only way of getting there though. If you're loaded, lazy, short of time or a combination of the above, you can go to Macchu Picchu by helicopter from Cuzco in no time flat. This has its advantages and flipsides. Such options have the advantage of opening up sites of interest to people who would not otherwise be capable of getting there such as the disabled and frail, which is great. The flipside is that the world becomes a checklist of places that you have to go and see which you tick off without taking the time to fully appreciate when you get there.

Walking there tends to up your level of appreciation upon arrival at your goal. Believe me, because I've done it. If you arrive at the Sun Gate of Macchu Picchu at dawn with twenty kilos in your rucksack and four days of incessant rain and stomach cramps behind you, the time you take to stop and appreciate what is before you is a lot longer than it is if you've stayed in a five star hotel overnight in Cuzco before hopping onto a helicopter and doing the trip in a whirlybird. Mind you, I've never been jealous of the high budget, big camera and big belly travellers. I've been jealous of their hotel rooms and their hot showers every now and then, but never of their method of going to see stuff. That is not to say that it is in any way wrong to do it their way; not everyone has a lot of time on their hands, and the less time you have to go and do something, the more finances you have to inject into doing it. I'd sooner go up to Macchu Picchu by helicopter than not at all.

Macchu Picchu is a perfect example because it is at fairly high altitude. Some folk will spend ten hours on a plane getting to Lima at the end of which the older and less fit ones are probably teetering on the brink of Deep Vein Thrombosis anyway. After a night in the Intercontinental, they then fly straight up to Cuzco and get spirited up to Macchu Picchu with less than a day to get used to the altitude. No wonder that loads of them die of heart attacks and all that sort of stuff.

I'd like to think that my method of travel will never change, even in the very unlikely event that I ever accumulate enough money to travel in the style to which I have not yet become accustomed. You get to see so much more if you slum it and do it on a low budget. You shop in the markets, sleep in hostels in the more back end of town places, and you take more time to get where you're going. Our train and footslog four day method of getting to Macchu Picchu was not only healthier, but also cheaper and more interesting. The fact that large parts of it were miserable is just an unfortunate aside. You have to take the rough with the smooth when you're in the cheap seats.

Misery is a word which I would use while recounting several walking contracts I've completed and the unexpected crops up on pretty much every outing you make on foot. Macchu Picchu was by no means the first time I'd made pedestrian forays to interesting and beautiful parts of the world. It was also not the first time I'd endured hardship while doing so. A combination of the two was the result when Charlie and I set off on a four day walk around Mount Ruapehu on the North Island of New Zealand. I should have known it wasn't going to go totally according when the back left suspension of my motorbike collapsed on the way there from Lake Taupo.

Digression No 20 – New Zealand

Ruapehu sums up the geography of New Zealand to a T. A big mountain with big rumbles and ructions which blew its top with very little warning in September 1995. The eruption was of such a magnitude as to make the headlines worldwide, and it wasn't the first time. A previous eruption had made the international headlines a good long while before they were invented. Ruapehu erupted so violently in God-knows-when-BC that the fallout was visible in Rome and recorded on a block of marble or something for posterity.

We got there eighteen months after the latter of these eruptions to do the four(ish) day walk around the aforementioned and volatile mountain, which is in the heart of Tongariro National Park. Tongariro is a lovely spot and contains many of the variations in terrain and climate which makes New Zealand one of the most diverse, changeable and beautiful countries on earth. At roughly the same size as the UK, New Zealand is diversity personified and has pretty much everything the planet has to offer. The 'land of the long white cloud' boasts fjords with some of the highest annual rainfall in the world, a desert, glaciers, sub-tropical and temperate climates, and pretty much every other climate and geographical variation you'll find on the planet. It's the geographical equivalent of going to see Elton John or Cher in concert; seven costume changes in two hours.

End of digression.

A four day scenic trek through some beautiful and ever-changing unspoilt back country. Sounds fantastic doesn't it? Didn't quite go like that though. As happened on Macchu Picchu a couple of years later, it all started so well. The first day was a lovely if hard walk during which we started our clockwise circumnavigation of Ruapehu. It was good but hard

157

going with rucksacks and all, but the stunning scenery takes your mind off the physical side of things. For a large majority of the day we had stunning views of Mount Tongariro itself, which is a beautiful and almost perfectly isosceles triangular mountain. We got to the first night's hut in plenty of time and cooked up some grub before hitting the hay. All was well, as it was the next morning when we headed out on day two.

The highlight of the second day was just before the arrival of the tropical cyclone. Having walked a good way further round the girth of Ruapehu, a lot of it spent looking down on New Zealand's only desert, we arrived at a five meter wide river. Charlie fell in it. Now it's obviously for the companionship and banter that you go travelling with other people. It's also for moments like that though. It's a sorry world if you can't thrive on your mate's misfortune, which is what I was busy doing. The Germans even have a word for this activity; 'Schadenfreude'.

My laughter came to an abrupt halt when I realised that Charlie had fallen in and got back out of the river completely dry as a bone. He'd spent all summer working in an outdoor sports shop in Kingston-on-Thames and had bought all the kit. Mr 'All the Gear and No Idea' had got out of jail for free thanks to a pair of Gore-Tex hiking boots and a pair of posh leggings. Life just isn't fair sometimes. When he slipped in I thought I was going to get a hefty amount of mirth mileage out of it.

Any mirth we had enjoyed up to that point very quickly vanished with the arrival of a low front which it was quickly apparent was a lot worse than your communal garden low front. The weather got so bad, so quickly that we spent the rest of the day staring at our boots and trudging doggedly on to the next stop.

The first thirty-six hours of that trek were glorious from both a weather and scenery point of view. The following twenty-four were not. We experienced every single type of weather you can encounter on earth during the course of a single afternoon's walking; sunshine, snow, fog, rain, hail, sleet and cloud, all in very quick succession. The whole lot was blown into us by an ever strengthening wind which, by sunset, had reached gale force.

By the time we got to the Massey University mountaineering lodge it was blowing a right hoolie. The winds must have been gusting at seventy or eighty miles per hour and pitching our tents was out of the question. So, wet, tired and miserable, we got installed in some public toilets and tried to get warm and dry things out a bit before cooking something to eat. A miserable night trying to keep off the wet floor was ahead of us. After half an hour or so I decided to go over to the mountain lodge for a look and found exactly what I was after. It was only a log shed and had very little space in it, but it was very well built and totally windproof, more than could be said for our current camp. It also didn't smell like shithouses which was a bonus. Before going to get Charlie I nipped round the corner to find the door of the lodge itself open! Jackpot! I was so tired and so wet that I punched the air all the way back to Château Shithouse.

An hour later and we had a roaring fire going, all our clothes hung up and drying, and a gargantuan amount of pasta which would have fed a couple of dozen on the flames. After a cracking night's sleep we set off again into the storm the next morning, having left a note for the next university trip to say that it wasn't us who'd bust their window, but thanks anyway for the hospitality. Little did we know that although we were now in the tail-end of it, that storm would become the first of two tropical cyclones to hit Fiji in the space of two months that year.

We were going along at a fair lick and could probably have finished the walk on the third day. Instead, we finished early and put our feet up at the last of the refuges on the tour. Charlie spent the evening correcting all the spelling mistakes of an over critical complaint entry in the visitors' book before signing it 'Smartarse' at the end. I contemplated this and that. At least we weren't alone in having a hard time of it. A Danish chap who was a day ahead of us had signed the visitors the night before after writing the following; 'What a terrible day. I neither saw or enjoyed anything'! My god did we ever know how he felt.

Another banging night's sleep and a well deserved lie in, followed by a bright morning and things were definitely on the up and up. The weather improved somewhat and we got back to where we'd started and got pitched and set up in the campsite we'd stayed in the night before heading out. A shower and a scrub up brought us up to early evening at which point we went out and got battered on alcohol after having a good meal. Can you see a pattern emerging? Four days of misery and then a big piss-up.

We'd pretty much agreed that we deserved a big piss-up after such an arduous Ruapehu trek despite the fact that we were on a pretty tight budget. Sometimes you've just got to go big and have a blowout. The plan was to go out, have a good meal, get leathered and have a lie-in before doing a few hours riding the next day.

With that you'd have thought that our ordeal was over. Well, for Charlie it was. Despite being plastered we successfully weaved our way back to the campsite and into our tents. Each of the plots was separated from next by little dwarf privet hedges, so although in my own little bit, I was only about three yards from my next-door-neighbour's tent. He turned out to be them; a couple; two blokes; two very vocal German blokes. I was just slipping into and very much looking forward to another night of reverie when the lovers returned to their love tent. They proceeded to bugger each other senseless

160

all night complete with sound effects. They grunted, groaned, panted 'ja, jA, JA', and generally really pissed me off by kicking each other's back doors in all night and keeping me very much awake. No matter how loudly I or others close by told them to shut up, they just carried on hanging out the back of each other, and I really couldn't be bothered to get up and set fire to their tent. Charlie was some thirty yards away and slept through the whole sordid coupling but that didn't stop him laughing for a good long while when I told him of my sleepless night the next day. 'Schadenfreude' is a two-way street, and it gets even worse in the next animals section.

Despite the ardours of undertaking big treks, walking is a great activity as you'll know if you're a lover of discovering new places and satisfying your curiosity on foot. It's not just the scenery along the way and the adventure of discovery which makes it so fulfilling though. The best bit about walking is the getting there. Arriving at the place you've been toiling to get to for X number of days, or if you're in the big boys league, X number of weeks. Not only can you sit down and relax for a while and take a well-earned rest, you can also take solace in the fact that being at the top, it's all downhill from there on.

That's how I felt at the top of Point Lenana, the highest place I've ever trudged up to. At 5199 metres, it's the highest point you can get to on Mount Kenya without full mountaineering equipment, and is it ever worth it. We were very lucky in that we happened to get to the top on a morning when there wasn't a cloud in the sky. The view was truly unforgettable. Kilimanjaro, the highest mountain in Africa a couple of hundred miles away to the south and the Great Rift Valley winds its way between the two mountains.

It's when you've got a view like that in front of you that you develop a selective memory and suddenly forget all the toil you've gone through to get there. Such stunning scenery gives aches, pains, blisters, cold feet and other mild discomforts a real feeling of irrelevance. I just sat there with Charlie and Simon and we were all dumbstruck for ages. Silence is a rare event with us three together but the combination of fatigue and the scenery before your eyes can shut even the biggest of motor-mouths up every now and then.

Digression No 21 – just doing it

Mount Kenya is living proof that life used to be more straightforward and spontaneous than it is today. Before we left for Africa, Ellie's dad was telling us about his trip up Mount Kenya during his national service with the British Army. Him and some of his colleagues decided to go skiing on the glacier we'd just walked up on the way to Point Lenana. They took route one though; a helicopter. Now heading up to over 5,000 metres in a helicopter is a risky business nowadays, let alone in the sixties and, although the whirlybird got them there, the air was too thin for it to take off again. The pilot had to slide down the glacier on his runners with the rotor going full pelt until he was low enough to get some lift! How cool is that? Bet you a fiver his arse was puckering a bit though!

It must have been ace to live through an era when there were less rules, less forms to fill in, less health and safety officers and more risks taken. As the saying goes on the No Fear T-shirts; 'If you're not on the edge you're taking up too much room'.

End of digression.

In the scheme of things, the Mount Kenya expedition was quite successful by our standards. A few problems were encountered though, mainly caused by the miniscule brains which the three male members of the party posess. Problems encountered were;

1) Coldness-- Charlie was well pleased with himself at Heathrow airport as he proudly announced that the summer sleeping bag he'd brought with him weighed just over half a kilo. A month later and he was in my tent at the last camp before the summit of Mount Kenya so cold that he'd put on every single piece of clothing he had with him before getting in his sleeping bag, and shoved the foot end in his rucksack for good measure. That'll teach him.

2) Hyraxes-- Strange little animals really. Hyraxes are a breed of African rodent about the size of a small rabbit whose nearest genealogical relative is the elephant. I thought that was a wind up to start with but it is in fact true. Strange though considering that the two animals, apart from both being quadrupeds and living on the same continent, couldn't be much more different if they tried.

The problem we had was that they were using our tent as an adventure playground and as a food source. The little blighters were running clean over the top of our tent and making a good amount of noise while they were about it as well. Charlie was too cold to get to sleep and I was kept awake by our rodent friends. The other sound effect which wasn't helping was Ellie's screaming, which happened every time a hyrax ran over her and Simon's tent.

When we came to take the tent down a day later we also noticed that hyraxes appear to find nylon straps tasty. They'd eaten a couple all the way through on my tent. Generally pretty annoying little critters, those hyraxes.

3) Coldness part 2 – none of us had gloves. Ellie had decided not to go to the summit and remained at the last camp to play with the hyraxes. The three of us remaining set off to the summit of a 5,200 metre mountain with no guide, no gloves and no common sense. Being pikey, tax-free, grubby and penniless students we would rather have died a cold, miserable and frostbitten death than fork out some coins for such

essentials as gloves. We're the sort of people that mountain rescue teams around the world dread the most. Just a thought, but why is common sense called 'common', because there's not a lot of it about? As you've probably worked out, I have none whatsoever as far as I'm aware. It just goes to show that higher education is overrated. Top five percent of the population my arse. Back in those days we were all undergraduates but a decade later, we've all been graduates for a good long while, and we're all still stupid.

4) Geography – Mount Kenya is one of the most frustrating places I've ever walked up. That's mostly due to the second day, much of which is spent in a steep and strange terrain full of pampa-like reeds on little hillocks. It's known as the 'vertical bog' and it's very hard work, and pretty slippery just to make matters worse. The real bummer though is that it's got loads of false horizons on it and just when you think you've got it licked, you're in fact just getting to the brow of another hill and another 500 yards of vertical bog appears before you. This happens about twenty-five times during the course of the day, and becomes more and more demoralising each time.

The morale-sapping powers of this terrain are compounded by the guides and porters who overtake you all the time. Not only were they twice our age but they were carrying twice as much kit as us as well. We would be huffing and puffing our way up with no breath spare to talk to each other and a couple of chaps would gently overhaul us with that comfortable African gait. It looks totally effortless but is also surprisingly quick. Before you know it they're out of sight and long gone.

5) Memories – the saddest thing about the East Africa trip is that I got caught offside in Mombasa a week or so later and was mugged at sword and machete point by a pack of bastards who nicked all the photos of our trip up to that point, including all our snaps of the Mount Kenya expedition. I was well pissed

off with myself because it was one hundred percent my fault. I was dithering along about ten yards behind the other three and that was it. Before I knew it, I was on my back and it was all gone in a flash.

What really worried me was that after they'd got the small rucksack off of my front, the bloke standing over me with a cut off sword complete with scabbard, started to wave it about. Up to that point he'd stood as still as stone and remained very calm. When he started waving the sword about I thought he was going to stab me with it. Luckily, he didn't, and what was strange was that the prospect of being stabbed didn't stress me. Maybe I didn't have time as it was probably only five seconds between him starting to wave it and him running off with the rest of them. I just laid there like a turtle wallowing around helplessly on his shell. My big backpack was performing the shell role in my case.

I'd let the side down big time but the loss of a few replaceable possessions was nothing compared the other possible outcomes from the mugging, such as death. Life is very, very cheap in Africa and why not kill someone if you have nothing to lose anyway? At least then there's no chance of them identifying you. It was the photos I regretted losing as they could not be replaced.

The best thing of all was that Simon didn't get injured. I would never have forgiven my stupidity if he had. He ran back up the road when it all kicked off and started rucking with a couple of the muggers. I'd been shouting at him to stay away, that they had knives, but he didn't hear me and, because the sword wielder standing over me had his back to Simon, he didn't know that he had a sword. Luckily, neither of us were harmed. Well, I was on the inside. Pride for one. My lungs also took the brunt of the attack as well. I still smoked back then, and, once the shock of it all kicked in, I smoked a whole packet of fags in about an hour, I reckon. We were smoking a lovely local brand with toasted tobacco called 'Sportsman'; a bit of a contradiction really.

By now, you're probably thinking 'why doesn't this idiot just give up walking to places?' The simple answer is that despite a few disasters, bits of bad luck and near misses, I have actually done a lot of very enjoyable walking as well.

The highlight of all these was going up Uluru, the extraordinary natural edifice that is Ayers Rock. This is another place on earth I've had the luck to have been at the top of for daybreak. It was in about February 1999 when me and Foxy were touring Australia in a beaten up old Mazda 626.

Uluru is very dangerous. It's a very steep, hard lump of rock. Therefore, if you fall while climbing up it, you tend to die. The numerous plaques at the start of the climb are proof of this and we also set off in the dark just to complicate things. With my track record of walking disasters, you'd be justified to think that a major life ending catastrophe ensued, but as it goes, we got up and down without any worries at all and also timed it perfectly, getting to the top about five minutes before daybreak. It really was pretty spectacular sitting on the top of the world's largest natural monolith as the 'beast from the east' bathed us in early morning sunshine. To top it all, the dawn sunshine wasn't the only thing Foxy and me were basking in.

Digression no 22 – Peoples of the world part 3 – pretty victories and Germans

Germans are known worldwide for their ugly language, beautiful cars, gas chambers, meticulous planning, driving ambition, naked frolicking, and extremely early sun-lounger reservations. To say that Germans are competitive is no exaggeration. If you need any proof of this I refer you to the chapter on transport by animal and the Austrian donkey thrasher. Germany and Austria are of course permanently and indelibly linked, even if it is a case of one Anschluss and one bad bugger ruining it for everyone.

Considering this national will to win and succeed, imagine the disappointment of a panting, sweating German chap coming over the last brow hot with the excitement of being the first person that day to reach the top of Uluru, only to realise he was in fact third. He saw me and the Fox, went grey and said 'scheisse' in a very resigned and frustrated tone. We knew why he was so disconsolate and pissed ourselves laughing. Fritz's depression plunged new depths when he found out that not only were we British but we also couldn't have given two hoots whether we were first to the top or not. It was abundantly clear that being the day's first summit conqueror was his first and only goal for the day. Scheisse indeed.

What is it about Germans? Being British I obviously have a 'them versus us' approach to the relationship and any self-respecting Englishman or woman knows where he was on the evening of the 1st of September 2001 regardless of whether or not they're football fans.

Although there is no love lost between our countries, I rather like Germans. I don't like them all but then again you'll never find a race or creed which you like in its entirety. A good example of two Germans I don't like are the two whose high volume bum sex kept me awake earlier in this chapter. For the most part they're okay though, just like any other race on the planet. Around these parts (I'm back in the Alps) they're renowned for their organisation and preparation. If you want to know how long a ski lift is going to take from bottom to top, ask a German. I consider myself too interesting and not nearly anal enough to know that much information about the ski resort in which I live. It's what I call Bernhard Langer syndrome. The legendary golf commentator Peter Alliss was talking about the German love of precision on the TV one day and was recounting a time when Langer had asked his caddy how far it was to the pin. 'A hundred and fifty seven yards,' the caddy informed him. 'Is that to the front of the hole or the back?' was Langer's straight faced response!

That's not to say that Germans are not capable of laughing, because they are. More importantly, they are also capable of laughing at themselves. Monty Python is pretty big in Germany and the team even did sketches in German. *'Allo 'Allo*, the BBC comedy set in Nazi-occupied France, was popular in Germany but flopped in France. This is testament to the Germans' ability to laugh at themselves and the inability of the French to do likewise.

Germany and its population are slowly emerging from the shadow of war guilt which is a good thing. We met this lad in South America who said he was German in a low voice while looking at the floor. Someone told him not to beat himself up about it but he said that he was ashamed to be German because of his country's history. That was, as you can imagine, a bit of a conversation killer!

Why should he be ashamed though? At the ripe old age of twenty-something, he had nothing to do with the atrocities of sixty years ago. There are a few Germans left in Latin America who did, but he isn't one of them. True, the worst human-on-human atrocities in history were carried out in Germany's name, and having visited one of the camps in which they took place I can confirm that it's pretty horrific stuff. What a lot of Germans forget is that a lot of bad shit has gone down since, as well as before, the Holocaust. It doesn't in any way condone the Nazi's behaviour but we've all done it. I'm British, we invented the concentration camp. I'm also English and we've been slaughtering and starving our immediate neighbours for centuries, since before records began, in fact. Stalin boasted to Churchill that he'd killed twenty million of his own people, far more than Hitler ever managed. Mao killed about 75 million of his own people according to some estimates. What about Pol Pot in Cambodia, Idi Amin in Uganda or Mengistu in Ethiopia and Pinochet in Chile for that matter? The list goes on. They all made Attila the Hun look like a kindergarten teacher. The current leaders of the free world, the Americans, systematically betrayed and wiped out the majority of the North American indigenous population with gusto and in no time flat – see Bury My Heart at Wounded Knee – and only kicked their own apartheid in to touch relatively recently. The list of bad bastards mankind has produced is endless and is certain to get longer.

Germans beat themselves up about the twentieth century and their large (albeit mostly negative) contribution to the forging of its history, but every other country on the planet has got a good dollop of shit on its shoes as well.

Having said that Germans are okay, it is good to beat our old foe at footy every now and then. There's something very satisfying if wholly immature about petty victories, whether they take place on grass, mountains, monoliths or deckchairs at dawn.

End of digression.

Lastly on the subject of walking is how to make it easier. I have the answer, no word of a lie. All you have to do is break your leg. I mean it. Do that and you get a pair of crutches and walking becomes well, easy. It's not all good news though. There is a bit of suffering to endure as the skin is flayed from the palms of your hands and you experiment with a variety of pads to cushion your hand grips.

However, once you've got new thicker skin and you've worked out how far in front of you you need to plant your crutches for optimum pivoting, you're off. I was on crutches for the majority of 1988-9 and loved it. Even better is when you realise that hopping once between two conventional crutching strokes pretty much doubles your speed, and suddenly you can get from home to the Red Lion in Alvescot in under ten minutes! Fantastic.

Languages

If you believe in that sort of thing, God at some point decided that he'd had enough of all the different peoples of the planet bickering and arguing with each other. There are of course much more plausible explanations of why we don't all speak the same language, but hey, what's the point in letting the facts get in the way of a good profit-making yarn?

God's solution to the problem was to give each race a different language so that they couldn't understand each other, and therefore couldn't argue. And, it works. God – existence and gender to be confirmed – may have taken a bit of a rash decision as a kneejerk reaction to the high levels of annoyance incurred by the humans of the planet, but it's all worked out pretty well. Languages are one of the things which make travel worthwhile and which bring about some of the most hilarious moments in daily life.

When asked why he and his French girlfriend never argue, a Dutch-American friend of mine here in the Alps simply says, 'because we can't'. He's right. She doesn't speak English and he doesn't speak French. Problem solved. The next question this raises is obviously how the hell did they end up in bed together in the first place? Not the sort of gory details we need to be told about. It is a good example of the language barrier though and very carnal proof that no linguistic problem is insurmountable.

Languages are also a growth industry and an area in which there is a lot of money to be made. My very existence here in the Alps is financed by the fact that not all people who come skiing know how to speak the language of the country in which they are practicing their sport. Up here in the middle of nowhere, not everyone speaks French but everybody needs access to information about the resort and the mountain. Therefore there is Radio Will. Not the sharpest tool in the box as anyone in town will tell you. Not always registering a high score on the sobriety-ometer either, especially on the morning show. BUT, in my defence, I do speak English and French, which comes in handy every now and then. Having said that, I'm not making a lot of money out of it but who cares? Your bank balance is the last thing on your mind when your skiing chest-deep champagne powder off-piste in the sun with not a cloud to be seen. Unlike all those interpreters you see at the European parliament who are earning about national-debt-of-Mexico-an-hour, I'm in the roof of Europe with the earning power of a seven-year-old Pakistani sewing Manchester United footballs together in a Lahore sweatshop. It makes all those years of higher education seem so worthwhile!

While it is undoubtedly a great asset to be able to speak more than one language, it does also have its pitfalls. It's usually at times when you're winging it that you end up laughing uncontrollably. 'Winging it' in the linguistic sense means that you're trying to translate words for which you don't know the corresponding word in another language but give it a go anyway. This does not present a problem if you're translating say, English into Japanese or French into Hindi, as the two languages you are using are not derived from the same source and don't even use the same alphabet. Take two languages with the same origins, however, and the water is deeper, the cliffs higher, and the scope for disaster infinitely greater.

My worst moment in this respect came in the chic Norman coastal resort of Deauville in France in 1988. I was a sixteen-year-old virgin working with my dad on the market selling typically British clothing, such as Barbour jackets and knitwear, to holidaying Parisians. We were the only British stallholders in the market and as a result, if another stall holder was asked something by an Anglophone tourist, we would occasionally be asked to translate. Just down the way was the formidable and scantily clad Madame Lopez, who was Venezuelan. She sold mariner's bread but all the other stallholders said that she supplemented her income providing sexual services to the masses. Having observed the severity of gossip in market culture, there's no doubt that the chances of this being true are very slim.

Mariner's bread is made to an old time recipe which would allow ships in the old days to preserve it by keeping it in a damp rag. By this method and with the special recipe, the coarse but tasty bread would not go stale for about a month. Mme Lopez used to use all of this as her sales pitch when flogging bread to the tourists of Deauville.

She asked me to come over one day as she had an English woman who had a question to ask her. 'Are there any preservatives in the lady's bread or is it totally natural?' asked the tourist. Now it's at times like this that 'winging' comes into it. I didn't know the word for preservatives in French. However, at times like these you have to remember that there are 3,000 words in French and English which are written the same and mean the same thing. This knowledge gives you the chance of a shot at the title without really knowing what you're doing. The accepted method is to take the English word and say it in a French accent. On this occasion I had a pop and missed in a way only mullet-sporting Geordies in Italia 90 have done since. I asked Mme Lopez, 'Est ce qu'il y a des préservatifs dans votre pain?' She erupted with laughter and repeated what I'd just said at a volume capable of reaching several postcodes. 'Il vient de me demander si j'utilise des préservatifs dans la fabrication de mon pain,' she laughed. Everybody else erupted with laughter as well, tourists and stallholders alike. I proceeded to go telephone box red and retreated to the Bar des Sports for a tactical coffee. As I quickly surmised, I'd asked her if there were any condoms used in the making of her mariner's bread!! As a sixteen-year-old innocent, I didn't know the French word for 'Mr Happy's business suit' was 'préservatif' and the result was much hilarity for everyone else and much blushing for me.

In nine out of ten cases you guess right because French and English are so similar so much of the time. BUT, it's the one out of ten which is not which is fraught with danger, and can go disastrously wrong. When it goes wrong, it goes badly wrong. In Deauville, not only did the wheels fall off but the engine blew up as well. It's a lot safer to stick to languages with no similarity as, at least then, you're not remotely tempted to give 'winging it' a go. Being from the Basque Country is the way forward in this sense as their language bears no relation to anything else on the planet.

Our dad had first-hand experience of this problem as well. He first worked in France when it was still very rare, at the end of the sixties. Having had a few rudimentary lessons to pick up the basics, he arrived in Normandy to start up a pig breeding unit. Sitting down for supper on his first evening in his hotel's restaurant, he noticed he didn't have a fork at his place setting. 'Je n'ai pas de fourche,' he said to the waitress who had a bit of a smile on her face when she came back with a fork a second later. A fork and a hayfork perform similar tasks but on a slightly different scale. The old man would have looked pretty silly trying to eat his grub with a hayfork but that is what he'd asked for. *Fourche* and *fourchette* are pretty similar words, but not that similar. However, despite his error he had achieved the primary objective in all such situations, which is to get what you want.

Anyway, day two comes around, as does supper on evening number two. The hotel, the Soleil d'Or in Montfortsur-Risle, also doubles as the main drinking establishment of the village, and so the bar, which adjoined the restaurant, was full of locals drinking their apéritifs, and probably quite a lot more besides. Lo-and-behold, the old man sits down and there's no fork at his setting so he again asks the waitress for a 'fourche', as he had done the night before. Of course, this time it was a set up and as soon as he said it, a large eruption of laughter took place behind him. He looked over his shoulder to see the whole of the bar's custom sticking their heads around the door to wait for the English man's error. Having achieved the desired result the night before, i.e. getting the use of a fork, he assumed that he'd got his French right; and he wasn't far wrong, just not a hundred per cent right.

He's not the only member of our family to take foreign language classes. Tom very sensibly took some Spanish lessons for a week when we were in Quito, the capital of Ecuador. It's not a bad place to do so, what with its good nightlife and World Heritage Site old town. Charlie and myself, being a bit more basic, decided to travel down to Baños, a spa town down south, for a week of partying instead. Tom arrived a week later to find us in full party mode and having aged a lot more than a week's worth due to a lot of partying. Off we went for lunch. 'You learnt a lot then,' chuckled I; 'Good language course' added Charlie, laughing. Tom thought he'd ordered a pizza for lunch but was brought two glasses of orange juice instead! As it goes it was only a minor glitch and he had actually learnt a lot of Spanish during his week at school.

The language gap takes on new dimensions in different parts of the world. Alphabets can cause a lot of trouble. There are a lot of different ones and it doesn't make things any easier if you can't read or speak. That's not to say that it's automatically easier if you're in a country which uses the same alphabet as your mother tongue. Hungary; what is that all about? Lovely people and very beautiful women. Generally a pretty fantastic country, but the language, well, what a nightmare. Pottering through Eastern Europe on a motorcycle is a pretty good way to spend a few weeks. From a language point of view it had all gone pretty well. France, Germany, Czech Republic, Poland and Slovakia are all a bit complicated but not insurmountable. I'll give you an example: Police. Same in English, French, *polizei* in German. Okay, so it's changed a touch but still okay. Same goes for all ensuing countries until you get to Hungary. *Rendõrség*. What sort of a word is that to describe your law enforcement community? I knew I was in communication difficulties before my first human contact with a Hungarian citizen.

That happened to be a prostitute who spoke very good English. Thanks to her language skills we were able to establish that I didn't want to have sex with her. I just wanted to confirm that I was on the right road and she was able to give me that confirmation. Then she reiterated that if I wanted to pay her for what was on offer, the act would not be a roadside knee wobbler but a much classier visit to a barn on her uncle's farm, complete with straw to cushion any thrashing about which may occur. I should probably have said yes as she was very good looking, but thanked her and rode ever onward toward Budapest.

I had a great time in Hungary but never really made any improvements in my knowledge of the Magyar language. I used to eat lunch every day in a mama and papa stand up joint which are typical of Hungary. There are no chairs but high counters and a pot of paprika powder. Hungarians, like all humans, have to have oxygen and water to survive. Where they differ, though, is that it would appear that they have to have paprika to survive as well. They put it on everything. The food was invariably delicious. Deciphering the menu was a different matter though.

The old, very small lady owner used to start talking to me as soon as she spotted me joining the back of the queue. As I got nearer the front I used to have a look at what people had selected and point to something that took my fancy. If I got to the front and shrugged my shoulders, the old lady would simply give me a bread knife and I'd point at something on the menu. This would make her laugh to the point of tears while she put my lunch on a plate. It was usually about 50 cents and always absolutely delicious. Central and Eastern Europe is a fantastic part of the world from every point of view. Gastronomically, it is a true delight. I remember one day in that place in Budapest I pointed at this chap's plate which had mash and some pork chops on it with green gravy slopped across the top. It remains to this day the best pork I've ever eaten despite not having a clue what the gravy was. The language barrier just made going out for lunch an even more interesting experience.

Digression No 23 - advice for people with vowelophobia

While in that part of the world and on the subject of languages, it must be said that Poland deserves a special mention and a brief digression.

Like all countries and peoples in that area, the Poles and the country they populate are both interesting and certainly merit visiting and meeting. On the language front, however, not all that easy to get your tongue around is it?

There are some strange phobias on this planet with folk all over the place shit-scared of anything from ice cream, palm trees, water and the colour purple to cars, cats, heights, depths and carrier bags. The chances of finding someone who's got a phobia of vowels however, is pretty slim, but, if you are that person, I have a simple solution; just go to Poland. The place is purpose built for your average vowelophobe. Not a vowel in sight, especially in a famous sentence in Polish which has not got a single vowel in it anywhere. Can I find the book it's in though? To look at, Polish is very difficult. But, in practice, it's not actually that bad, especially with the help of the friendly population, a lot of whom are stunning women. Poland definitely gets the thumbs-up.

End of digression.

David Niven has written the two funniest autobiographies that I've ever read, but what has this got to do with languages? Quite a lot actually. David Niven was a great advert for our nation to the same degree as our football fans are not. A true Brit and a 'good sort' in general. I was bored in France, having finished work for the day with the old man, having probably made some glaring and embarrassing linguistic error on a market somewhere. I picked up D. Niven's first autobiography and have never looked back. It was so captivating that I've been into reading ever since, despite not being a terribly good reader. A real rollercoaster of hilarity, personal tragedy, 'professional' ladies, thwarted military careers, and cars with dodgy tax disks. Moreover, it made me laugh out loud on a number of occasions. For a book to do that is a major achievement and a lot more difficult to achieve for its author than it is for a film director.

The highlight of the two books for me is when they're filming *The Charge of the Light Brigade* and the director gets a bit angry with the cast. They all start giggling and laughing. This makes the director explode into a blinding rage, a rage which doesn't help the quality of his already pretty broken English. The year was 1936 and the director was none other than Michael Curtiz. The reason the long suffering Curtiz's English was broken in the first place was because, as a Hungarian, English was not his mother tongue. With the red

178

mist of imminent rage descending on him faster than it does on Irish midfielders in the number 16 Manchester United shirt, Curtiz decided that they would all benefit from a bit of high volume advice from his good self. Wanting to do this in the form of a discourse which would let them know that he was, contrary to their belief, right up to speed with what was going on, he opened by telling them that; 'You all think I know fuck nothing. Well you're wrong,' he continued, 'I know fuck all!' At this point, the previously giggling and laughing cast disintegrated into a heap of helpless actors crying with laughter and physically incapable of moving, let alone acting.

By this point I was on the brink of pissing my pants and the old man asked me what I was laughing about. When I told him which point I'd got to in the book, he understood my mirth and narrowly-avoided incontinence.

If you're looking for a linguistic giggle on your way around the planet there are two places you can guarantee a good rib tickler. The first is menus. You see some extraordinary things written in them in all parts of the world. A restaurant in the lowest village of our ski area has a delicious salad on its menu which contains bits of smoked duck, liver and other delights. It also has *gésiers* in it which are the gizzards of any piece poultry – I think. In the English translation of the menu it just says 'guts'. What with the Brits not being the most adventurous race of eaters anyway, I would venture I'm one of the few to ever have ordered it. Many other such linguistic oddities are out there for your mirth; you've just got to find them. That doesn't usually take too long, especially in Thailand, where restaurateurs always give translation into English a go and rarely get it right.

My other favourite piece of translation was on the border of Ecuador and Colombia. As is usually the case at borders, it took an age to get from one country to the other, this time over a rickety bridge on a narrow river. Charlie had just been called the devil by a beggar. She obviously wanted money and he gave her a bag of chocolate coated peanuts. It took her a couple of seconds to react, at which point Charlie got a good tongue lashing. Anyway, sitting on our rucksacks in no man's land, Tom started laughing and unleashed his camera. He pointed out the 'Bienvenido en Colombia' sign and the English translation of it underneath. I hope to God he's still got the photo otherwise I'm going to have to go all the way back to that border crossing to get another shot of it.

Languages not only provide incidents of massive hilarity but are also just generally interesting. My favourite word on the whole planet so far is 'jambo'. What a great way of saying hello to people. It's a really happy word and is Kiswahili for 'hello'. Not only that, but it has the honour of featuring in Lionel Ritchie's classic hit 'All Night Long'. It's great that whole countries can put you in a good mood before you've even tried to have a conversation with them just by virtue of having a good word for hello. The Greeks are not far behind with 'yassoo'; another very colourful way to greet someone. The other end of the stick is saying goodbye. The cloggies of Holland win that one for me with 'dooey'. I don't know how you write it in Dutch but it sounds great.

That's one sense in which us Brits are fairly unlucky. Our language is not all that much to shout about. English is much more of a means of doing business and communicating than it is an expression of national psyche as is the case in other countries. Despite its seemingly unstoppable march towards global domination, English has failed to grasp the hearts and minds of Anglophone communities around the world. The Anglophone world is notable for its pretty much universal disinterest in the origins of its main method of communication.

The Americans have even gone as far as to consider it a pretty major inconvenience. On the other side of the pond English has been simplified so that it is easier to spell correctly and easier to use. This makes a lot of sense in some ways but it is also sad to see in another sense. That's progress for you though. How far back do you go and where do you draw the line? Do you go back as far as getting everybody talking in Shakespearean English or is 'through' changing to 'thru' a natural evolution of our language that we should embrace? What is for sure is that the majority of the world's Anglophone community is not overly interested in the nuts and bolts of the language.

Also beyond doubt is the interest which the non-Anglophone world has in learning our language. It may not be due to an undying love for the English language but it is undeniable that English is spreading to become the first truly global language since we came down from the trees. English is spreading like wildfire, largely through a necessity brought about by the mercantile nature and financial ambitions of peoples in different parts of the planet. Realists are starting to learn English in droves because to make money you have to be able to communicate. The more clients and customers you can communicate with, the more money you have the potential of making. A high proportion of the planet speak English and, just as importantly, a lot of Anglophones live in the richer parts of the world. Mandarin Chinese is spoken by a lot of people, but the vast majority of them are in one country. English, much to the chagrin of some, is everywhere. Some, the realists, are jumping on the English bandwagon. Others are digging their heels in. The willing participants have called this one right to my mind. I'm not just saying that because I'm an Anglophone and I can't be arsed learning everybody else's languages. It's because, no matter what the language is, it'd be a lot more convenient if we all spoke the same one at some stage in the future. At the moment, English is the horse to back.

As mentioned, and it's only an opinion, but English is not the most beautiful language on the third stone from the sun.

Having said that, it's not the worst. That title goes to German. Anybody arguing? No? Good.

Some countries have the luck to be home to truly beautiful languages. My personal favourite is Italian which flows with the same smoothness as the curves of the bright red Ferraris that country produces. Never got round to learning how to speak it but I like the sound of it. Any language which is spoken as much with the hands as it is with the tongue is pretty cool. Italians are capable of putting such emphasis and inflection on certain words, and syllables of words, as to turn their mother tongue into a veritable linguistic rollercoaster ride. Not having spent enough time in Italy to find out either way, I can only assume that they're very passionate about their mother tongue.

That is certainly the case with other Latin-based languages such as French, right here next door to Italy. To the French, their language and the use of it is a national obsession. France is, like Italy, lucky enough to have a language which is very pleasing to the ear. French is a beautiful, flowing language in the throat of the right person. The accents and rolling guttural inflections it contains put its full powers of expression out of reach of a lot of the world's population and the scope for error is huge. I don't just mean that from a calling-sodium-benzoate-a- condom point of view but just by the sheer complexity of it. It takes years and years and years of formal education to be able to write a sentence in French to a very high standard. I spoke much better French as an eight-year-old than I do now as a thirty-four-year-old, and that's frustrating. It's not that my French is that bad, but when Charlie and I were at primary school in Brittany, we were taught seemingly endless different verb tenses and exceptions to the rules that boggled the mind. It was all done in a very boring and parrot like fashion but in their defence, any other way would be pretty much impossible.

A lot of folk say that English is the hardest language in the world to learn. I quite simply do not believe it. Do we have all that grammar? Not as I'm aware of. I could of course be wrong. Your mother tongue may just seem easier, and I'm sure that we do have a lot more verb tenses than most of us are aware of, but we either don't use them, or use them without realising it. The complexities of French are apparent to a lot more Francophones because they are made aware of their existence at school and encouraged to use them. This nurtures the interest the French have in their own language which is much less common in Anglophone parts of the world; it's a national obsession for them. They consider their language to be as much a part of their national identity as the Arc de Triomphe, croque monsieurs or Joan of Arc. They consider the beauty of their language to be a reflection of their country and its populous – something to be savoured and enjoyed, by those who speak it as a mother tongue, in the same way as a good glass of red wine and a nice ripe camembert.

The French enjoy speaking their language, which is great. That may explain why it takes them a long time to say something. Just watch President Chirac on the telly and you notice two things. First, well, he's patronising in a bullshitty sort of way. Of course he is, he's a politician, so both come naturally to him. That's not a uniquely French trait, that's politicians the world over, our very own 'dear leader' Mr Blair, who can patronise with the best of them, being a case in point. No, the second and different thing about Chirac is the seemingly interminable pauses he makes in the middle of sentences. In Chirac's case you have to assume that it's pause for effect and an attempt to pass for a 'grand savant'. But as with a lot of discourses in French, the slow, measured and passionate delivery is a sign that Chirac cares about making sure that what he is trying to say is said with a certain level of beauty, even if what he is actually saying is a crock of shit. By the French rationale, there's no point in saying something in fifteen words if you can use thirty. To their way of thinking, the short route to explaining something is more likely to be blunt, brash or less flowing. French is the adjective's best friend.

Digression No 24 – Peoples of the world part 4 – the French

You have to give it to the French, they've got life sussed. Having been in their place for a good part of my life I've developed a healthy respect for them. The inhabitants of the most visited country in the world mix a healthy dose of arrogance with a *laissez faire* attitude to life which basically involves a selective application of the laws governing their country. This is their greatest attribute and one which must save them millions of pounds a year, especially where European law is concerned. Fair play to them, whether it's a surrender document in the Bois de Boulogne or a European treaty, the French will sign anything put in front of them. Getting them to enforce it is a totally different matter.

That's the way they play the game. Sign it and forget about it. It's no more legal to smoke behind the bar in a French café than it is in an English pub or a Greek taverna. We apply the law and they just carry on regardless. None of that refrigerated cabinets and scale-proof fish stalls in French markets; bung it on a wooden table and flog it as passing cars spew exhaust fumes all over the produce. Always play to the whistle like the French do. If you're getting away with it, don't stop until someone notices.

Their practical application of rules and regulations applies to almost every facet of daily life. Look at the now deceased President Mitterand. It was common knowledge that Mitterand had a lover and that their relationship had produced a daughter. If he'd been British the PM he'd have had to resign. If he'd been American President he would have endured years of moralising which would have impaired his ability to do his job. Instead of enduring what Clinton went through, the French looked on Mitterand as a good President, so as long as he did his job, who cared about his private life? Same for Clinton; he may have had an away fixture with a White House intern but he was actually clever and good at his job, unlike the idiot who replaced him, so let him get on with it. The shrug of the shoulders is probably sums up the French approach to life.

Another of their better qualities is that they are so openly workshy. The thirty five hour week may be slowly dying a death, but it's had a good run in France. Bank holidays are as common as bicycles in France, and if the calendar falls favourably in May and August, you can go nearly the whole month without the inconvenience of going to work. This is the country which invented what is called a 'bridge' day or a *journée pont* as the locals call it. If one of the multitude of bank holidays falls on a Thursday, Friday is declared a *journée pont* which is carte blanche for everybody to bunk off work on the Friday and make a long weekend of it! Same goes for Tuesday bank holidays. Bunk off on the Monday and another long weekend is the result.

The great thing about the French is their togetherness and that revolution has contributed to a national identity in which they have no qualms about getting out in the streets and demonstrating their opposition to something. You'd think that the unions are strong in France when you see the mass protests on TV every couple of weeks but that is not the case. French union membership is among the lowest in Europe. The way they look at it is that why should the fact that you're not in the union stop you from going out in support of those who are: i.e.; skiving off work for the day.

France is bankrupt. It has been for a couple of decades at least, and has unemployment benefit and pensions it cannot pay for. Despite this, a quick collective shrug of the shoulders, and life goes on. Another Prime Minister who thought he could reform the rigid and stagnant labour market had to wake up to the reality of mass street protests and drop the whole idea earlier this year. Can you imagine that in Britain? God no! People protesting in the streets? How vulgar. It's happened about twice ever. In France it's virtually a weekly event.

France's food, which is something else it can be proud of, will be discussed later; which leaves the last of France's great attributes to be discussed in this digression, the cars it produces. I'm not into cars but I am aware that the Citroën DS is the most beautiful car ever produced. This, however, is not the best thing about French cars. That would be that they're always driven by fit women – well, the small ones are anyway. This is a phenomenon called 'SFCF' or Small French Car Factor. Check it out, it's all true. Spot a small French car and it'll usually be driven by a good looking woman.

End of digression.

Back to beautifully spoken languages. Anybody who's ever heard Alasdair Cooke's 'Letter from America' will say that English can also be spoken beautifully, and to a certain extent this is true. Compared to French though, it's a fairly rare occurrence. The majority of the time, when English is being spoken, it's a case of the shorter and more concise the better. Time is money and it takes time to talk. Therefore, cut down on the talk time and profits are optimised. The big loser, and there always is one, is the beauty of the language.

It's largely due to these factors that the onward march of English globally really, really pisses the French off. They've got a right bee in there bonnet about it and 'Le Sulk' is only going to get worse. While the rest of the world just gets about its business, France spends a lot of time and energy moaning about the fate of its language. It was replaced as the official world language of diplomacy in the dying throes of last century. What's worse as far as the French are concerned is that English was the replacement. The French dummy was again spat out when the announcements at the summer Olympics in Athens were not made in French for the first time in the games' history. Greek was of course one of the languages but that accursed English came up to bite French on the arse again. Anything but English.

This leads to some ridiculous laws which they put in place to protect their language and customs from what they call the 'Coca-Cola culture'. This is an all-embracing term for things they feel are eroding the Frenchness of French as a language and France as a country. It leads to people not being able to listen to what music they want to, for example. I have to take their laws into account when deciding what to play next on my radio show because if I don't play enough French language music, I'm in the poo. The law dictates that I have to have 40% French music in every hour of programming. I think that what is played should be dictated by the wishes of the listeners and not by the government. Same goes for advertising. How can the use of the word 'Walkman' possibly destroy French culture? It's not that you get carted off in a police car if you say Walkman in the street, but if you're advertising a product for sale in a shop or magazine you have to put the French *balladeur* in instead of the English. Ridiculous in the extreme.

The 'Coca-Cola culture' is a phrase which has been banded about for a long time in France but is it really the great evil it is perceived as? France gives huge grants and subsidies to its (very good) cinema industry and protects its musicians with a guaranteed amount of airtime, but are they any less influenced by all things American than other less defensive nations as a result? Not really. I'm British and we've had the added ingredient of American military personnel in the UK for over sixty years, as well as sharing a common language with the Americans. Why then do we not feel the need to put up defences? Maybe we consider our culture and traditions strong enough to be capable of defending themselves.

French is currently the official national language of forty countries on this planet, which is quite a lot if you think that there are two hundred odd countries in total at the moment. With organisations such as the Maison de la France and events like World Francophone Day and the periodic Francophone summits, the French government does go to huge lengths and give a big budget to ways and means of promoting French as a language all over the planet. While there is beauty in diversity, English looks to be the way forward at the moment. English does have equivalent self-promoting organisations like the British Council but as a language, English is spreading globally without any help at all, really. The current big expansion is in Asia where the rush to learn English is only matched by the rush up the GDP league by a lot of Asian countries' economies.

With laziness comes trouble though and if, like a lot of Brits, you don't speak a foreign language, you're going to get in a tight spot at some point. The British answer to this is quite irritating and involves talking to people in their own country, in English, but louder and slower. You see it the world over. Why would anyone assume that someone is more likely to understand something if it is said at higher volume and in the sort of patronising childlike way in which you'd explain something to a four-year-old at home? It's a very unfortunate trait of the British for which we're infamous rather than famous. The alternative, it's unfortunate to have to admit, is even sadder.

What can you do to defend yourself against the potential and ultimately inevitable linguistic tight spots? Export your whole culture abroad of course! That's what a lot of populations, especially those richer countries in Northern Europe, do instead of putting up with the inconvenience of interacting with the locals. Another shining example of the Dead Kennedys' expression 'give me convenience or give me death'. It works in a lot of respects and is the holiday equivalent of painting a room white instead of being a bit more adventurous.

Being hypocritical, I am currently sitting in a hotel on a Greek island which is full of British families. Not my usual method of travel but I'm visiting a friend from skiing who works here. The people who are accustomed to coming on such holidays want to go on holiday in the sun without the hassles that go with it. So, they get to an airport at home having booked a holiday in Britain. They get on a plane and four hours later they're in Greece or somewhere else hot. They're met off the plane by British staff, who are out in hotter climes to do a season in the sun, and get on a coach. They head to entirely self-contained hotel resorts staffed by people who speak the same language as them, and never have to leave the confines of the resort which they are holidaying in. When their time is up, they do the reverse journey on the coach and plane and a lot of them will arrive back at the airport in the UK without having had a single piece of contact, let alone meaningful interaction, with any of the locals in the place they've just visited. Yes, they've got a lot out of it. They've got a tan, had a nice relaxing time, played a bit of beach volleyball, eaten good food, had a few drinks of an evening and maybe got lucky. They've also avoided getting the shits by drinking bottled water and have not had to eat anything too 'bizarre', which comes as a great relief to the largely unadventurous pallet of your average Brit. So, that's alright then, isn't it?

Well, yes it is, and the money-paying customer is always right. If a belt-and-braces holiday with people to look after your kids is what you want, it's your money, and that is what you can have. But you'd like to think that with so much out there, people would like to do a bit more than just transport their own place abroad. To get out there and see different cultures and meet different people; to try the local cuisine and the local firewater. In a lot of cases, if not a majority, people just don't want to. This is not just a British phenomenon either. The Germans, Americans, French and loads of other nationalities do it as well as us.

The reason? Fear. Fear of the unknown in general, be it food, drink, geography or language. It's fair enough that people want to have a trouble free time when they go away on holiday, and for climatic reasons some people, notably North Europeans, have to go away on holiday. As much as I love Britain and Jürgen the made up German loves Germany, a week on the beach in Cleethorpes or Kiel just isn't the same as a week in the real sun. Of course, the sun does shine in Northern Europe in the summer, but you wouldn't put the savings on it, would you?

Apart from good weather, tourists want other essentials. A lot of people take their kids on holiday to places where they can guarantee the quality of the drinking water. Picky eaters would look pretty miserable if you transported them to Ecuador and stuck the national dish 'Cuy' – a gutted, grilled guinea pig cut in half with the head still on it – in front of them. Others want the chlorine-scented safety of a swimming pool and fresh water showers, soft towels and a good bed.

The only crap thing about my brilliant Autumn of 2003 was Gran Canaria, or parts of it at least. When arrived it was brilliant. We were all pretty tired and looking forward to a bit of a chill out and getting away from the motion of the boat for a while. We were moored in Puerto Mogàn, a quaint and compact little port and marina on the south end of the island. Cals had some mates who lived on the island and they showed us a lot of the interior which was pretty striking as well as some good beaches and mouth-wateringly good restaurants. There's nothing like a bit of local knowledge.

The flip side is Puerto Rico and the only thing which I didn't like about Gran Canaria. After a windy fifteen kilometre drive round some beautiful coast from Puerto Mogàn on a billiard table of a road which makes you cry out for a motorbike, you're in Puerto Rico, which is pretty dreadful. A half-moon beach full of bars selling transported England. Or more like 'Ingurrrlund', 'Ingurrland', 'Ingurrland' than England though, I'm afraid. All day fried breakfasts, pubs called the 'Red Lion' and the 'Royal Oak', tattoos, wife-beater vests, lager, football colours, shepherd's pie, shell suits, sunburn, turbo shandies and no sun-cream. That pretty much sums up Puerto Rico. Awful is the shorter version. Go inland a bit and it gets worse. An ugly building obviously put up as a shopping centre has been invaded by more bars and shops selling football shirts, postcards and 'my brother went to Gran Canaria and all I got was this lousy t-shirt' T-shirts. I am proud to say though that I did come away with a 100% polyester nipple-scratching Hawaiian shirt in the most gorgeous shades of bright yellow, radioactive red and British sunburn pink I've ever seen. It's got lovely silhouetted palm trees on it as well. I couldn't resist it.

What do you learn on your way to school in the morning when you're seven? Not a lot. It's usually a short trip to primary school by foot or in the old dear's car. For me, in September 1979, it was nine kilometres from our hotel to our first morning at school in France. Charlie was nine and the old man was trying to teach us how to say 'est ce que vous pouvez parler un peu plus lentement s'il vous plait?' Can you speak a little bit slower please? Twenty minutes later and the parents were gone and we were right in amongst it. That first day was a bit of a blur, really. We could both already count to ten and say 'yes' and 'no' in French but that was about it. We'd forgotten how to say 'est-ce que vous pouvez parler un peu plus lentement s'il vous plait' before the parents' car had got out of sight. Then they were there again to pick us up. It had gone so quickly. The three things I really remember from that first day are;

1) Asking myself (and then Charlie) what all these people were going on about, as I couldn't understand a word.

2) Why do they want to have a conference in the middle of a football pitch all the time? As it turns out, 'coup franc' means 'free kick' in French. I thought they were saying 'conference'.

3) Having a slight altercation with some lads who thought they'd better explain who was top of the playground food chain to the new arrivals. To modify a famous Brian Clough quote, you could say that, after a swiftly played out disagreement including physical blows, they decided we were right, and all was well.

And that was that. What a doddle. Walk in the park, but what isn't at that age? You'll give anything a go, won't you? Later that evening, the lads who were our 'welcoming committee' were sent round to our house to invite us down to the park to play footy and what followed was three years of great fun. We didn't go and play three years of non-stop football. We had nearly three years of school and play in Brittany in north-western France and loved it. Down the scrapyard with Bruno Aubry and Marc Guillemet smashing up the cars, throwing still-green maize plants at each other in the fields down the road, looking on proudly as the lads jealously admired my metallic green 'Strika' and Charlie's bigger red 'Grifter' pushbikes, coughing like a bastard when you nick one of the old man's Gitane cigarettes.

We spent three years doing what kids do. The difference was that we did it in a foreign country and learnt the local language in no time flat. At that age you're like a sponge for knowledge and in six months we were right up there on the pace and pretty much fluent French speakers. I remember very clearly the day when I thought; hang on, this all makes sense; I can speak this. All the parts and bits you'd learnt over the past months suddenly slip into place and knit together in sentences you seem to be able to construct without too much thought. It's the linguistic equivalent of being on the road to Damascus I suppose – not that I've ever been on any of the thoroughfares leading to the Syrian capital, mind.

Back in Oxfordshire, I went to school with a lot of kids whose parents were in the armed forces because we have always lived near RAF Brize Norton. I always thought what a waste it is for so many people to go and do a tour of duty in Germany, Holland or wherever, and not immerse their whole family in local life, and their kids in the local schooling. That's in hindsight of course, and you have to consider that forces' families are probably kept on camp for security reasons, but it's been a huge advantage to me and my brother to speak a foreign language.

Last but not least in the languages section is the ultimate problem which is of course two people speaking the same language who can't understand each other. Then you really do know that you're in the poo. Coming back up into France from Spain in the summer of 1981, Charlie and I both spoke fully fluent French by that point, but were really only familiar with the accents of the north. Upon arrival in the South West, I asked my dad why all the people spoke as if they had a spring in the back of their throats. We'd never before been right down in the south-west corner of France and were amazed by the accents of folk as we chomped on our first ever battered squid rings in St Jean de Luz. Calamari really are all that. Despite being full on ninth dan French speakers we had to really stick an ear out to understand the Basques.

This can happen to you all over the world and especially being a native English speaker because so many people are learning it and speak it with their own accent. This is only to be expected. But in your own country? Surely not, ref? Well, it does if you're British. If you're a Kiwi, you're pretty much in the clear with your own country folk. As far as I could work out there, are no accent variations at all in New Zealand. Most other countries have at least some regional dialects and inflections. New Zealand is the only exception I've ever found to date.

Britain is full of regional accents, and the rapidity of the change is incredible. My highest levels of concentration here at home were needed when I started university in Dundee. Being a higher education establishment, it is a richly international seat of learning to which people come from far and wide to attend. I was 426 miles from home; believe me, you count every yard when you do the journey in a Communist era, engine-in-the-boot Skoda. That was nothing though. The Greek chap in the room next to me was from Crete and a lot further away from home than me. Good accent though. Manos he was called, reading Accountancy, and he spoke very good English. There were a healthy number of Irish students as well, mostly from the north, some of whom had pretty challenging accents.

The hardest of all the accents I encountered in Dundee was in fact from right there, though. Kathy, our cleaner, was an absolute diamond. She was from Hawkhill in Dundee and was born and bred. Could I understand her? No is the short answer. If I really hung on in there and shut my eyes for maximum concentration I could pick out the odd word, but then it looks like you're asleep anyway which is just as rude. In an academic year I did work out that she was; A) a lovely lady, B) from Hawkhill, C) that her son was serving in the army, D) err, that's it. She had the most indecipherable accent going. I didn't feel too guilty mind. Tom, Lindsay, Keith, Simon and Paul, the

Scottish contingent in our house, all said they had a hell of a time understanding her as well!

Things to see and do

Boredom

Here's a negative but realistic thought before getting into the bare bones of the chapter. There's more to travelling than standing on top of mountains and trekking through jungles. Some of the time you'll be bored. Whether it's on a bus in the middle of the night or sitting waiting for a boat, train or one of your party, at some point you're going to be bored stupid. There are certain essentials you'll need to avoid going mad. The first of these is a book. Always have one with you and never miss the opportunity to use a book-swap, as found in most hostels and backpackers.

A pack of cards should be one of the essentials your bag contains as well. A pack of cards will prove their worth by the state they're in after a couple of months. You'll play so many games of five card brag and 'shithead' that your cards, whose crisp edges once proudly shone with glycerine, will be as dog-eared as a porno mag in a boarding school dormitory after a matter of weeks.

A board game is the last anti-boredom device I would suggest. Something really vindictive I would suggest, as thriving on your fellow traveller's board game misfortune is the source of raucous ribaldry which further makes you forget the boredom of your current location. To this end, Backgammon and Ludo are the best. They are the board game versions of the world's most vindictive sport, Croquet. Forget Scrabble because you have to take a dictionary with you and argue a lot. Backgammon and Ludo are the way forward.

Digression No 25 – 38, Ruthven St, Bondi Junction, Sydney, NSW, Australia

In a terraced three-bedroom house in the eastern suburbs of Sydney, Ludo finally took over our lives. A load of us who had met in South America all ended up in Sydney and despite being aware of each other's behaviour and habits, ended up sharing a house together. It was the perfect combination of great fun and hell on earth, 24/7. God knows what the neighbours thought. Over fifty people lived there on and off during the course of the year we rented it, and there were always a couple of unknowns kipping on the couch when you got up in the morning.

Ludo had been a distraction in South America. We'd had others such as cards, backgammon and all the usuals, but Ludo was favourite. In Sydney it ruled our lives, though. As we could never decide who was going to do the dishes, or any of the other domestic chores for that matter, every household decision was made by Ludo. Stef the Dutchy didn't have a job and spent one day turning the coffee table in the lounge into a permanent Ludo pitch, which was the scene of some truly emotional sporting moments.

At the time I was a motorbike dispatch rider in Sydney and would come in at six in the evening absolutely knackered. It's too hot for leathers and a helmet in Sydney during the summer but it's the law. Not only that, but it's too dangerous to not wear all the kit. I used to finish the day having sweated about half a stone, with a black soot mark all over my face from the car fumes. I pulled up one evening and turned the engine of the bike off and removed my lid off, enjoying the silence of the killed engine and the wind on my newly liberated head, and looking forward to collapsing prostrate on the couch for a while. It lasted about four seconds. The front door of the house was open and the lounge absolutely erupted in a cacophony of shrieking, laughter, clapping and abuse. 'Drink you bastard! Drink!' was an all-too-familiar utterance in our lounge. Some unlucky sod had just lost a chores game big time. The shouts of drink related to the other disadvantage of losing. We used to force wine from a wine box down the loser's throats. The real cheap stuff you get in Australia for ten bucks per three litre box. Thoughts of an hour's veg out on the couch were unrealistic.

End of digression.

For the vast majority of your trip you're going to be having a lot of fun, seeing some amazing stuff and meeting some great people, some of whom you'll know for the rest of your life. Get out there and make the most of it. Be safe and stay healthy but don't hold back. Grab the planet by the horns and wrestle the best out of it. The whole place is great fun and the good bit is that a lot of it is free!

Free stuff Part 1--People watching

Free stuff is a great release for the average budget traveller, and being on a tight budget doesn't stop you seeing the best bits because the best bits are the cheapest. People watching is amongst these. Sitting on a bench in the main square of a town and watching the hustle and bustle of daily life is uninterrupted fun. The wedding procession in Port Saïd (chapter five) will stick in my mind forever. There are plenty of others as well, though. Jaw dropping moments aplenty all around the planet.

South America's fascination with all things military is quite a rich source of this. Charlie and I were sitting in the Plaza de Armas in Cuzco on a particularly action packed day in 1998 which warranted a mention in a letter home in those simple uncomplicated days before email took the world over. It must have been a Sunday because everybody came piling out of church into the main square which was, of course, as if often the case in South America, named after military firepower. With that a few open-topped troop transports came round the corner and pulled up outside the church, disgorging a few dozen soldiers. The head honcho started barking orders and the troops fell into groups of about ten. Some others produced some musical instruments and without so much as a tune up launched into a full on military march-type tune. After a few bars, the soldiers in formation started to perform what I can only describe as Morris Dancing with guns. It was another pinch yourself moment and after that didn't work, I looked at my brother to confirm the reality of it.

The soldiers continued to prance around each other in a very Monty Python type way, but the whole thing was taken very seriously by the participants and, in particular, the self-important officer. Then they were gone. Just like that. The last bar of music blew weakly out of the end of the trombone and the squaddies were back in the lorries quick smart. Polite applause continued from the church goers as the lorries disappeared around the corner and then everybody walked off. Wild. It was all over within a matter of about four minutes.

The South American fascination for all things military is the cause of much hilarity but you have to be careful. They all take the whole thing very seriously and like the Italians, they're a lot more worried about looking good and doing a bit of chest beating than they are about actually going to war. All of them have been to war with all the other countries on the continent on numerous occasions, even the ones they don't actually have a border with. The trouble is that no one ever seems to win. Everyone seems to lose all the wars they're in with the exception of Chile.

Down in the jungle one day, another fanfare struck up in a barracks and out stomped a procession of the Navy to very

199

melodramatically raise the frayed and fading Bolivian national flag for the day. After observing the ridiculously serious pomp of it all, I found myself asking what Bolivia has a Navy for. In fact, not only is Bolivia landlocked but it actually feels the need for an Armada, not just a Navy. Lake Titicaca is pretty big, but the Swiss seem to cope on Lake Geneva without an armada. Down in the jungle, well, I mean, how many fast pursuit boats can you really need on the upper reaches of an Amazon tributary or on the highest navigable lake in the world? Despite this, 'Armada Nacional' was what they had written on the shabby board outside their barracks.

It goes for the law enforcement communities as well. La Paz is policed almost entirely by small men on Suzuki GN250 motorcycles. They wear brown waist length jackets and beige outrider trousers tucked into highly polished leather boots. They all wear (fake) Ray Ban aviator sunglasses, some are heavily moustachioed, and they all think they're really cool. They all think they're Baker and Poncherello out of 'CHiPs' except that their uniforms are a bit frayed and they're on GN250s, not proper motorbikes like the 1000 cc Kawasakis that Ponch and Baker rode.

Same with the police in Peru. We were again in the action packed Cuzco one day when a bloke ran past waving a pistol in the air very non-proficiently. Fifty yards behind came the first of the cops, looking over his shoulder and encouraging his colleagues on, weapon drawn. The sheer comedy of it. You'd have paid for the privilege.

The peculiarities of the military down there or the unorthodox driving techniques of wedding cortèges in Northern Egypt are just two examples of the fun you can have watching daily life. Board games played by old men in town squares is another one. Old men who sit there looking feeble and then slap down a domino piece with the ferocity of a founder's sledgehammer. Daily life is as much as part of a country's make up as is its wildlife and history. It's also free. Very important to the average budget traveller.

Moving continents but sticking with people in town squares, I have to take you back to Croatia and to the capital, Zagreb. This time we're not just talking old people playing dominoes, but whole populations. I was there trying to buy a ticket for the 2003 Rugby World Cup final on eBay, something I ultimately failed to do. Coming out of the Internet café after another futile couple of hours I came out into one of the squares in town to find a massive TV screen had been set up with a bar next to it. It transpired that three things were being combined which proved not to be a particularly good idea. These were a football match, politics and alcohol. What were they thinking of!?

Someone in a political party had had this really bright idea when considering how to get people to vote for their party in the forthcoming elections. Croatia was playing its neighbour and rival Slovenia in the play-offs to get into the 2004 European Football Championships. 'I know,' cried some bright spark hoping to impress the party hierarchy with a moment of clarity, 'why don't we take over a whole square in Zagreb and erect a giant screen for the electorate to watch the game on? Even better, we could further confirm their allegiance to our banner by plying them with free beer and wine during the proceedings!' Brilliant! That's exactly what happened. The square in which the Internet café was was packed with people who were making the very most of the free bar and were being warmed up by some traditional Croatian dancing. By the time the football match started a lot of the electorate were starting to get a bit top-heavy.

Having nothing better to do, I watched the first half and had a couple of glasses of very good red wine. At half time I decided to go and get some food from a good little spot I'd discovered in town. It was at that juncture that I discovered the full scale of the giveaway in progress. I had watched the first half in one of the smaller squares and had to go through the biggest square in town, Ban Josip Jelacic, to get to the eatery I was headed for. A bigger political party with two giant screens and, more importantly, a bigger bar budget, had occupied this square, named after Croatia's national hero. As I walked through it, things were noticeably rowdier than the square I'd been in. I went off to my preferred little eatery and walked back through Josip Jelacic Square to find things had gone downhill badly in the intervening twenty minutes. The second half was just underway and everybody was absolutely plastered. There were people lying spread-eagled on the floor, a woman threw-up all over her husband and the whole square was a complete fiasco. Not in the opinion of the police though. They seemed to think it was totally normal by the looks of their casual supervision of the revellers. I strode on through thinking I'd get back to the tamer square where I'd watched the first half. None of it though. The square had also degenerated into the same sort of affair as the main one. As Zagreb drowned, the bar staff kept serving. I beat a retreat to the Internet café to make another unsuccessful attempt at getting to Sydney's big game.

Croatians must be kicking themselves that they put up with Communism for half a century. They could have had countless elections in those intervening fifty years, and had missed out on the massive amounts of free alcohol which would appear to go hand in hand with a trip to the ballot box in those parts. Errors all round!

The great thing about people watching is that you can do it whilst getting on with something else as well. The scope for hilarity is massive, and this seems to be especially true of supermarkets. A lot of strange people go food shopping and it's often people trying to keep control of their kids who provide the hilarity. On my first ever day in the US, I was fourteen, jet-lagged to hell and we went to K-Mart on the way back to my hosts' house. It culminated in this woman going totally hysterical after accidentally dislocating her young daughter's elbow and screaming, 'Oh my god, I've killed my child!' while kneeling in a pool of her own and her daughter's tears. Strange country this is, I thought, as I watched the episode unfold.

Twenty something years later and I was loading shopping into the back of our old Mazda 626 with Foxy and Arjen the cloggy. We were at Woolworth's supermarket in Gimpy, Queensland, Australia. The woman who came out of the shop's sliding doors was the epitome of the local population. Up country, foul-mouthed, white trash; a thoroughly unpleasant cow. A really evil country hick who looked like the nasty, domineering mother who was leader of the Fratelli gang in that modern classic 'The Goonies'. Every country has them and in Australia there seem to be a fair concentration of them up in rum country in Queensland.

She was pushing a shopping trolley and her daughter was following at her heel like a faithful hound. We heard her well before we saw her as a tirade of expletives and crying preceded the opening of the doors. Her other child, a scrawny little boy of about ten with a mucky face, was whining very loudly and bawling; 'Mummy, I want to go and see the toys, I want to go and see the toys!'

'Come here you little bastard, we're not going to see the fucking toys,' devil woman screamed at full volume with no hint of shame, while she crossed the car park zebra crossing. We'd stopped loading our shopping to take in the incident and, after pleading once more, and getting a death threat from Devil Woman for his trouble, the boy realised he wasn't going to get his way. He bolted across the road and nearly got run over by a Ford Falcon. 'Watch my fucking child,' Mrs Fratelli screamed at the entirely blameless driver. She grabbed her son and took one step before turning round and shoving him back towards the Falcon and saying to the driver; 'No, no, on second thoughts, run the little cunt over!' That was it, we were all doubled over laughing, as was the rest of the population of the car park. She started ranting at us to the effect of what the fuck were we staring at, which just made things worse. I really did think that I was never going to stop laughing ever again and that I'd die of dehydration from crying so much. People watching will make a reappearance in the next chapter, but in the more expensive guise of watching sport.

Meeting the locals and having a laugh with them is good fun, whether they're sober or not. Take the above case or that of the Romanians in the petrol station (you'll have to wait till the end of chapter fifteen). Petrol stations are usually pretty good places for me whether in Romania or in the Gaza Strip. My bro was in Morocco and told me about a chap who gave him a rooftop tour of Fez. I had a similar bit of local knowledge thanks to a lovely bloke in Dubrovnik in Croatia. He talked me through the finer points of the town after I got chatting to him on the walls of the old town. His account of living there during the Civil War was fascinating.

My favourite ever hanging out with the locals was in Fiji. They're such a friendly nation of people and they'll do anything for you. We got to the cyclone-ravaged island of Mana on the day the latter stages of the 97 Rugby Sevens World Cup took place. I ended up watching it on the only TV on the island in someone's living room. There were about thirty of us in a very small room and we had a great time. I was the only tourist there but they made me very welcome and I was supporting Fiji which put some popularity on top of the novelty value. Fiji beat South Africa in the final with the help of Mana Island. One of the squad was from the island. A celebration of suitable raucousness ensued as we partied all night long to celebrate their victory. It really is great when the locals involve you so totally that you lose the inhibitions of a stranger in a strange land.

Free stuff part 2 – The beach. The beach is another great source of free fun. Do try and avoid drowning, though. This is a feat I very nearly achieved on Ipanema beach in Rio de Janeiro in 98. That would have spoiled it really. Apart from rip tides the beach is a great place to hang out and check things out. For a start, there is the big blue wobbly thing which you can go and jump in should you get too hot at any point. The sea is great fun, but as I said, don't drown.

Every facet of beach life is super-double interesting and nowhere more so than Rio. Brazilians, like Australians and other nations with a beach culture, have life on the beach sussed down to the last minute detail. They dress right, they bring the right kit and they respect the dangers of the sun. They dress right in that everybody wears as little as possible. Brazilian beaches are a great place to perv, whichever way you swing.

As to the activities taking place on the beach, they are hives of activity in countries where people know what they're doing. Brazil is the geographic opposite of a day on the beach in the UK, which is looked on by older beach-goers as a battle quite frankly. British people over the age of thirty consider sand to be an inconvenience which gets between your toes and in your sandwiches. A day at the beach means sticking up the windbreak and trying to keep warm. If it's sunny, it's a race to see who can sunburnt first.

Digression No 26 – great sun cream moments

UV – don't mess with it because it'll kill you. Skin cancer is a massive problem and no one knows this better than the

Australians. So seriously do they take it that they fine parents who send their kids to school without hats. Rightly so too.

Don't think you're immune because you're an adult, either. I was working for a rendering firm in Sydney of which I was the only employee who was not Irish. We'd been on a site over the bridge for a couple of weeks and I was mixing muck next to the brickies. This old fella in a big slouch hat who always had a fag hanging out of his mouth had never said a word to me in all the weeks we'd been there. I nicknamed him 'Wile E Coyote' because he never said a word and he looked sort of wizened and weather-beaten like driftwood, and sly.

The Irish lads were all taking the piss out of me one day for putting sun cream on for about the eighth time that day. Every site in Oz has to provide it by law, but the Irish were all far too macho to put any on. (The sun cream's-for-poofs club is alive and well in the southern hemisphere as well). 'Don't you worry about them mate, you keep slapping that cream on.' I turned around from my mixer to the unlikely tones of Wile E Coyote talking to me for the first time ever. 'I've been having melanomas burnt off my skin for the last thirty years,' he continued while taking off his hat and rolling up his sleeves to reveal the white laser marks all over his skin. His crocodile-like sun-ripened skin was testament to how important it is to cover up when in the sun. Brits tend to be a bit ignorant of this. The sun shines so rarely in combination with enough heat to merit the removal of a shirt that as soon as the two do combine it's as if someone sets a suntan stopwatch going. It's a race to see who can get a tan the quickest, but all anyone gets is sunburn and peeling skin. This problem is made all the worse because a lot of Brits have exactly the same approach when visiting countries where the sun does actually come out. Go to any seaside resort in Europe and the pinkest, most sunburnt people you can find are usually from the UK.

Do people a good turn. Sunburn can creep up on you and you don't feel the pain of your skin burning until it's too late. Furthermore, what with the beach being a relaxing place and all, it is easy to fall asleep. If you do see someone on the beach who's starting to get a bit lobster-esque, why not do them a favour and point it out to them? Or maybe not.

A load of us turned up at the beach one day in Bondi to see a worrying sight. It was late morning but there was already one outstanding candidate for hospitalisation. Fair skinned, ginger and going scarlet very fast indeed. Tom, my cousin, took it upon himself to go and do her a good turn by telling her she was getting burnt. About a minute later he was severely regretting being a good Samaritan. He went over and told her she was getting burnt and, well, we might have been a good twenty yards away but she launched into Tom with such a tirade of abuse that we had no trouble hearing at all. 'Don't you fockin' tell me what'aye fockin do you' this and that. Tom retreated with his tail between his legs but laughing like hell as she made a complete tit of herself in front of everybody within range of her sexual swearwords, which was anyone within about a kilometre. We all had a good laugh. She was young, Irish, and had obviously just got off the plane. Her skin was so fair before going scarlet it had probably looked as if it had never been exposed to direct sunlight. One night in the Cock and Bull in Bondi Junction and then straight down the beach to get frazzled.

Posh and pompous bloke walks into the English Medical Centre in Val d'Isère. Leaning on the counter is yours truly, in for a chat with Nursey Sue. Nursey was the nurse on duty. Not the politest, he says; 'I say, I've had an allergic reaction,' very matter-of-factly, standing there with shining lips the size of life-rafts. 'You've got sunburn,' says Nursey without the slightest trace of sympathy. She's like that, and rightly so. If they don't bother being polite, why should she bother showing sympathy? He persisted in interrupting our gossip-mongering by saying, 'Impossible! I put sun cream on this morning.' It turned out that he'd put on some Factor 4, practically cooking fat, before going skiing in the morning. No surprise that nine hours later he was in a world of trouble. You don't have to be in a pair of swimmers to get sunburn. Out skiing you see some really bad cases. Combine the sun, altitude and the reflection off of the snow, and you've got a recipe for disaster.

End of digression.

Back to Brazil. In Rio it's walking down the steps while peeling most of your clothes off and getting straight into some sort of game; the miles of beaches are alive with people playing beach games very well. Brazilians are so good at football that they play foot-volleyball instead of volleyball at the beach. The person receiving the serve does so in the middle of their chest so that all the players have a big red spot on their sternum. Players are not allowed to use their hands, and the skill involved is out of this world, keeping you mesmerised for hours. Any of these chaps or the players in any of the many normal games of beach football going on would get a start in the Premier League.

Other high levels of aptitude are displayed in the two other favourites, Frisbee and bat and ball. Even the dogs are good at Frisbee. As to bat and ball, it's incredible how hard these people can hit a ball at a friend holding a wooden bat twenty yards away. Equally incredible is the coolness with which it is returned at equal speed.

Beaches are free, fun, hot and have a free swimming pool complete with wave machine. Be there soon.

Wandering around is often, if not always, free. A lot of the culture of a country is open to be explored for relatively little money, and often for free. Plenty of low budget activities are out there. Museums, art galleries and other cultural places are quite often free, especially if you're in a fairly wealthy country. The stuff you learn about the place you're in is worth the expense, should you find that there is an admission fee. One museum which sticks in the mind was in Perth in Western Australia which had a fascinating exhibition about the history of the rabbit in Australia. It turns out that some joker brought twenty four over from Europe to Adelaide in the nineteenth-century for a bit of target practice for him and his friends. A few years later there were millions of the little lettuce-crunching blighters. That museum also had a meteor in it the size of my motorbike, which weighed eleven tons. The gold museum in Lima in Peru is pretty special as well, as are any of London's many brilliant free museums. For sheer tackiness you have to go back to the earthquake town of Napier in New Zealand which, understandably, has an earthquake museum. The museum itself is very interesting but the tackiness comes from the fact that they got none other than Shakin' Stevens over from the UK to open it! Good money well spent.

Some bits I'm better at than others where culture's concerned, and I must say that art galleries are not really my thing. Some are, but far from all. You can't like everything.

Now monasteries and churches, that's more my thing. I very nearly got a bit of a church overload in South America where there are more churches than there are petrol stations in Turkey, but they really are incredible edifices. There's one in Quito which has around seven tons of gold in the ceiling! Wild. Monasteries are pretty incredible places as well, and the Buddhist monasteries of Asia really do take the biscuit. Mosques do it for me as well. The Blue Mosque in Istanbul is my favourite so far.

My only problem with all these religious edifices is the noise they make at the crack of dawn. Again, I don't wish to become the recipient of a Salman Rushdie-style fatwa, but why the hell are mosques allowed to amplify their calling folk to prayer at dawn? If some bloke wants to give everybody a reminder from the vantage point of a minaret, well, so be it. Not entirely unselfish in itself, but verging on acceptable. To amplify it to the point of producing feedback and distortion is plain rude.

However, just to keep things even and fair, Christians are no better. It's Sunday and you're enjoying a nice lie in when some load of campanologists start ringing the bells of the local church. Why should they be allowed to do it when me putting a Motörhead CD on would be considered anti-social?

Take the whole religion thing a bit further back into history and you can't help but be impressed by everything that Egypt has to offer. In both life and death, the Egyptians thought big and built big. They built beautiful as well. Big outside doesn't mean big inside, though. The good thing about going into one of the pyramids at Giza is that it's good training for the silver mines of Southern Bolivia. You head down this tiny shaft which makes you bend double but is well worth the back pain. The other thing about going in is that you'll be a lot more sympathetic to the next animal you put in your oven. That's because when you get to the central chamber, the temperature is right up there at Gas Mark 7. Move south and the Valley of the Kings, over the river from Luxor is no less impressive. The burial chambers have to be seen to be believed.

The other great thing about religious buildings is that is quite often an unspoken competition to see who can put one up in the most stupid place. The more inaccessible the place you put your church, mosque or temple up, the bigger devotion you're showing. Makes for some extraordinary views for us infidel non-believers. One of my favourites is the church above the town of Castellane in Southern France. Perched is the word.

Buildings in general are pretty fantastic and I reckon Flinder's Street Train Station in Melbourne is among my favourites. Others would have to be Battersea Power Station in London and the whole town of Napier in New Zealand which is Art Deco heaven. There's lots out there to see. Architecture is something else you can wander around looking at without hitting the budget very hard, if at all.

Other culture that you can experience abroad could be stuff that you may not get the opportunity to enjoy at home, not because you don't have access to it, but because you can't afford it. Opera is a very good example of this if you're British like me. It's not that Britain doesn't have world-class opera because it does. Seventy pounds to get into the National Opera is pretty steep though. It's something that I have not yet done in London, but I have done abroad. That was in Budapest, where a ticket for the National Opera cost me one dollar fifty in 1999, and it wasn't a hell of a lot more a couple of years ago in Zagreb in Croatia. Give it a go, it's a very moving experience, even if you don't know what's going on, as I didn't.

I can also strongly recommend going to the flicks in foreign climes. I was well amused in Egypt to go to the cinema and be the only person in there who was on their own. It was a massive cinema and it was pretty packed, with young people for the most part. They were all jabbering away for the whole film, it was very funny. I'd given up trying to watch the film after about five minutes because the noise was just too loud. It wasn't just people whispering, it was loud laughter and heated discussion. I spent the rest of the film watching the audience, which was probably more interesting anyway.

Then, all of a sudden, deathly silence. Conversations were abandoned and everybody shut up and started staring intently at the screen. I looked round to see what all the fuss was about and it turned out to be a romantic scene. It's incredible. Any hint of a kiss and the whole audience is totally enthralled. Then, at some point, the scene finishes and everybody gets back to their conversations whether a kiss occurred or not. It's incredible, and great to watch. Conversations continue apace until the next time the remotest hint of romance occurs on the screen, and so the pattern continues.

This is an international phenomenon as well. It's not exclusive to Saharan Africa. Down in Bolivia, the lovely town of Sucre is the judicial capital of the country. I went to a cinema whilst there which was proudly announced in the guidebook as the cheapest cinema on earth. Right enough, it cost me and Cockney Bastard fifty US cents for two of us to watch a double bill. Yet again, the audience spoke the whole way through the films except for the romantic interludes. The cinema was very frayed around the edges and the extra entertainment on this occasion came from the projectionist. Every now and then the light would start to fade on the screen and it must have been some sort error in the control room because the crowd would start whistling like hell and shouting until the bloke upstairs who had fallen asleep got his shit together and the film running properly again. Whenever this happened it was like a football match.

That wasn't the best bit, though. I remember that the second film was *Rumble in the Bronx*, the Jackie Chan film which was harmless enough. Before that was a very poor Anthony Hopkins offering called *The Edge*. It was made a lot poorer by the fact that there was a big five second gap in it which turned out to be where they'd taken a chewed-up bit of the reel out and somehow repaired it. How do I know this? Well, because there was a black bloke in the film to start with who was never seen again after the ripped bit. Then this thumping great big grizzly bear gets involved, so I deduced that the black chap had been gobbled up by the bear during the bit of the reel that got chewed up and spat out. What a great night out; I mean from a people watching point of view of course, not that it was good from a film point of view, obviously. Good fun, though.

Last but not least on the 'taking in the culture of the place' front is festivals. These are an absolute must wherever you are. I'll give you a couple of examples if you need convincing after reminding you of Los Nevados in Venezuela which was right in the middle of nowhere. Loads of fun, lots of great music and dancing in the moonlight.

At that point we were thick in the middle of festival country and shortly after the New Year's Festival in Southern Colombia, we moved down to Popayàn and Pasto for the Black and White festival. This is a two-day gig which used to be representative of slavery. It was the only two days of the year that the slaves got off work, and the first day is spent with the owners getting 'blacked' up to look like the slaves. The second day saw the slaves get covered in flour to look like their owners. The highlight of the first day was some little kid running up to Charlie and smearing two handfuls of axle grease down either cheek. Axle grease is what they use to 'get black' for the day. Could he get it out? Could he hell. He had to shave his beard off, much to mine and Tom's amusement. It was the first time Charlie's chin had been visible for about five years.

The second day is the real eye-opener, though. Moving south to Pasto, we were in a 'porpueso' minibus and came round a bend in the road to see that the town of Pasto was covered in a cloud of flour. We got into the middle of town and dumped the bags – which took a couple of direct hits – off in a hostel and got out in the street with everybody else. The whole town is full of drunk people throwing flour at each other and there's so much of the stuff that all the terracotta tiles on the roofs are white. The next day, everyone has sore heads and the council hose the whole town down.

What with south-west Colombia being festival central, it'd be a bit rude not to mention Cali. We spent Christmas there and it was a hell of a lot of fun. There's a massive music and bull-fighting festival put on by the city, although a lot of people say it's financed by the cocaine cartels which isn't overly surprising. So, we had Christmas amidst the gunfire and celebrated the day itself by sitting down to a roast chicken each in a *pollo loco* sort of joint where it took us a while to convince the girl that we wanted a whole chicken each.

Last of the festival scene is Gay Mardi Gras in Sydney. You could not wish to go to a better festival if you scoured the planet for decades. As long as you're tolerant of all persuasions and not easily shocked and it is the most incredible night out. The floats and the effort put into the whole thing are out of this world, and it certainly seems like the whole of Sydney is out on the streets to revel in the atmosphere. It's got to go on the 'must do' list.

Countries have a lot of history and it is from this that festivals, museums and all that other cultural stuff are generated. Whatever you do when on tour, don't be afraid to investigate the darker elements of cultures as well. Somebody once said to me that going to Auschwitz was morbid and that I shouldn't have done it. I couldn't disagree more. It was very moving and is one of the crossroads of twentieth-century history. Why not go there? Admittedly you feel like crying a lot of the time, but why would you not go there? The same goes for the Killing Fields in Cambodia, the slave caves of Zanzibar or the carnage of the Gallipoli Peninsula in Turkey.

The most depressing place I've been where the human suffering is current has to be the Potosi silver mine in Bolivia. Adults and children alike work underground for up to thirty six hours at a time in mines where methods are primitive, work is dangerous, pay is abysmal, and life expectancy is low. It's real life though, the same as Auschwitz-Birkenau is real history, and to try to cocoon yourself from it is selective living and partial reality.

Geography

Right, that's culture covered, or at least as covered as it's going to get. We're now getting onto the hard physical realities of the planet, the permanent aspects of our home. Amongst the peaks and troughs of our planet you're going to find some amazing stuff to visit, and the beauty of it is that there's something for everyone. No matter what your thing is, get out there and fill your boots. It's so good it begs belief.

Waterfalls your thing? Well, go big and go to Iguaçu on the tri-nation border of Argentina, Brazil and Paraguay. We had a good giggle there and it was right in the middle of El Niño as well so the water was as high as it gets. I had a butterfly hitch a ride on my head for a few minutes as well. Or, you could go high and go to Angel Falls in Venezuela which is the highest free-falling waterfall in the world at 979 metres. There's a single drop of 807 metres and a good swim-hole at the bottom where you can hang out and get battered by the water. We were really lucky to get the last boat up there before the onset of the dry season. We were in a big dugout with an outboard on the back and a bloke with a big oar at the front. We still had to get out and walk at times, but it was well worth it, and a very exciting ride to get there.

How about white frozen water instead of free-falling blue water? Head down to Franz Jozef glacier on the South Island of New Zealand.

Digression No 27 – people of the world part 5 – Israelis

'I don't care if it's the fastest moving glacier in the world, the cricket's on,' was my reply to Charlie's suggestion that we go and see Franz Jozef. We'd turned up and got installed in the local backpackers' before retreating to the pub to plan our next few days. The thing is that all this travelling is all good and well, but you can't let it get in the way of the cricket. Call me a philistine, but cricket is a matter of national importance. New Zealand were hosting England in a three test series and the first match was drawn in Auckland. All was to play for in Wellington and I was ready for a hard day in front of the TV watching every ball.

After a couple more beverages, Charlie had persuaded me to get up early and go and see the glacier before the start of play at eleven in the morning. I must say it was great. The fastest moving glacier in the world and a huge wall of ice at the bottom of it. What an imposing bit of natural beauty.

Back at the hostel and I'm in front of the telly at five to eleven with everything you need for a day of cricket. Tins of chilled cider, nibbles and dips, a full national newspaper and other essentials were all there. As the first ball was about to be bowled, this Israeli girl walked in waving a videotape at me. 'I want to watch this movie,' she announced to the room which contained me and my cricket viewing essentials. 'Sorry,' I said, 'but I'm watching this. It's live,' I added helpfully. 'What is this?' she asked suspiciously. I explained that it was New Zealand against England to which she informed me that she was going to get her boyfriend.

She did as well, and he told me that his girlfriend wanted to watch the movie. I told him I knew that but that I had been here for an hour getting ready for the cricket and that it was on live. 'Now!' she suddenly blurted out, more at her boyfriend than me by the look on his face. They had a discussion in something I assumed to be Hebrew. At its conclusion, he asked me when it would finish. I looked at his scowling girlfriend, who had had a right hissy fit and said 'Monday'. I could have said six o'clock this evening but Monday was an equally factual answer as that would be the end of the game, not the end of the day's play. I thought that considering she was being so nasty with him and me that she might as well have both barrels. She stormed off and he followed, after giving me an apologetic shrug of the shoulders. I was going to advise him to get a new girlfriend but thought better of it. He could've done better though, and not a lot worse, by the way.

Israelis are a funny bunch when travelling. You meet all of them or none of them. They're often brash, curt and arrogant. Rude, some would call it. Not always though. One of the most affable people I've ever met was an Israeli paratrooper who was travelling alone in the Bolivian interior. His parents were Indian Jews who had moved to Israel and, like a lot of his countrymen travelling the same continent, he'd just finished his National Service. Alone, Israelis tend to be more bearable than when they travel in packs. The only sign I've ever seen banning a race of people from a hostel was in Cali in Colombia where a sign outside said 'no Israelis or Germans'!

You have to admire the Israelis and their nation. When you go there, you get an idea of just how small it is. This makes it all the more incredible that they were invaded by three countries simultaneously on their biggest national holiday and totally routed the lot of them. Their will to survive is high as Joe Simpson's on Siula Grande. What you don't have to appreciate is their complete disregard for the wishes and enjoyment of those outside their group. More about them in the fauna section in a minute. As to cricket, that will reappear later on as well.

End of digression.

Glaciers not your thing? What about canyons? The three gorges across the bottom of France, the Grand Canyon, King's Canyon in the middle of Oz, how many more do you want? The list is never-ending. Of course, if you want to go for biggest is best, or deepest in this case, head to the Colca Canyon in Peru; the place where the condors fly for so long non-stop that they sleep in the air. Or is that a wind up I swallowed whole?

How about mountains? You've already had my top mountains wish list. Why not walk up a volcano such as Chimborazo in Ecuador, or the magnificent Fogo which me and my brother have just been up in Cape Verde?

Two things which have stuck with me above all are in Africa and on the Isla del Sol in the middle of Lake Titicaca. In Africa, the Great Rift Valley is one of our planet's most incredible features. It actually starts in the Lebanon and goes right down the Eastern side of Africa all the way to Mozambique. It is the only one of its kind and is basically a big tear in the top layer of the earth's crust. Seeing this disappearing into the distance in both directions from the top of Mount Kenya at dawn is a memory which will stay with me for the rest of my life. You're there thinking how privileged you are to witness such a view. The grind and misery of getting there are suddenly totally insignificant.

The second is a bit random. I've been to a few famous folks' birthplaces, such as Freddie Mercury's on Zanzibar and Nostradamus' in Salon de Provence. As I was in Copacabana on the shores of Titicaca, I thought I'd better go and see the birthplace of the sun. That's the famous, hot, gas ball Sun; you know the one which keeps our planet alive, not the crap xenophobic newspaper with 'Zoe, 23, from London' on page 3 with her tits out. I mean, Freddie was famous, but the sun is one of the most famous things ever. Apart from this claim to fame, the Isla del Sol also has the largest football stadium on the planet. There's a footy pitch which is surrounded by natural terracing on three sides which has enough room to sit at least a million supporters. The things you remember, eh?

Want to feel what it's like to be on another planet? There's the 'Craters of the Moon' in both New Zealand's Wairakei or Idaho in the States. Death Valley or any of the locations for *Mad Max* films, Devil's Marbles in Oz, Capadoccia in Turkey for weird mushroom-shaped houses and lava tubes in Queensland and Jordan. You could almost say it's like being on another planet on the salt flats of Uyuni in Bolivia as well, especially at night when the moon is shining on the salt.

All of these are, of course, natural phenomenons of our planet, but there are some equally eerie manmade ones as well. Right next to Uyuni is a place called the Cementerio de Locomotivos – literally translated, the train graveyard. That's exactly what it is as well. It's on a plain in the middle of nowhere where thousands and thousands of plastic bags, the tumbleweed of the Third World, are blown about by the winds of the high Andean plains before getting snagged on the thorns of bushes. The result is that all the bushes look like they're genetically modified giant cotton plants.

Too far away from town for noise to carry, you're there in the cemetery, surrounded by redundant, broken skeletons of stream trains built in Coventry amongst other places, with nothing but silence for company. Very surreal. The silence is as total as it is at Auschwitz where the birds never sing.

Moving on from infrastructure to planet 'furniture', the next section goes headlong into the things which fill our planet's physical presence with a more refined beauty; the plants and animals. See you there.

Things to see and do – mid range

From a financial point of view, it's worth mentioning that a lot of the plant and wildlife is going to cost you a fair bit of money to see. You tend to take organised tours to go and see a lot of it, even if just so you can fully appreciate it by way of a guide. It's worth it though. The natural wonders of our world should be a budgetary priority.

If geography is our infrastructure then flora and fauna are the meat on the bones, the aesthetics, which fill the large hulking frame which is the geography of planet Earth. They make the place look beautiful and they make it breathe. The majority of it is pretty regional so if you want to see the animal and plant life of planet Earth you're either going to have to get a big expensive haemorrhoid-friendly couch and a job lot of David Attenborough videos or, get off your arse and get out there and see it all. It's impossible to go through the whole lot but here's a few highlights.

The Amazon Basin – I went on a trip out of Rurrenabaque in Bolivia with Cockney Bastard and it was unforgettable. We had such a great voyage of discovery that I felt like kissing Silvio our guide for what he had shown us. We pottered off out into the middle of nowhere in boats and the amount of wildlife is the first thing that strikes you. The river you're on, the skies above you and the bushes on the banks of the river are all constantly moving. There are so many birds in the sky that it's claustrophobic, and you couldn't count the different species if you had all day.

Night fell and we'd set up camp. That was when things started to go pear shaped. The sky empties of birds but fills up with mosquitoes. It takes a while to get used to eating food with mosquitoes on your lips. You can brush them away but it really makes no difference as they're back a second later. Silvio ignored them but then I suppose he was used to it after putting up with it all his life. A good bit of advice I got then which I've stuck to ever since is to take a long-sleeved white round neck T-shirt away with you on every trip. Mozzies don't like white, and the long arms and round neck cover more of you up. If you don't like mozzies, it really is worth trying to put up with them in Amazonia for what follows.

After eating, we went out in the boat to see what was lurking in the dark. Lots, that's what was lurking in the dark. It's pretty simple, really. You shine a torch under the bushes on the edge of the river and see what reflects back at you. Eyes, lots and lots of eyes. We caught a caiman in those bushes that night. Silvio liked a bit of danger as we found out the next day. A caiman is like a crocodile or alligator. It's prehistoric, nasty and eats flesh. The differences with a caiman are that they're the smallest of the three species, have different body armour and are much more unpleasant. Great. Like being in a pub in Glasgow, it's the smaller ones you've to watch.

The next day, Silvio really excelled himself. The sky was again full of everything imaginable and we saw loads of pink river dolphins in the river itself, one of only five freshwater dolphins species in the world. Then it all got dangerous again. Silvio and his mate driving the other boat we met walked off saying that they were off to find some snakes. Sure enough, they came back twenty minutes later clutching an anaconda and a cobra! The cobra was pretty upset. Even the amateur onlooker could deduce this by the way venom was dripping from its fangs. No wildlife expert by any means, I still made the assumption that this meant it wasn't very happy. The anaconda was about a metre long and wrapping itself around anything and anybody in sight.

221

After everybody had had their photos taken with the snakes accompanied by a lot of screaming from the Israeli girls on the other boat, Silvio thought he'd show us the classic cobra pose. This he did by chucking the snake on the floor and prodding it with a stick! What an idiot. Israelis scattered and screamed, and I stood there thinking that Silvio was the one prodding it with a stick and the one with no shoes on. If someone was going to get the good news, it'd be him. 'Ça và Jacques' as we say in France. He was withdrawing his feet every time the cobra went for one of them and eventually it was at such a speed as to make him look like he was moonwalking. Save for the mozzies, that trip was perfect. Silvio is one of those guides who really make the trip for you.

Digression no 28 – Flying things

Don't worry about mosquitoes, they're just mildly irritating. A lot of flying things are terrible and frightening. True, evolution has given us animals we need and every species of the planet's intricate and complex web of fauna has a role. Personally, I am shit scared of wasps. Stupid I know, but there you go. Despite scaring me, I do realise that they do have a purpose. Wasps eat other stuff like ladybirds and contribute to keeping the planet's ecosystem balanced, so hats off to them.

Australia is another matter, though. I popped my head out of a swimming pool on my way up the middle of Australia a few years ago only to see this thing flying towards me. Bearing in mind my aversion to wasps, imagine my alarm at seeing an insect which was about the size of a swan flying towards me, five millimetres above water level. What's more, it had a stinging bit hanging off its arse end which looked like a nine inch nail fresh out of a blacksmith's forge, so bright was it glowing. I was so convinced that it was there to kill me that I disappeared underwater with the fear of re-emergence keeping me under for a period of time which would have got me a part in *The Big Blue* alongside Jean Reno.

Big flying things very nearly brought about my demise a couple of years earlier in Ecuador. Right enough, I was assisting in my own downfall by riding a badly maintained Honda Paris Dakar CR 250cc motorbike down the Pan-American highway with no helmet on. Not very clever. The other factor was this massive flying bear. If I hadn't had a pair of sunglasses on, I would probably have lost my left eye. I did a shoulder check before pulling out to overtake a truck and on looking back front ways had this big flying thing about three inches from my face. Wallop! it hit me right in the eye and I damn near came off the bike. The rest of the ride was completed at a much lower speed as the bloody thing broke my sunnies. If they'd been real Oakleys instead of fake 'jokeleys', they may have lived to tell the tale. Oh well, on the bright side at least I didn't end up as mashed up as my sunglasses, despite my own stupidity. Charlie came out of the trip unscathed as well, thank God.

End of digression.

Kakamega Rainforest in Kenya will be further visited in the tenting section. Charlie and Simon had made up for their tenting errors by finding us a great guide called John. He showed us the animal and plant life of the forest and what was good for healing which ailments. I just about jumped into Charlie's arms in the style of Shaggy into Scooby Doo's when he sees the big bad ghost is behind them. This made John laugh. He'd pointed out a very sinister-looking Forest Cobra which was retreating into a hole in a tree to patiently wait for its next unwitting victim. I was incredibly scared.

Further south in Kenya, we went to Lake Nakuru National Park where the father of the nation Jomo Kenyatta had a retreat while serving as Kenya's first President. Who can blame him? What a beautiful place. It's huge at 188 square kilometres, although tiny compared to some of the vast reserves and parks elsewhere in Africa. Simon managed to fall asleep as an albino giraffe ran in front of our vehicle. Good skills. Again, like in the Amazon, it's pretty hard for your brain to cope with the amount of wildlife your eyes are taking in with warthogs darting left right and centre with their tails bolt upright like car aerials, baboons scurrying up rocks everywhere with their red arses and frightening bark, and the flamingos on the soda lake which number anything up to a million in peak season. Add to this the rhinos, water buffalo and all the other big movers and, if you're a wild animal, you probably need to have pretty good peripheral vision if you want to survive.

One of the enduring images of that trip was a water buffalo. Being bovine in origin, he wasn't very clever. Water buffalo are one of the most dangerous animals on the continent, which, considering that Africa is a continent full of dangerous wildlife, is quite an accolade. The huge set of horns they have lying across their thick, heavy boned brow is a major piece of armoury not to be messed with. Masters of using these to the best and most lethal effects, water buffalo can open up a fatal wound in the flank of the biggest, thickest, skinned animals like a tin opener on a can of pineapple chunks, with a mere shake of the head.

This particular beast was on his own. He was standing in a wallow hole which was in the latter stages of drying up but still wet enough for him to be buried to the top of his legs. He looked really bored and depressed and, as if to confirm this, he would inhale deeply every minute or so and sigh with such a deep air of resignation that you wondered why he didn't just gash his own side open and get it all over and done with with a good suicide. It would be nearly a decade before I would see another animal looking so pissed off.

224

That was here in France and it's happened quite a few times since. Up here in the Alps, the wildlife is pretty exceptional and in Val, we're lucky enough to be right on the edge of a National Park which spans the Franco-Italian border. I was walking up there a few years ago in pretty bad weather. It's nice to go out and about when you don't feel like skiing and walking is good for you.

So there I am, walking up the valley to the St Charles Bridge and I see an Ibex up on the side of the mountain about 150 yards away. An Ibex is a big old unit; a mountain goat of sorts with a huge set of horns which rake backwards from the head. A very impressive beast and a beautiful sight. It's also very lucky to see one from that close up – they don't actively avoid humans but they do get up and walk off, or even run off, if they feel threatened or you're getting too close. This male was down so low because it was quite cold and that tends to get them down the hill a bit. Like my old mate the water buffalo in Kenya, he looked manically depressed, shoulders hunched, head down and facing into the wind. Every thirty seconds or so he would emit a huge sigh and I was stood there watching him for quarter of an hour wandering why he didn't go and find a bit of shelter, or at least go and stand in a bus shelter or something. But no, this beautiful creature had been born, had grown up, and was now standing somewhere really cold. He wasn't very happy with his lot by the look of him.

Just as amusing as Simon falling asleep in Kenya was a hike in Litchfield National Park near Darwin. As well as having one of the best swimming holes and rock jumps I've ever been to, it also provided a great comedy moment. Our guide was a proper brash Aussie with his Akubra hat and Hard Yakka khaki shorts. He really knew his stuff as well. The comedy was provided by a couple we came across in the middle of nowhere who were taking Adam and Eve photos of each other. As we burst out of the surrounding bush, the lady was reclined on some rocks in the middle of a flowing stream of about five metres width. The bloke doing the snapping was also in his birthday suit. We chanced upon them again later in the day taking some 'together shots' with the timer. Very amusing and the subject of some very forthright comments from our guide.

The 'Valley of Longevity' in Ecuador provided some indelible wildlife memories as well. It's a place which is famous for two things – hallucinogenic cactus juice which a lot of gringos go there for, and old people. Eastbourne and Bournemouth are famous for old people, but only because there are a lot of them. This place in Ecuador is famous for having people quite regularly living to be a hundred and twenty. It is constantly arguing the claim to the title of Earth's longest living people with somewhere on the Russian steppes. Probably a load of cobblers.

As to memories, well, Tom provided one of them. He provided the rest of us with a lot of entertainment while trying to control a pony considerably more rapid than the one he'd been on in Colombia a month or so earlier. The highlight of the day on the horses, apart from the beautiful valley we were in, was the nature around us.

The other moment was a lot smaller than a pony; about as small as you can get, in fact. We had a break from riding somewhere and I looked at the bush I was lying next to to find a hummingbird hovering right next to my head. It's one of the most extraordinary things I've ever seen. It was so small that it took me a while to realise that it wasn't an insect but in fact the world's smallest bird. Ten seconds of my life I'll never forget. Moments like that make the crap buses with no legroom, puking, shits and hard beds worth enduring.

Back on Zanzibar, I can't talk the place up enough. Even its name has an air of mystery about it. There's been a bit of bother there in the last few years but that goes for Motherwell on a Friday night as well. It's a great archipelago where Africa meets Arabia in a lot of ways. The slave trade left an Arabic tinge on Zanzibar which is part of the feel of the place. Zanzibar is not just known for slavery but also for its spices. It and its neighbours are collectively known as the 'Spice Islands', and the cloves are particularly famous. We went and visited a spice farm while touring the old slave caves on the east coast of the island. I honestly thought it was a wind up, I really did. I'd never given much thought to what sort of plant a pineapple came from but I was convinced it wasn't the thing I was being shown. It looked like the hairdo of Sideshow Bob out of the *Simpsons* with big pointy leaves fanning out a metre in every direction. It was like the plant in the *Little Shop of Horrors* without the head. This massive plant had one pineapple sat right in the middle of it! It looked totally ridiculous. The bloke finally convinced me that it was the real deal.

A third of our planet is above water and that means that two thirds of it is covered in water. Clever aren't I, eh? This obviously means that a huge amount of what there is to see on our planet is underwater. Time to get all Jacques Cousteau.

I suppose the first thing to say about scuba diving is that it's not really necessary a lot of the time. As often as not you'll see as much marine life snorkelling as you will scuba diving. Most of the stuff you want to see in the sea lives in the first ten metres of depth and snorkelling is a lot cheaper and easier to do, so if you are confined to the cheap seats, snorkelling is a good option. I was pottering about in Fiji, once watching a huge manta ray roaming the sandy bottom. So transfixed was I by the elegant and graceful glider that it wasn't until it was twenty yards away that I saw a seasnake coming towards me. They're proper dangerous apparently but it swam harmlessly behind me, thank God. Snorkelling concludes the cheap and free things to do section because as soon as you put tanks on

227

your back to go underwater, it gets a lot more expensive. See you in the far-from-free things to do section.

Prior to departing for the expensive section of things to do, animals warrant further discussion from a domesticated angle. Animals are useful for getting around the place, as discussed previously. That apart, they're also prolific contributors to the richness of our daily lives. Can you imagine how little atmosphere our planet would have if it was only inhabited by humans? No dawn chorus from the bird population to bring in the new day, no crickets outside a Mediterranean taverna of an evening, no lions' roars filling the African nocturne or no peacocks regally squawking around the palaces of Europe? All parts of daily life which you'd soon notice if they weren't there, and we have our wildlife to thank for that. A planet with just us on it would be like a classical concert hall with a single violinist in it, instead of the fully armed orchestra of dozens, with all its different sections. Life is audio as well as visual, and the atmosphere of our planet is provided by all its inhabitants, not just the human ones. Even camels and sea lions add to the richness of our planet's diversity.

Animals can also make as great a contribution to our lives when domesticated. By this, I mean that farmed animals and domestic pets have a role to play, as do wild animals which use the surrounding humans to make their own lives easier.

Take our last dog for instance; he was called Joss or 'Joss the dog' as he was often called, for obvious reasons. Absolutely thick as pig shit that dog was, may his soul rest in peace. Thick he may have been, but he was a good companion and a great friend.

He stopped being a great friend in April 2002 when the old man shot him in the back of the head with a .22 rifle while Joss was pottering around the garden. Before all you animal rights people start filling envelopes with shit to post to my

228

parents' house, here's a defence of the execution; 1) The old man is half-Scottish and half-Yorkshire and therefore about as tight as a British person can get. The vet was going to charge £70 to give the poor little bastard the good news! 2) Joss the dog had been to the vets that much in his life that he'd have worked out that he was going to get a lethal injection. 3) It's better for him to have died in familiar surroundings. 4) Fair play to the old man, I couldn't have done it.

Joss loved routine. Two walks a day, a good siesta on the couch in the living room, as much food as he could beg, steal or borrow and the rest of the day patrolling the borders of his domain. Basic requirements for his basic brain.

Digression no 29 – cats and dogs

My friend Charlie introduced me to the cats and dogs theory, which is explained thus by cat lovers; a cat and a dog are sat down watching their owner put up a set of shelves. The cat is sat there, bored, thinking, 'I hope to God he puts a spirit level on that before drilling the holes, it's low on the left.' The dog is sat there, with his tongue hanging out and his tail wagging excitedly, thinking, 'I haven't got a clue what he's doing but it looks brilliant!' That to cat lovers is the difference between cats and dogs, and the reason that they consider cats to be superior. Namely, because they're more intelligent. I'm not arguing that fact, it's true, but does that make cats better than dogs?

Of course not, as any dog lover will tell you. A pet is just that; a pet. A pet is supposed to be a companion and a friend and some non-human mate you can have a laugh with; a sight for sore eyes who gives you a big welcome when you get home. A pet is not some smart-arse animal which eats what you put out for it when it feels like it and leaves the mangled remains of some animal it's been torturing all night on the doorstep for you to clear up.

Cats are a lot cleverer than dogs but are too selfish to be pets; 15-love to the canines.

End of digression.

Joss the dog loved routine because the thicker the animal, the more they rely on routine. I'm not speaking ill of the dead, but that dog could have won a hundred caps if there had been a British Canine-Being-Thick team. No lights on at all.

Watching him eat breakfast was a right fiasco. He'd have a slice of toast with nothing on it cut up into 16 squares on the doormat. First of all, he'd bark at it for a couple of minutes until it cooled down a bit and then pick up the first bit, trot off between the front legs of the kitchen table, over to his bed, get in, and eat the bit of toast. Back to the doormat for another piece via the front two legs of the table, and so on until he'd finished the whole slice. What an idiot.

His next routine was dogged by lack of stealth. You can't be stealthy if you're a quadruped with a leg in plaster. He'd been badly messed up by a Renault 5 and had only survived through strength of character. Being thick, he'd taken a liking to raw Brussels sprouts. It was very amusing to hear him come out of the carpeted living room onto the tiled floor of the hall and tap tap tap tap tap, thud. The thud was sign that he'd headbutted the pantry door open and selected himself a raw brussel. Tap tap tap tap he'd head back to the living room to consume his ill-gotten gains. Joss! someone would occasionally shout from the kitchen for a laugh, a couple of taps into the getaway run. The tapping would stop for exactly eight seconds and you'd not hear a sound. Eight seconds was obviously what he deemed to be enough time for anybody who was going to spring him to come out of the kitchen. Then the tapping would resume as he made his bid to get to the living

230

room and we'd all laugh like hell. The main problem with that unstealthy routine of his was that despite the comedy value and hours of fun it gave us in the kitchen, it gave Joss the dog nerve gas-like flatulence. He used to lie in front of the TV and emit 'silent but violent' farts of crippling smelliness.

That dog's crowning achievement came thanks to another of his likeable habits. He used to bark like hell whenever the garden gate opened and then welcome in folk he knew and eye suspiciously those he didn't. One day the old man came back in from the farm. It was summer and we were all out on the lawn. Now, Joss wasn't the biggest of dogs, being a little pocket battleship of a Terrier, and he'd get under your feet a bit in the excitement of welcoming you home.

Joss and the old man had got off on the wrong foot. It wasn't that they didn't like each other, but just that they didn't spend a lot of time together. It could well have been because the old man wasn't really in favour of getting another dog after the Red Setter he'd loved ran out of steam a few years previously. They got on like a house on fire in the end. The dog ended up going down the farm one day for some reason and the two of them became inseparable from there on in.

That day when the old man rocked up in the garden, him and Joss were still in their 'arm's length' stage. The dog liked the old man enough to say hello and the old man would give him a pat hello. As already mentioned though, Joss did get under your feet a bit, being small and all. That day he got between the old boy's welly boots and tripped him up. Talk about David slaying the Giant; the old man lost his footing and did a sort of reverse pirouette, landing on his back on the lawn. Joss the dog decided that it was time to show him a lot more affection and pounced on the prostrate bloke on his back, with docked tail wagging aplenty and genitals in the old man's face. 'Get your fucking tool out of my face!' commanded the old man, eventually peeling the dog off his face. The rest of the family were on the lawn as the fiasco unfolded and we were killing ourselves with laughter even before the old man delivered that classic line. Granny got the giggles and went bright red, unable to breathe. I thought she was going to die but she gulped in some air after thirty seconds or so.

Exceptions exist for every statement. Ginnie was one such exception, to the 'all dogs are thick' argument. She was the cleverest dog I've ever met. Ginnie, like most of the cleverer canines around, is a mongrel. She's got some Border Collie in her and probably some description of fast thin thing like a Lurcher or thereabouts. The surefire thing is that she's a hell of a clever dog and good to have around, being very mild mannered as well as clever. I met her in New Zealand when I was working on a 400+ cow dairy unit just outside of Rotorua on the North Island. It was a great job. Not the most financially rewarding job I've ever had but good all the same. It was hard work but also a good, clean living lifestyle. I was working for and living with a lovely couple called Dave and Jo and getting up at first sparrow shit every morning to go and get the cows in. I could hear Ginnie getting revved up out in the garage where she slept, as I ate my porridge oats. We were out the door at four-ish, down to the shed to get the quad bike, and then off to the milking parlour.

I used to love that time of day. We'd race along, me on the quad with the lights ablaze, and Ginnie running alongside, almost capable of outrunning the Honda. We'd get to the paddock in which the herd were and I'd just have to open the gate onto the track, a function which marked the end of my participation in getting the cows in. That dog used to go and get all the cows for you while you just sat there smoking your first fag of the day. All 400-odd. I used to sit on the quad and smoke a big heart starting King Edward-size roll up which was a great way to spend creeping dawn every morning. Ginnie would run around busy with her favourite pastime; telling cows what to do.

I thought that getting the cows out of the paddock was clever until after the end of the artificial insemination season when I nearly burst into applause. Every cow in the herd was artificially inseminated with high quality bulls' semen as part of New Zealand's program to improve the quality of its bloodstock. After a couple of rounds of AI some cows are still empty – not pregnant. As with most farmers, Dave had a few random bulls to bung in with the cows thereafter on the off-chance of getting any of the cows which were still empty in calf. The resulting calves are no good for the herd but good eating.

Getting the six bulls up to the main farm from rough land called the 'run off' had been a fiasco. Six sex-crazed bulls who've been living with other bulls for months running down a mile and a half of straight road. A car was nearly written off when one of the bulls took a swipe at it with its hind legs, luckily just missing it. We finally got them to the farm.

So in the morning, Ginnie and I went down to the paddock to get the cows. I sat on the quad smoking a fag, and she went in to get the cows out as usual. I assumed that she'd get the bulls as well. What she did, in the pitch dark, was separate the six bulls out from the 400 and odd milking cows, push the cows down the race towards the milking shed and leave the bulls in the paddock. I was dumbfounded. I knew she was clever but that really catapulted her into the canine genius hall of fame. One dog in the virtual pitch black of dawn.

It's also safe to say that Ginnie was by far the most intelligent animal on that farm. That is not only testament to her intelligence, but also to the fact that virtually all the other animals on Dave and Jo's place were cows, and cows are thick as two thick things stuck together. A dreadful invention are cows and sheep. They get on your tits as well. Calling them a

233

bad invention is probably a bit harsh because they produce milk. Oh yes, and they're useful; dead and in the oven or on the BBQ. (See food chapter)

Being a much bigger fan of all things porcine than all things bovine, it was a surprise to me that there were a couple of cows I liked. Number 196 was actually quite clever and used to nudge me for a hello at every milk, a substance she produced vast amounts of. Number 229 was so bozz-eyed and worried-looking that she got the name Foghorn Cleghorn. The rest of them were all thick as you like. 175 used to be first in the parlour at every milk, trap 1, right-hand lane of the milking shed. She'd walk to the shed in the morning because she had heavy udders, but the afternoon was another matter. The herd used to be put in a faraway paddock between milks because their udders were lighter for afternoon milk and so they could therefore walk further without discomfort. On her way to the shed in the afternoon, 175 used to come bursting over the brow of the hill at a full trot like a champion racehorse. She'd jog all the way to the parlour and get there about 20 minutes before any of the other cows, and stand there waiting to be milked in trap 1, right-hand side. Idiot.

By far my worst day on the job was Christmas Day 1996. It's bad enough having to work on Christmas Day but that didn't really bother me. It was the getting shat on that affected my enjoyment of work a bit that particular morning. Having just put the cups on a cow, I heard the faint internal plopping sounds of a ruminating animal about to unleash, a bit like porridge bubbling when it's on too high a heat. With only a microsecond's notice, I initiated evasive action, but it was too late. I was hit in the chest by a tidal wave of sloppy shit which poured from the cow's arse like the blood gushing from the lifts of the Overlook Hotel in the Stephen King thriller *The Shining*. It poured down the inside of my milking apron and shirt. I'd wrongly assumed that things had reached a low point

234

for the morning. Unfortunately not. Screaming and using a lot of swearwords involves having your mouth open and it was while swearing that some of the cow's 'bum gravy' shot up off a fold in my apron and into my mouth. It was turning into comfortably my worst Christmas morning since I'd tried to hack my thumb off with a sword I'd found in my Grandparent's attic aged about 12.

Cow shit is nice and warm. If you were dying of hypothermia you'd urge as many cows to shit on you as possible. The trouble is that it doesn't taste all that good. I managed not throw-up, but only just. It was a very disappointing turn of events as far as I was concerned. Not so for Dave who had trouble controlling himself and his bowels, so all-consuming was his mirth. We were a man down for a couple of minutes or so and I was on my own, covered in shit, milking cows with Dave incapable of any contribution towards completing the task at hand, namely milking the herd, because he was laughing too much to be able to work simultaneously. Too busy thriving on my misfortune so he was. I took a dimmer view of the whole episode. Cow shit is fairly harmless but I'd just as soon have avoided getting to taste it really.

The day did get a lot better though. We had a fantastic BBQ Christmas lunch (after a very long shower in my case) and the beer and wine flowed like shit out of a cow's arse, but for longer and at less pounds per square inch. Afternoon milking took about twice as long as usual due to our levels of inebriation.

In the same way as some animals do a lot better in the wild than they do when exploited by humans, some also use the human lifestyle to their advantage. Look at foxes, really clever buggers who certainly have the measure of humans. We used to go down to the pig farm at dusk and shoot a few every now and then. They used to trot casually onto the farm at dusk, kill loads of piglets and then walk off with one. It was very rare

235

that we got close enough to them to shoot the buggers because they're so clever. They either see you or smell you. They give a hell of a lot of thought to which way to approach from and other things essential to survival. Me and the old man were in the hedge one night and I unloaded my little 20 bore shotgun at one fox, broadside from about 20 yards. I was only young and couldn't cope with anything bigger than a 20 bore. The fox viewed me with a look of mild annoyance, more pissed off with itself for not noticing us than the actual being shot. If it had fingers, it would surely have stuck the V sign up at me but, lacking the necessary digits, turned round and casually walked off instead. Not for long though; the old man unleashed his new cannon, a .22 rifle which he'd bought to replace his 12 bore, and blew the back of its head off. That'll teach it! That was a country dweller, a traditional fox if you will. Urban foxes are now as common as countryside ones and the shift to the 'burbs and the big bad city just proves how adaptable and clever foxes are.

This also applies to other animals as well, though. The most frustrating example of this I ever suffered was in Kenya, and more specifically on Mount Kenya. The four of us had camped the first night and were finishing breakfast before a back-breaking day of false horizons and hard trekking. Packing up, Ellie suddenly started shouting and screaming. I looked up to see a Colobus monkey scampering off with a loaf of bread. We were all four of us within a few feet of where the raider had struck and I couldn't believe the nerve of the simian thief. That monkey had more front than Dolly Parton. It then proceeded to take the full piss out of us by sitting on a branch about three feet out of our reach and eating the whole loaf of bread right in front of us. 'My kingdom for a shotgun' was my immediate thought. That'd have wiped the smile off its face. You couldn't help but admire its cunning and courage though.

Top of my benefitting from human existence league though has to be the possums of New Zealand. Most of them would appear to be pretty thick judging by the amount of roadkill you see on the roads, especially on the South Island. It's quite off-putting on a motorbike when you're laying the bike at an angle in a tight turn and start bouncing around on roadkill. But one possum at least has bucked the trend for lack of intelligence among the species. This particular possum lived in Taupo. I say lived because it was seven years ago, so I presume its dead by now. Having said that, I don't know the life expectancy of a possum so he may still be on the go. Anyway, me and Charlie had just done a bungee jump at a beautiful place called Devil's Gate on the Waikato River and I was walking back up the track from the river bank. Passing a litter bin, it was making noises which litter bins shouldn't really make. I investigated and found to my amazement that the rustling noises emanating from the bin were coming from a possum who was lying on his back in the bin, just finishing a packet of cheese and onion crisps! He looked up at me with his paw in the bag as if to say; 'What? Haven't you ever seen a possum reclining in a litter bin eating a packet of crisps before?' I hadn't.

You have to feel quite sorry for animals which have been domesticated in a lot of ways. They all have relations in the wild which may live a shorter time after being horrifically torn to pieces by something bigger and harder than them, but at least they can have a laugh while they're alive. Think of those warthogs running merrily around Africa with their tails bolt upright like chimney sweeps' brushes and compare it to the plight of other pigs. More specifically, I'm thinking of a town called Otovalo in Ecuador which has a huge market every… I can't remember how often. The regular market later in the morning is pretty good in itself, but for someone of farming extraction it's the dawn livestock market which is the highlight.

Tom is great at getting arty black and white photos and is a very good amateur photographer. He's really captured the moment on a number of occasions on his travels, but rarely better than one morning in early 1998 in Otovalo. He got a photo of a woman trudging up a dirt road with a piglet of about a month old on a lead. The great thing was that the piglet was sitting on its arse with its back legs lying flat on the ground. It had no intention of cooperating with its owner's intentions, and she was forced to drag the porcine friction-maker up the hill with her. The poor pig eyed us as it was dragged past with that fateful look of resignation that Wile E Coyote gets when gravity is just about to take hold of him, having just run over a cliff – that mournful look of inevitability as another ACME-inspired attempt to despatch Road Runner to the afterlife fails miserably. It was a great moment but we did feel sorry for that piglet.

I felt sorry for Tom as well. It said in the guidebook that it's polite to ask the locals before photographing them. Conforming to politeness, Tom had asked the first person he'd wanted to snap that morning if he could and she said yes. As soon as he'd finished, she stuck her hand out and said, 'That'll be 3,000 sucres please.' Tom went green and me and Charlie collapsed in stitches as our cousin was taken to the cleaners by a harmless looking woman not an inch over 4 feet 9 wearing a bowler hat and dragging a pig to market!

It's not just in the Third World where animals are badly treated, though. I was walking to work one evening late last ski season when a car came swinging to a screeching halt in a bus stop just up the road. Two blokes were there holding a Border Collie by the collar, and waiting for the driver as it transpired. An irate woman got out of the car and started bollocking the dog, saying stuff like 'where the hell have you been?' to it in French. She then took a piece of climbing rope with a full size carabina clip on it out of her coat pocket and swung for the dog

238

just as I passed the scene. Luckily for me, she just missed my head with the clip as it started on its arc. Not so luckily for the dog, she hit it with extraordinary viciousness right across the hind quarters. Then she hit it again. Then she thanked the two men with a lovely radiant smile. From what she said it was clear that they'd rung her to tell her where her dog was. What was strange was that they seemed to find her behaviour totally normal.

I didn't. I told her that she had just very nearly hit me in the face with her homemade dog-lead-cum-torture implement and that if I ever saw her treat an animal like that again I would report her to the police for animal cruelty. In the following ten seconds, I learnt about fifteen new French swearwords. My comments had not improved her mood. I'm only assuming that all the words she used in that sentence which I didn't already know were swear words, but considering the venom of the delivery, I'm fairly certain they were.

I'll never forget the look on that dog's face and my God do I feel sorry for it. This is not to say that all French dogs have a hard time of it. The French are certainly crueller to their dogs than most Europeans but, contrary to popular belief, France does have its own animal cruelty charity. It also has citizens who like dogs, some a little bit too much.

One of these was Monsieur Tico, who lived opposite us in Brittany. He owned the hotel in the village and was the next door neighbour of Madame l'Hospitalier, our school dinner lady. Monsieur Tico loved his three dogs – not in the way Welshmen love sheep, but he was very fond of them.

Old Tico also liked to mow his lawn wearing his slippers. Not a good idea as he found out when he pushed the mower over his foot and gratuitously hacked most of the top of his foot off. Ouch. Errors. So there's Tico, an ambulance ride, several hundred stitches and a few skin grafts later, lying in bed recuperating. Our dad suggested we go round to see him like good neighbours do. Off we went and found Tico lying there looking a bit pasty but otherwise okay. While we were talking to him I was distracted by thinking about how all the lumps and contours of his covers could not be formed by the body of a five-foot-something Frenchman. Then, as if to confirm this, an Alsatian's head poked out of the bottom of the duvet! To add to the comedy value of the moment it was quickly joined by the head of a sausage dog. Both dogs were panting and it was becoming clear that the obviously high 'Tog' rating of Tico's duvet and the combined heat of one French bloke and two dogs was creating a lot of extra heat. Then, some sort of Heinz 57 mongrel-looking thing, vaguely similar to a Welsh Terrier, popped out of the headboard end of the bed, raising the dog-in-bed count to three, and started licking Tico's face! Yuck.

Now, call me old-fashioned, but despite my lifelong love of dogs, I would not have three dogs in my bed, especially if one of my feet was covered in deep lacerations. MRSA was not on the same scale as it is now in the early eighties but even I know that the addition of an Alsatian, a sausage dog and a fake Welsh Terrier are not going to increase the hygiene levels of your bed.

Things to do – more expensive

I was never in a big rush to go scuba diving but am glad that I got round to it on my second visit to the Great Barrier Reef. The swimming test nearly killed me because I swim like a brick, but once actually full of new knowledge, I was okay at the actual scuba bit. Since that initial foray, I've been diving again in Thailand and Greece amongst others. The Barrier Reef is a cut above anything else I've done, though. Let's hope it's around for future generations to see and experience. I'm sure that thousands of people out there with greater literary powers of description could and have put on paper something vivid enough to adequately describe the sheer riches of the Great Barrier Reef, but I don't consider myself to be one of them; you'll just have to go and see it.

Very interesting though that a chap who came in to give us a talk during our course should say that out of the thousands of dives he'd done around the world, Scapa Flow in Scotland was the best of all.

Things take on a slightly more laidback approach when you're diving in Thailand. In Australia they will do anything to protect the Reef which is admirable. They ask you not to apply sun cream before going on a dive and little attentions to detail like that will hopefully preserve the natural wonder which is the Great Barrier Reef for a good long time to come. Back in Thailand, me and Foxy went for a post-full moon party chill out on Koh Tao. The first difference from Australia was that we got to the first dive site and the skipper's mate just lobbed the anchor straight off the front of the boat and onto the reef! He'd have been straight to Cairns Prison if he'd done that on the Barrier Reef. Second thing, the skipper was crying. The dive master explained that he'd had a domestic with his wife and was always like this on the many occasions on which they argued. What he failed to mention was that he also drank his way through the tears. By the time we came up from the first dive, during which we went through a really cool underwater tunnel, there was an empty bottle of Sang Som rum in the bin. By the time we got back to the island, he could barely stand up.

Extreme sports tend to be fairly expensive things to do while you're away travelling, but a lot of them are a real buzz. I'm not sure that scuba diving qualifies as extreme sports but it's getting a lot closer to being so. It's now possible to dive in a cage off the coast of South Africa, and go down to the depths where Great White sharks are lurking. That's pretty extreme. Another similar thing I'd love to do is to dive in Flores in Indonesia where a mate of mine says there were an estimated four hundred Hammerhead sharks between him and his buddy lying on the seafloor and the surface. Very cool indeed and no cage. That's the weird thing about Hammerheads. Although they are on the 'danger to humans' list, attacks on humans are almost unheard of.

Take the salt out of the water and you can go white-water rafting all over the place. In my case, this was in New Zealand at a place called Taihape (pron: 'thai-happy'), on the North Island. 'You can't die happy unless you've been to Taihape' as the locals claim. I'm not sure about that, but it's got some great Grade 5 rapids on the nearby Hautapu River and I only went and fell in. It all got a bit hairy for a while until I got dragged back into the boat. It's not the only extreme sport you can give a go in Taihape. It's also the world capital of welly boot throwing!

Gaining further in altitude, you can jump out of a plane, which is something else I haven't got round to yet. I've had the opportunity to do quite a few skydives, but never had the funds at the time. I'm going to give it a go at some point though; it's

242

just something else still hanging around on the ever-expanding 'things to do while on tour' list. Like a lot of budget travellers, I have to put up with having a long wish list; it's all part of the low budget lifestyle.

In the same vein but coming back down a bit, why not try leaping off of something such as a platform up in the air with a bungee attached to your ankles? A word of advice if you are going to go bungee jumping though. Don't do what I did and allow your hands to drift apart as you hit the water. I had a very sore face for a couple of days as my fists hadn't broken the surface of the water properly. As with most extreme activities, bungee jumping is going ever higher and more extreme. The one I did at Devil's Gate on the banks of the Waikato river in Taupo, New Zealand was a mere forty-seven metres; the current highest is a monster of two hundred and sixteen metres in South Africa. That's a long way down. Alternatively, why not run down the side of the Novotel in Auckland or do a rap jump somewhere else? Still a fast loss of altitude and a big rush but without the diving into space.

Two things I can definitely recommend on this front are; a variation on the above bungee jumping which goes in the other direction. Up at Tauranga in New Zealand they had a bungee 'catapult', which was a right buzz. It's simple; two big tower masts and a sphere. Two people sit in the sphere and a big hook is attached to the bottom of the sphere while they run the bungees up the masts. When the bungees are tight, they let the hook go. One point not a lot of hundredth of seconds later you're about sixty metres in the air and the G-force is wild. Give it a go. That goes for bobsleighing as well. My God it that quick and made to feel even quicker by the fact that the run you're going down is so narrow.

Extreme sports really go in the category of things that you should do if you can. It's all a matter of what you consider more important. Extreme sports are here to stay and you'll probably be able to do them for evermore. This could well not be true for things you can go and visit and if I had the choice I would much sooner go on loads of excursions to the jungle and stuff like that than the adrenalin side of things.

The trouble with excursions is that they usually cost a good couple of hundred dollars, so you could be limited to the number you can do. As is always the case in the cheap seats, you just have to wring as many activities as you can out of the financial resources available to you, and then hammer the credit card like hell for the last few weeks before going home.

If you find yourself in the perfect world where you can do everything, then get on and do it. From there on in it's all a matter of compromise. If you don't have to compromise, fair play to you. Not everyone with a backpack on is a pauper. Some people are already doing what I hope to do forever, which is travel the same way no matter how much money I may have in the future. It's more fun, it's more of a challenge, and you meet a wider spectrum of people.

Last but not least in the expensive things to do is shop. Shop till you drop is my advice. What's the point in filling your house with soulless IKEA and Habitat stuff when there's a whole world of superb stuff to buy out there? I'm not particularly good at shopping because I haven't got the organisational skills to sort out what to do with the stuff. I'm sitting in my cousin Tom's house and it's full of lovely stuff he's harvested from all over the place. I won't be more specific about where it is in case you come and burgle it. He's always been very good at buying stuff and getting it taken home by him or someone else which is one option, or shipping it home which takes more organisation than I'm capable of.

That's the main problem with buying stuff; you have to carry it and if you're backpacking you've probably got enough to carry as it is. Buy it and post it home is your best option. How and when you go about it is secondary to actually getting involved, though. Do go shopping if you can. It's great fun and often done in a great atmosphere. Markets in the Third World, whether at night or in the daytime, always have a great, intense, loud and claustrophobia atmosphere. The bazaars of the Arab world stand out in this respect, but it's an unmissable experience everywhere.

The other thing to remember, especially if you're British, is to haggle. Watch Monty Python's *The Life Of Brian* before leaving home to get an idea and get into it. Why do the Brits not haggle? If you go into a shop in Britain and try to haggle, they look at you like you're an alien or something. Everywhere else it's not so much allowed as expected. Haggling is a mutual enjoyment activity and the stallholders enjoy it as much as you will. It becomes a battle of nerve like a game of poker. It's very good sport and everybody does it, except the Brits.

Talking of sport, it really does bring the planet together and although you'd have to put it in the expensive section of 'things to do', do go and soak up the atmosphere of a live sporting event if you can. At the cheaper end of things, you can just go and see the stadiums in a number of countries, which are very impressive and more often than not free to visit. I've never been to a match at the MCG in Melbourne, but I've had a look around when it's empty. With a capacity of over ninety thousand, it really is a cathedral of sport. A hundred thousand is even more impressive and that's the capacity of the Nou Camp in Barçelona. A mate of mine has a photo of one whole three tiered side of the ground with no one but himself sat in the middle of the middle tier on the half way line. Pretty cool.

Next up the ladder is the Maracana in Rio where they packed in a hundred and ninety nine thousand for the final of the 1950 World Cup. It's a beautiful place even when empty. With that said, the idea is of course is to get into these places when there's something going on, such as a game. Here are some of my favourites sporting moments.

245

Lancaster Park, Christchurch, New Zealand.

Cricket is a game of which most people on the planet are aware, even if only because it is famous for taking five days to play. It's only the populations of about fifteen countries who know what's actually going on on the pitch, though. The French are all aware of it and it is a source of great mirth. I'm forever reading out the cricket scores on the radio in the winter, and as soon as my French colleagues hear the word 'cricket', they are ribbing me about it live on air.

While touring New Zealand, Charlie and I stopped in the great city that is Christchurch and saw England win two games of cricket in the space of three days. A rare event in itself.

A half-full stadium is better than an empty one but that was as full as the ground got in the last two days of the five day game we saw, which England won by four wickets. We all went out on the town to celebrate on the night the England player Phil Tufnell got caught smoking dope in the bogs of a Christchurch bar and my mate Charlie nearly managed to nick a whole uniform out of the staffroom in McDonald's. A raucous night out indeed.

For the one day game a couple of days later though, the ground was transformed. The place was packed and the beer was flowing. England won a good game of cricket but it's the crowd that made it. In the cheap seats the banter was incredible. It was in the early days of mobile phones and every time one rang, the crowd would boo loudly until the owner would hold it up in the air and hit the red button. Loud cheers would ring out as the owner acknowledged that it is sacrilege to take your phone to the cricket.

One bloke got booed at and the booing reached a crescendo when he answered the call. With that, a bloke who'd been playing the trumpet very badly throughout the day started playing 'When The Saints Go Marching In' right behind this bloke's ear. A mate of the bloke on the phone grabbed hold of the trumpet and threw it down onto the pitch some ten rows in front of us. With that the crowd became inconsolable and started booing the bloke and pelting him with plastic pint glasses. It was such a comic moment and the sort of thing which makes going to the cricket so worthwhile.

Things degenerated as the beers flowed, the Mexican waves started and England's innings was the first ever under floodlights in Christchurch. As night drew in and the beer clouded judgements, the streakers started to have a shot at the title. The police had anticipated this and there were special pursuit coppers in tracksuits dotted around the edge of the pitch to intercept the runners. The biggest laugh of the day was earned by a fat English bloke who had a shot at the title while worse for wear. He'd managed to get his Sheffield Wednesday shirt off but tried to take his pants off and vault the advertising hoardings at the same time. The result was that he tripped over his underwear and ended up sprawled on the floor at the feet of a very unimpressed looking policewoman with his knob hanging out. Needless to say, that was the last of the cricket he saw that day, as the legendary John Arlott would have said on the commentary. Let's go to Australia.

Digression No 30 – The best day of my life part 2 – Sydney cricket ground – 17th of January 1999

It was looking like we were going to see England lose two games in a row at the same ground in the space of two weeks. Normal service had resumed. We'd lost the test match by ninety eight runs but the England fans sang on regardless, loyal to the cause come rain or shine. Losing at three in the afternoon, the 'Barmy Army' were still in full song three hours later when the police told them to bugger off home on the loud-halers. England's legendary away support can turn a cricket match anywhere in the world into a home fixture.

Now it was a one dayer and the place was packed to the rafters, the difference from the five-day game was that the crowd were all Australian. The 'Barmy Army' had all gone back to the UK leaving us Sydney-resident expats to support the boys. Fifteen of us were in the cheap seats on Yabba's Hill and surrounded by Aussies who were in fine voice as England slumped to thirty nine for two wickets. From there on in it was all England and the Aussies all shut up one by one and eventually left.

What you have to remember about Australians is that, like the French, they're interested in victory more than sport. It is said that France won the Football World Cup in 1998 and celebrated on the streets of Paris for thirty hours. England won it in 66 and are still celebrating to this day! The same goes for the Aussies. If their cricket team was as bad as England's has been for most of the last twenty years, none of them would turn up. We turn up rain or shine to support the boys, and let's face it, it's more often been rain than shine.

The SCG was testament to this. We were singing songs at them all day and they couldn't take it. At one point we started getting on at Shane Warne who was fielding near us. Warney may be the best bowler in the world, and a great ambassador for cricket, but he's not very good at giving up smoking. Nicorette had sponsored him a hundred thousand dollars to give up and after nearly three weeks, he was biting his nails a bit. We were singing songs about ovine sex and chucking Winfield cigarettes at him and, lo and behold, three days later he was caught by the paparazzi having a fag and had to give the dosh back!

The closer Australia got to defeat, the bigger the sense of humour failure the home fans suffered. In the end we were forced to change from singing 'we're shit but we're beating you' by the numbers of them leaving before the end of the match. We changed to 'we can see you sneaking out'. What a

248

great day out. To top it all off, the team had as big a sense of humour failure as their fans. Batsman Ricky Ponting went out drinking after the game to drown his sorrows. Elbowing his way rudely to the bar at the Beefsteak and Bourbon nightclub in Sydney's King's Cross, he made the mistake of elbowing a bloke from Hull out of the way. The bloke turned out to be the hardest bloke in England and proceeded to knock the little oik right out! The next day Ponting, complete with black eye, was on the TV admitting that he had a drink problem! He's now the captain, and led by example again in the summer of 2005, when seen swearing at the England coach after being run out at Trent Bridge.

Beating the Australians on the 17th of January 1999 was great. Taking the mickey out of them all day was just as enjoyable.

Digression no 31 – The worst day of my life part 1 – 7th of August 2005 – Cowes regatta

The stress which sport in general, and cricket in particular, can invoke, is incredible. Never more has this been so than at the conclusion of the Edgbaston Test, 2005. England had lost the first at Lord's, but after a good day for England on the Saturday at Edgbaston, victory was but a formality on the Sunday morning. We all went out on the town to celebrate. It didn't quite happen like that though. I peeled myself out of bed and went to the legendary Egon's cafe for a fried breakfast before heading to The Globe pub to watch England mop up the last two Australian wickets.

However, an hour into the day's play and I was standing in front of a gambling machine having just put a pound in it. The only thing was that I didn't have a clue how to play it. I never, ever play gambling machines. It was the stress though.

As the Aussies got closer to the improbable target, I started biting my nails harder and harder. Eighty needed. Then I started pacing around the pub, and when that didn't work, I went for the surefire haven which is bouncing my bouncy ball on the floor. Thirty needed. I eventually got so out of my mind with worry when they needed about ten to win, that I shoved some money in the puggy. Needless to say, I lost. Everyone does on those things which is why I don't use them. England didn't though. They won, with two runs to spare as Harmison dug a vicious bouncer into the pitch which was gloved for a catch by the unlucky Kasprowicz.

End of digression.

For those of you who don't watch cricket or sport at all, this will all be complete gobbledygook. For those of you who went through it, it will have made you nearly pass out with relief when we won. Nothing else mattered. It's the passion, the anguish, the joy and sorrow and the rollercoaster of emotions which make sport the human race's greatest invention.

If you need any proof of this, go to a football match in South America. It's a pretty intense experience and a load of our travelling entourage even got on the front cover of a Bolivian newspaper under the headline 'La Paz side get foreign support'. I was down in the jungle and missed out on the fame of it all, but my brother and cousin and a few of the other lads were there with whistles and all the gear.

In Chile, we went to a Copa Libertador game which is their version of the European Cup. Colo Colo lost but the local fans never stopped singing and banging their big bass drums. Whether they scored, the opposition scored, it was half time or full time, the drums played on and the fans kept on singing. This was a pretty strange sight in Chile which is populated by people notable for their fairly reserved behaviour.

In Argentina, the whole thing is taken to a new level. Boca Juniors is one of the two big Buenos Aires clubs and is in a bitter rivalry with River Plate. A load of us went to a league game at Boca's ground, La Bombonera, against Espanyol. The visitors went three-nil up before Boca eventually drew back to three each. The football was a bit of a distraction though, to be honest. The ground shakes as you're approaching the stadium which is a very impressive three-tiered shrine to football. When you get into the place it gets even more full on. The chanting Boca fans are all jumping up and down well before the first whistle. The experience is made even more intense by the proximity to the pitch of any given seat. The tiers are so steep that it feels like you're right next to the pitch no matter where you're standing. I say standing because the whole place is terraced. None other than Diego Maradona turned up on a balcony at half time and everyone, except us gringos, were chanting 'Diego! Diego!' Even the away fans who'd had the courage to turn up. The man might be a cheat, but there he's also a God.

So there we were behind one of the goals on the middle tier and having a great time. Three-nil down and Palermo scored Boca's first. We just weren't ready for what followed. The crowd surged forward and you could almost hear the stadium groaning under the strain. The whole place went totally mental and down on the ground floor tier, folk are trying to scale the ten-metre-high fences with fireworks ablaze in their spare hand. Then there's a bit of a two second row in front of me as some bastard ripped Daz's watch clean off of his wrist. It took a couple of yanks to get it off, by which time I realised what was going on. As the thief ran past I tap-tackled him, just tripping him up, and set off after him. A couple of locals grabbed me and stopped me from following him up the stand as I saw him disappear into the throng of 'loco' Boca fans. They asked me where I was from and I told them I was

English. They asked me what the hell I was doing in this bit of the ground. 'If you go up there they will kill you,' one of them told me. I believed him. I got talking to my saviours and apparently, we were in with the worst of the worst. They couldn't believe we'd been sold tickets for the middle tier behind this goal. That was an interesting night out!

I'd like to say that I was in Homebush Stadium in Sydney but I wasn't. God knows I'd tried to get there. From Zagreb, I could have ended up in Sydney but I ended up in Val d'Isère.

That was good in some ways and less good in others. It was great to get home after a few weeks swanning around the Adriatic. I'd had a great time but getting back up into the roof of Europe and the expectancy of the ski season which was about to start left me full of the joys of living. The other good thing about watching the final in Val were as follows. A drunk bloke from Bradford, the number of Aussie ski bums, and the result. However, before the positives, let's get the negatives out of the way. Those were another drunk bloke from Yorkshire, insomnia, Beaujolais Nouveau and crossing international borders. These will be addressed in reverse order.

Customs Officers of the world part 5 and we're in Slovenia. You may recall a brush with a hefty, powerful and scary Croatian female Border Guard in the dim and distant past that is the maritime chapter. I didn't have to wait very long till the next one. The only person I met while in Slovenia was a border guard. I boarded a train in Zagreb bound for Venice and never even set foot on Slovenian soil. The border guard I met was horrible though. He slid the door of my train compartment open with such force that I thought it was going to fly clean of the end of the runners. He looked down at the till-three-seconds-ago-sleeping me, with his mean, pasty little ferret face and almost screamed 'PASS!' in a hysterical but impressively baritone voice. I reached into my back pocket and produced it.

He examined it for at least half a second threw it nonchalantly onto the middle of my chest and without a word, slammed the door shut with such ferocity that I expected to be covered in the shattering glass. I don't half pick them.

Having successfully made it into Italy I proceeded to France by way of Milan, which has a lovely train station, by the way. The next problem I encountered en route to the World Cup Final was in Chambéry, the very scenic capital of the Savoie department, complete with its multi-elephanted monument to Hannibal. It was there that I hooked up with my brother Charlie who was also on his way back to the Alps after mountain biking down one of France's best kept secrets, the Ardèche valley. As luck would have it, he is also my bestest drinking wingman. Combine this with the fact that it was the first night of the year's Beaujolais Nouveau and you can guess what happened.

Beaujolais Nouveau is dreadful stuff, it really is. Even worse is the hangover it gives you. Beaujolais night in France is a good night out though. We got proper muddled up with all the locals while swilling down glass after glass of the already identified paint-stripper and bunging in the odd bit of charcuterie traditionally offered by bars on Beaujolais night.

Insomnia was the next problem and the night before the final I didn't sleep a wink. Lying there staring at the ceiling, mulling over the infinite scenarios of what could happen the following day in Sydney, and trying to cope with the guilt of not having got on that plane in Zagreb and just risked going to Sydney without a final ticket, hoping to pick one up from a tout.

Digression No 32 – The best day of my life part 3
November the 22nd 2003- Pacific Bar, Val d'Isère

At five in the morning I gave up and started drinking tea, heavily. By seven I was outside the pub, stressed right out. It is at times like these that you need your worry beads, security blanket, or whatever you use for this purpose. In my case it's a bouncy ball and I sought stress relief by bouncing it against the door of the bar for an hour.

Three hours later and we'd won the World Cup which is where the second of the day's Yorkshiremen came into the equation. Swearbox; a burly former squaddie from the shadier parts of Sheffield; a thirty-something customer-insulting, nanny-shagging muppet whose nickname was awarded after fitting a couple of dozen sexual swear words into a single sentence. The worse thing about winning the World Cup was Swearbox coming along to my end of the bar in tears and kissing me full on the mouth and then trying to hug me to death. Thank God he didn't use tongues, else I'd've been shouting at the floor. Let's move on to the good points before I start getting Swearbox flashbacks and get depressed.

The first Yorkshireman of the day was Guffy. He's from Bradford, owns the Pacific Bar, and failed to turn up to open the place. He got so ring-bolted on cider the night before that he no-showed. This was good news for me as it meant I had to help Swearbox out behind the bar. We were so busy serving thirsty rugby fans that I didn't have time to be stressed about the match.

The result was a second positive if you're an England fan because after getting reffed out of it in 91 by a Kiwi ref, the dodgy South African ref this time couldn't manage to swing it Australia's way despite being the biggest homer since *The Iliad* was written a few thousand years ago, or some fat bloke who works in Mr Burns' Nuclear Power Plant got famous.

Last but not least, the atmosphere was brilliant. As usual it was everybody supporting whoever England are playing but we're used to that. It was all great fun and the number of Aussies doing ski seasons certainly did a lot for the atmosphere.

End of digression.

Places to stay

Right, with that out of the way we can swallow dive headlong into the 'places to stay' section with no safety net.

No matter whereabouts in the world you're going, you're going to need somewhere to stay. In some places you're going to have a lot of fun and in others it'll be the endurance of complete misery. Travelling can be physically tiring and sometimes it's important to get your head down and have a good night's shut-eye. At other times it's reassuring just to have somewhere to leave all your belongings and to have a base from which you can go out and explore the environs of the place in which you find yourself.

This is made more complicated if you're doing it on the cheap. If it was just a case of checking into the Waldorf Astoria every night and having a bubble bath it wouldn't be a major problem. That's not always the case though. For most of us, money is the main problem. I've never stayed at the aforementioned New York hotel but I'm assuming that it costs more to stay there a night than the entire budget of some of my six-month-long planetary wanderings.

This is not the only problem with accommodation you'll encounter, though. Depending on where you're going your options may well be limited. My first experience of this was in the scouting movement when we were sent off into the wilds of Cranham Woods in Gloucestershire, England to spend the night in a construction of our own making. Bivouacing is great fun until it rains. I'm sure if you're SAS trained you'd make a better job of it, but ours leaked. Wet sleeping bags are misery.

Of course the thing with living outside is that if you try to do it in the higher reaches of Europe, the bit where it pisses it down all the time, you really do need to know how to make a waterproof shelter out of sticks and leaves and stuff. This is because it's never very long until the next shower.

The other options are;

A) Get drunk and then just sleep outside anyway, keeping your fingers crossed that you don't get wet. This has limited success in the UK due to the less-than-good general weather synopsis. It's not without success, though. Three of us went out on the bevvy in a local market town one night and got as far as the roundabout on the edge of town before deciding that we couldn't be arsed to walk the six remaining miles home. As luck would have it, it was the death throes of the Thatcher era and public spending was so non-existent that the council had stopped cutting the grass in the middle of roundabouts. I was enjoying a good, rain-free sleep until I was rudely awoken by the toe-end of PC Rocky Stallard's boot in the side of my ribs. Rocky was a beat bobby in the true old style and was a very nice chap. Needless to say, it was not the first time our paths had crossed. Rain is not the only peril attached to sleeping rough.

B) The more sensible option is to go and sleep rough in a country where it rains less than it does in Britain. This of course includes the majority of the planet.

Digression number 33 – the British weather

There are probably a good number of places where it rains more than it does in the UK in terms of centimetres of rainfall per year. But, at least in a lot of those places it comes down in short, heavy deluges. The heavens open, it pisses it down with proper 'get wet' rain and then the clouds disappear, the sun comes out, and everybody can get back to enjoying themselves and getting a tan. The trouble with the UK is that we get the first bit right. Proper, crop flattening rain is pretty common in the UK which is why the place is so verdant and lush. It's the intervening bits where the UK lets itself down. Whereas a lot of other countries revert to sunshine, in Britain we get drizzle. Mention drizzle in a lot of countries and they don't know what you're on about. The word is not in their vocabulary because the stuff doesn't exist. Lucky old them. In the UK, not only does it exist, but it falls with alarming regularity. According to the Romans it fell with depressing regularity. The Romans had to invent psychotherapy in the last few decades before Christ because quite a large percentage of the legionnaires who came back from a tour of duty in Roman occupied Britain were depressed due to the shit weather they'd had to endure over there, and had to go to the shrinks and spend a few sessions on the chaise longue. Chaise longue is French for 'sofa invented by the Romans to lie depressed squaddies on'.

I'll concur, drizzle is depressing. It doesn't get you proper wet but it's damp, dull, dreary and the sky is full of cloud which stops the advent of anything exciting such as the sun coming out. Britain is a lovely part of the world but the weather does let it down somewhat. People in Cornwall will say 'what's he going on about?' and it is true that it's not non-stop misery.

The summer in Britain is lovely. It doesn't last very long, but what we get of it is pretty damn good. It's hot but not unbearably so, and you can get out and enjoy all the things you've been yearning to do for months. Britain is so verdant and the ripening ears of corn swaying in the breeze in the summer fill you with 'joie de vivre'.

It's short lived though. Two days of sun in a row and everybody is burnt to a crisp and full of sausages whose BBQ burnt exteriors conceal an interior of raw swine. Brits are totally incapable of dealing with anything other than overcast weather. Then it's all over. The cloud is back, the drizzle sets in and cricket matches are rained off. It is said that there are two seasons in Britain; the 7th of August and winter. Not all that far off the mark. Long or short, the British summer is well worth coming home for.

End of digression.

Back to option 'B' and to Venezuela.

I really like Venezuela. It was so named because the arriving Spaniards saw the houses on stilts on the Caribbean coast and it reminded them of Venice; hence the name which means 'Little Venice'. What's more, the place has got some great scenery, topography, wildlife and, currently, a very popular firebrand populist President who really pisses George 'Dubya' Bush off; Good old Chavez. If he's pissing Bush off he must be doing something right.

I was there in June 1998 waiting to take a flight back to the UK. I met my brother on the beach in a place where we'd been at the start of our trip. We were so broke that we didn't have the funds left to get a room at a great hostel run by a Québecois called Jacques so we resided on the beach. We pitched a tent to stick all our gear in and then just kipped on the beach. It was lovely. My brother's addiction to climbing trees was satiated every morning when I'd mill about on the beach and look after our gear while he went off to the mango trees which lined the high street and get us some breakfast. In the evening we'd potter on up to this old couple's house and have a big plate of grilled chicken as a sundowner. What an existence. In no way flash and very cheap. The good life personified.

Camping-- next up the ladder from making your own bivouac out of nature's offerings or sleeping rough is the good old tent. Camping is very handy because it is the most versatile way of keeping a roof over your head that man has yet devised. It's a lightweight, portable house that you can take pretty much anywhere. The fact that it is portable makes the tent a lot more useful than any hotel. You always need somewhere dry to stay and you don't get a hotel popping up in every corner of the planet you may wish to go and investigate.

Not only is it practical but it's also not all that bad. Okay, it may be a bit compact and bijoux, but that's not the end of the world. It just takes a bit of thinking about. I've just been in France for a week camping with my girlfriend and, yes I had a good time. We both had a good time. I had a hard time getting into bed but we didn't encounter any insurmountable problems. We were in a two-man tent with a porch and as anybody who has ever stayed in one will know, a two-man tent is not big enough for two people. Well, if you've got two people of five foot five or less lying flat and rigid with their arms pressed hard against their flanks in the style of a medieval Templar knight in his sarcophagus, you'll both fit in. How many tent frequenters do you know who fit that criteria, though? Approximately none is my first guess. And my second guess as well, for that matter.

So there we are in France and I'm having to clamber into the tent over the girlfriend's massive suitcase which is in the little porch bit on the front of our 'two' man tent. I then turn round, lean out and pull my clothes bag in and sit it on top hers in the porch. By the way, she's already in the establishment and snuggled up in her sleeping bag. After performing my hermit crab-like retreat into the tent, pulling our chattels in behind me as I go, I shut the zips on the porch and the mozzie nets that protect the sleeping area. Then it's a night of hard floor and lots of tossing and turning. But it's okay. It's not out of this world and it's not high luxury, but it's okay.

I've had some great times camping in lots of spots and some very funny times. Camp sites can be really sociable as well with everyone cracking a few beers in the fading evening light and meeting new folk from all over the place. It's also cheap, which is a major consideration to a lot of budget travellers. Tents are cheap to buy and cheap to pitch. Can't go wrong.

My favourite tenting moment ever was in New Zealand , about two weeks after my worst night in a tent ever; (see chapter nine and the German lovers) Since that unfortunate night, we'd swapped the North Island for the South and had made it to the fairly strange town of Greymouth on the West coast and were pretty knackered after a great day's potholing. To cut costs we were camping out the back of a backpacker hostel and I waited at the tents while Charlie hit the showers first. He came out of the building sometime later looking well freshened up and with a new spring in his step, which made me look forward to my own scrub up.

My tent was a veteran of the Africa trip of two years previously and was still just about holding together despite being eaten and used as a playground by a variety of African animals. Charlie's tent was a state-of-the-art Ferrino Colorado of which he was, and still is, very proud. I was lying in my tent while Charlie was in the shower and couldn't see what caused his uncontrollable swearing upon his return to his fancy tent. 'Fuck off! Get out! GET OUT!' was my first indication that there was a problem. I stuck my head out of the end of my tent to see a Shetland pony exiting Charlie's tent at speed ! Impressed with the quality of the tentage, the mini-horse had nipped round the corner and moved in while he was in the shower! Charlie had returned to find the Ferrino Colorado full of squatting pocket-sized equine! He didn't laugh, I did.

It's not all bliss though. There are downsides to camping as there are with everything. Cold is one. On the Africa gig, Charlie was very pleased with himself while we queued at Aeroflot check-in because he only had seven kilos of gear for six weeks, including his sleeping bag. It was a lightweight summer bag and he was much less pleased with it at the highest camp on Mount Kenya when he had his whole wardrobe on inside his sleeping bag, and his feet inside his rucksack for good measure.

The most addictive thing about camping though, is rain. If you're camping and it rains, the rain takes over your life. Even the most fidgety, hyperactive human being is capable of lying totally still staring at the ceiling for hours on end in a tent which is being rained on. It must be because tents aren't the most permanent of things and there is always that lingering doubt that it might leak. This has become a lot less likely with the advent of single-skin tents but it is still a possibility which keeps your attention focused on any possible leak for hours on end.

The other end of this problem is when you have to put the thing up in the rain. It doesn't make it any less damp, so if you got the chance to erect your tent in the dry you'd best grab it with both hands. This is the approach I took at the end of a long walk in Kenya. We'd got a 'matatu' bus to as close as we could get to Kenya's only rainforest at Kakamega, and had to walk the rest. My mates Charlie and Simon and I were pretty knackered when we got there. 'Good timing,' the warden said to us, 'you've got here just before it rains.' It was a Rain Forest after all. We were in a small clearing and surrounded by really tall trees so you couldn't actually see much of the sky. What you could see was a perfect deep shade of blue. It had been a lovely day and still was.

Digression No 34 – Always, always listen to the locals

I'm mocked all ski season, every ski season up in the Alps for getting the weather forecast wrong. The thing is is that I'm just the joker who reads it out and I have nothing to do with the actual predictions, which are made by the totally-devoid-of-talent French Met Office, Météo France, down in Bourg St Maurice. I just read them out, but I've given up trying to explain that to people and let them get on with their piss-taking.

Having already got the weather forecast wrong once at five past eight every morning, the Deputy Director of the ski patrol, a likeable chap called Jean-Pierre, comes in to be interviewed about the openings and generals dos and don'ts up in the ski area for the day ahead. Before he goes on air, I tell him what the forecast is according to the geniuses down the hill and ask him if he thinks they're right. He rarely agrees with their predictions, and when there is a difference of opinion, it is always Jean-Pierre who is right. He's a local and he knows the local weather patterns. He's also on the ground and not sitting in an office twenty miles away looking at a computer projection. Always listen to the locals.

End of digression.

Back in the only rainforest in Kenya and the current state of play is: 1) We'd been walking for a good long while and were a bit parched, 2) We were camping and had tents to put up in the clearing we find ourselves in, 3) The clearing also contained a little shop selling cold beers. Now not being a beer drinker I could still have sat down and had a bottle of the lovely grape-flavoured Fanta they have in those parts. I needed it but then thought about what the warden had said and started to unleash the tent. The other two knocked the top off a couple of 'Tusker' beers or some other local brew, happy as a couple of dogs scratching fleas. So used were we to putting our mobile homes up that I'd got the Millets twenty-quid tunnel-tent upright by the time they headed to the shop for a reload of beer, having declared that their own tent construction would launch into full swing after one more.

As if on cue the warden's prophecy came true and not the largest, but definitely the blackest cloud I've ever seen, appeared over the tops of the trees. Beers were forgotten about as Charlie and Simon started their race against time. And, in fairness to them, they did get within about two minutes of getting their tent up before the heavens opened. It was proper get-wet rain as well. I had retreated to the dry safety of a little round hut in the middle of the clearing and was giving them not-altogether- helpful tips on what to do. In some parts of the world, rain is a phenomenon. It falls so heavily that you are totally transfixed by it and Africa is at least joint first in this respect, if not outright winner. 'It always rains here,' the warden had said, 'every day,' and he wasn't wrong. Always listen to the locals.

Camping takes on a different dimension if you're in a particularly hot place. This quickly dawned on me one morning in Fiji. I was with the Ferrino Colorado-inhabiting Charlie and we'd moved on from New Zealand to the Pacific Islands. First night on the island of Mana, one of the many islands off the west coast of the main island, and we thought we'd better go out and get hideously drunk. This we achieved, in Charlie's case by imbibing the local beer, Fiji Bitter, and in mine by consuming spirits of dubious origin. We'd also both been on the Cava, a local drink which looks (and tastes) like muddy water. It's made from the root of a plant and is a natural amphetamine. Despite the taste it is strangely addictive in the same sort of way as Twiglets are.

Anyway, having got bladdered the night before the first opening of my eyes was a painful experience. I thought I was in the middle of spontaneous combustion as I was very hot and assumed my brain and eyeballs were bleeding. Then the sun hit my tent and the temperature doubled in about a second. That tipped me over the edge and I was scrambling out of the tent in a way not dissimilar to Charles Bronson's character in the film

The Great Escape, when he has a panic attack in one of the tunnels. Luckily I made it out of the tent before throwing up, but it was a close call.

Although it says at the top that we've moved from the 'getting around' section into the 'where to stay' section , we are actually going to go for a semi-regression into the 'getting around' section for a couple of paragraphs. Why? Because there is a phenomenon which requires highlighting which is a bit of both. It is half at home in both sections; it has a foot in each category like the giant Benandonner striding cross the Giant's Causeway from Scotland into Northern Ireland to take on his rival Finn MacCool. It's like a batsman skipping a step down the wicket into the 'places to stay' section, missing the ball and avoiding getting stumped by just sticking a toe-end back behind the crease which represents the 'getting around' section.

I am, of course, talking about caravans. Caravans have to be amongst the worst inventions our species has ever come up with. They have not a single redeeming quality. They're ugly, hold everybody else up on the roads and are often not roadworthy. The people who own and inhabit them tend to be pretty uninteresting and invariably pretty weird. As if Britons haven't been humiliated enough by their government in recent years thanks to joining Bush's blatant global oil stripping tour, the idiot in charge has now appointed a caravanner as Foreign Secretary! We are represented abroad by a big noise from the Caravan Club. It's totally humiliating. It doesn't help matters that Margaret Beckett is not a lot to look at, and that's being pretty kind, quite frankly. A harsher person would point to the fact that she is separated at birth with the very unattractive Rosa Klebb, one of the baddies in the best James Bond film, From *Russia With Love*.

Time to get those skeletons out of the closet quickly. I have been on a caravan holiday. I'm not taking the rap for it though. I was five and it was before I got to choose where I went on my holidays. My aunt and mother decided to take us three kids on a caravan holiday. It's the worst holiday any of us have ever been on. It may well have emotionally scarred the mumster and my aunt for life judging by the anguished, glazed look they both assume whenever it's mentioned. To top it all off, it was in Wales. Needless to say that now I do choose my holidays, they are not in a tin tent, but they are sometimes in Wales which, despite a lot of ribbing from the English, is a very beautiful part of Britain. Mind you, they give as good as they get, bless 'em.

The fair country of Holland has only three real black marks against its name. The first is that it's a bit too flat as a country and the second is the dubious phenomenon that is the 'inspection shelf' – see toilets' section. The third and by far most serious black mark is the number of caravanners in Holland. Very suspect. They even take their 'holiday chariots' with them skiing, for God's sake.

The only places you'll meet a similarly high concentration of weirdoes as in the caravanning fraternity, anywhere else on the planet, is at the Ski Club of Great Britain's annual ball in London (known to normal skiers as 'Weirdoes r Us'), and at Clapham Junction or Crewe railway stations.

Digression no 35 – Trainspotters

If you're not British, you may not be aware of trainspotting. I've been to a lot of train stations abroad but I've never seen a train spotter. It could well be a purely British phenomenon and let's hope that it is confined to this little island because, let's face it, it's pretty embarrassing and pointless. Crewe and Clapham Junction get a special mention because they're Britain's busiest train hubs and are therefore the shit which attracts the flies that are train spotters.

However, not until last summer did I realise that train spotters are no longer the big fish in the pool of sad bastards. There exists, unbeknown to me, a sadder creature called a coach spotter. I was busy asking a driver at Hampton Court Palace car park to move his vehicle to get access to a gateway when I was pretty much elbowed out of the way by a man desperate to ask the driver if he could nip onto his bus to check out the coachwork. Oh dear!

End of digression. Let's move on to less mobile forms of accommodation.

Hotels – bottom end

If you're penniless, tight, or travelling with the purse strings pretty much pulled shut, you're going to end up staying in some pretty awful hotels at some point or other. Camping is usually as cheap a way as you can get of staying somewhere, but then not everywhere has a campsite. If you're in town, hotels and hostels are the way forward, so be prepared. There are some good ones and a hell of a lot of bad ones at the bottom end of the market.

Before getting to the hostelries themselves, what about the ones which aren't hotels at all? Brothels is the usual name for these. 'Love hotels' is what they prefer to call them in the Third World; very dodgy establishments where you are looked at sideways if you say you want to stay for the whole night. Most of the clientele of these places rent a room for an hour or two. Some clients who are real sexual decathletes may take a room for longer but a couple of hours is the most common period of residency. Very simple; you rent a room, get a prostitute, put her (or him) to the sword, and then bugger off. Simple. Just to add to the convenience of the whole venture, you can usually pick up a 'professional lady' or rent boy on the spot or in the immediate vicinity.

As you can imagine, love hotels are not usually in the better end of town, apart from in towns so awful (see Maicao, Columbia, chapter three) that they don't have a better end. This doesn't make using them any safer as every type of dodgy individual, sex pest and weirdo you could ever wish not to meet is hanging around outside. We met a burnt out, cocaine-addicted Swiss stockbroker in Venezuela and ended up in the same hotel in Cartagena in the north of Colombia some time later.

The hotel itself was great. It was run by some Swiss folk and, as was the case in all hotels in those climes, you had to put down an occupation on the sign in forms. I used to put lawyer all the time and Charlie would put builder. Tom used to mix it up a bit and on that day chose nuclear physicist as his profession. 'Ah, you are scientist ja?' enquired the Germanic hotelier. 'I am an engineer by trade put particle physics are one of my favourite hobbies,' he further intimated. Sensing intellectual deep water, Tom went red and moved into a darker shade when the bloke started asking him a complicated, in-depth question about his profession; at this point Tom decided he needed the loo! Good hotel; clean, safe and friendly.

The Swiss stockbroker decided to go and buy some cocaine shortly after our arrival and off he went. He came back a couple of hours later. We thought he must have been arrested or killed but as it turned out he'd been offered sex outside the love hotel a few doors down and had accepted! Not only did he get it but he managed to buy himself some coke while he was in the love hotel! And women say men can't multi-task!

From a more optimistic point of view, 'bottom end' is probably a bit of a bad title for this section as it sounds quite negative. Just because you're staying in the cheaper hotels and hostels doesn't mean that you're always staying in poor accommodation. You find a lot of quality places to stay all over the world either by just turning up and getting lucky with your choice or by use of your guidebook. Usually though, you'll do it by word of mouth and follow the advice of someone you've met.

The advantage of this type of accommodation is that you're quite often actually staying in someone's house so your language skills are likely to improve and you're more immersed in local daily life. That may sound a bit 'at one-ish' but I don't care. Your aim is, after all, to see the country you're visiting and to my mind the daily lives of the people are as much a part of that as the scenery and culture. One of my favourite spots regarding living this way was in Peru where we stayed with a family up in the back streets of Cuzco. They were very welcoming and not just to us. They had a young lad working for them whose father had turned up on the doorstep with him one morning a few months previously and said; 'This is my son, he's a good lad but I can't afford to look after him.' The family took him in and he did all the chores. His father was right, he was a good lad and I hope him and his father are now together again. That's real life in the Third World though, and Peru is a lot better off than most countries as well.

Bottom end – Backpackers

Backpackers hostels are the next rung up the ladder and a slightly different kettle of fish where you usually get a lot for your money. You get a bed, somewhere safe to leave your stuff, although in this regard you should never really trust anyone – never leave your passport and valuables anywhere. Backpackers usually have a safe or a secure place for you to put such items which is very handy. They quite often run trips themselves or can recommend a company to take you where you want to go. They're also full of people doing the same thing as you – i.e., having a look around the place. The great thing is that you meet lots of different nationalities who've arrived from all points of the compass and you can exchange information about the dos and don'ts of the places you've come from, and the places you're going next. It's a great reciprocal thing which is of benefit to all travellers. It's also a free advice service.

The only real problems I've had with backpackers is that they're not all that good if you're trying to improve your mastery of the local lingo. I am speaking from an Anglophone perspective but it is a problem. You'll find a lot of people who speak the same language as you in such establishments but it's not a big problem. If you really want to master the local language you will make yourself.

The other is that people can get a bit bogged down in them and before you know it you've been there for too long instead of getting out there and seeing stuff. It's never happened to me but you do see people who've been in a place for a long time and are maybe doing a bit of cleaning or laundry to help subsidise their rent. They're having a good time going out partying and get into a rut. You can't have it all.

When on tour, always talk to as many folk as you can going in the other direction and you'll get some good advice. As previously mentioned, your chances of ending up in a dump are higher if you're travelling on the cheap, but it's by no means a case of going from one hovel to the next. I've stayed in some absolute gems in every corner of every continent and had some very good times. Places stick in your mind for different reasons. The backpackers I stayed at with my mate Charlie sticks in the mind, and not only because it's the only time I've ever seen someone have to kick a Shetland pony out of their tent! It was also because it had a sort of Noah's Ark-sized collection of animals out the back of which the fun-sized pony was but one in a family of dozens of animals. The other place which left a mark for the same reason was Hotel España in Lima, Peru, which has a little zoo on the roof with tortoises and all sorts. Very cool.

Other places you remember for different reasons. The backpackers of Cairns in Australia are notable for their party atmosphere, something which also goes for Adelaide. This is definitely also the case for the islands in the gulf of Thailand where the partying is good on Samui and Pha Ngan at full moon time, Tao being better for a post-party chill out. You'll also find some enchanted places where you can't quite believe the setting. We stayed in a place in Colombia run by a French woman who had 'wind tunnel effect', as in she'd had too much plastic surgery. It was in the archaeological town of San Agustín and was lots of little cabins up in the trees and stuff. Lovely place, scary owner. Some places are just plain helpful like Swiss Tom's place in Merida in Venezuela and the Merry V in Bangkok. Same goes for a place I stayed at in Talat Harb in Budapest, and the list goes on. For riot viewing, the Marsala on the cusp of New Town and Old Town Quito in Ecuador takes some beating. It was very clean and friendly and Charlie and I had a grandstand view of a full scale riot from there. Water cannons, tear gas, riot police; the whole nine yards. Very exciting, free entertainment. No idea what the riot was about, mind.

For sheer simplicity it has to be Jambiani Beach in Zanzibar. A lovely white beach on the Indian Ocean, no electric, salt water showers and earthen floor white-painted block huts. All you need really.

The short answer to the accommodation issue is that it's usually good fun, even when you're staying in a place which is less than fantastic. My favourite proof of this was in Ciudad Bolivar in Venezuela, an unfeasibly hot town on the banks of the Orinoco River. The Hotel Caracas was probably quite a grand building in its day and had a lovely first floor terrace overlooking the Orinoco. You couldn't see the river from our room though, not only because it was on the other side of the hotel but also because our room didn't have any windows. Yes, you guessed it right. My brother, my cousin and myself had chosen one of the hottest places any of us had ever been to rent a room with no windows. Not only that, but the fan in the middle of the ceiling didn't break any records. Any slower and it'd have been going backwards. Despite being run down, hot and without ventilation, we really liked the place. The managers couldn't really be bothered and just sat around watching telly. They left the running of the place to their daughter and her cousin who were probably about fourteen and eleven. They were lovely girls and made us very welcome. They were very good at the parents' jobs and made up for all their idleness.

It's for sure that, at times, the fun often stems from the fact that you are in a lower end establishment. We asked the girls running the Hotel Caracas if we could borrow the kitchen one night and they said no problem. We'd finished cooking and were sitting down eating when the girls came in. One of them went over to the cast iron range and went to open the oven door. Tom said, 'Don't open that, there's a rat in there!' with lots of panic in his voice. The girl turned her head to see that he was joking and went back and opened the oven door. There wasn't a rat in there, there were two! They'd obviously come out from somewhere to sample Tom's cooking. I seem to remember that we had 'albondingas' meatballs and spaghetti. I'd swear blind that someone took a photo of those rats but none of us have been able to find the photo since. They just sat there looking out at us with their noses twitching; it was very funny.

If you are going to do it on the cheap I'm afraid that you're going to have to get used to animals such as rats and in fact all types of vermin. You can be reassured though that if there are rats about, a place is not all that dirty. They're very clean animals. The biggest bugger I've ever seen ran straight up a set of curtains at a place I was in in Thailand; it was about the size of a Yorkshire Terrier. Good job the curtain rails were well put up otherwise he'd have had them down!

The good thing about some of these pests is that they can occupy quite a lot of your time and provide some good sport. While in Kenya, we didn't just constantly make errors and take the piss out of each other after the ensuing disasters. We also made some good calls. One of these was to not go to one of the bigger game parks but to one of the smaller ones; Lake Nakuru National Park, which has already had a mention in the depressed water buffalo section. Not only were the wildlife and scenery stunning but the accommodation was pretty funny. Nothing special and I can't even remember the name of the town or the hotel, but I do remember mine and Charlie's room. Small, two windows and one door. Two beds, no other furniture and a lot of wildlife. We used to go to bed and go in two waves. The first bedroom entrant would kill all the cockroaches, and the second person would kill all the mozzies. It's hard to say which was the harder of the two contracts so we used to alternate them. The mosquitoes were more numerous but the roaches were harder to kill. Those blighters cannot only survive nuclear winter (allegedly), they can also cope with blokes stamping on them repeatedly. They're born survivors and with me and Charlie both weighing in at around the thirteen stone mark, we still had all on to get through the Kevlar on the back of some of them, even with hiking boots on. It would quite often take more than one stamp to kill one. The question of which was the harder contract remained a stewards enquiry. The more important contract was definitely the mosquitoes. They carry malaria which is the scourge of the African continent. Fair enough, it's pretty unpleasant having cockroaches crawling across you in bed until you get used to it, but at least they can't kill you. Cockroaches may be physically a bigger animal but nothing and nobody has had a bigger effect on the destiny of Africa than the tsetse fly.

As for living up to its frightening name and reputation, there's only one place on my scary places to stay list. Crossing from Hungary into Romania you're actually in Transylvania before you hit Romania. This of course depends on who you ask and which map you believe. This is, after all, one of the most troubled and war torn parts of Europe which changed hands several times during the turbulent twentieth century. Just over the current border is Oradea. Regular sort of a border town really; pretty dull and made duller by the glum housing blocks put up by the Communist regime of Nicolae Ceaucescu. In amongst that was a lovely town centre though. My handbook mentioned a place called the Black Vulture. Had to be done really, didn't it? What a place. A beautiful if run down sort of place it was. Frayed carpets, dust all over the place, a grand piano which hadn't had the lid opened for years, dodgy plumbing and the overall look of the Addams Family house; or is it The Munsters? Doesn't matter, you get the idea. It was spooky. The folk running it were normal and welcoming, but this being Transylvania, who's to say they wouldn't turn into zombies or bloodsuckers?

It was great to start with. The bloke let me put the motorbike in the massive entrance lobby and my abode for the night was a beautiful Art Nouveau hotel. I went out for dinner and came back to the hotel refreshed and ready for bed. Then the heavens opened which I didn't really mind because I was just walking into the porch of the Black Vulture. With the rain came lightning though. I was totally scared witless the whole night in this creaky old hotel in Transylvania. At one point I plucked up the courage and went down the corridor for a pee and a huge flash of lightning lit up the whole cavernous stairwell. Spooky with a capital oo. I don't think the fact that the place was called the 'Black Vulture' helped any either.

Romania was also the country in which I've spent my most compact night ever; that was in the smallest little wooden cabin I've ever seen in a campsite in the picturesque town of Cluj-Napoca. I thought the bloke was joking when he showed me it. It looked like a wendy house but smaller. My Honda Transalp absolutely dwarfed it.

It's a great place, Romania. It's very beautiful geographically and the people are very friendly and welcoming. Considering that they've suffered one of the most tyrannical regimes the world has ever seen, they're doing okay. I was there in 1998 when the place was still pretty mixed up but, thanks to the people and the scenery, I had a great time. It was a bit dodgy though. There's a few people trying to fleece you but I suppose that's to be expected if you're in a country where folk are struggling to make ends meet.

Of all the dodgy folk in Romania, about half of them were on the border with Bulgaria. A mile before arriving at the bridge over the Danube this shady looking middle aged cove just wandered out of some bushes and into the middle of the road with his hand up. I should have just carried on but stopped. He had a fake leather tan, PVC jacket and a pair of jeans on, and was sporting at least two days' worth of facial hair. He said he was from the Romanian Environment Agency and that everybody leaving the country had to pay a motorway tax; he was asking for the equivalent of about ten US dollars. I kicked the bike into first gear and said to him; 'but there aren't any motorways in Romania.' I just rode off and said goodbye at the same time with the bloke left nodding his head resignedly and looking at his feet as if I'd just made a very good point in a debating contest.

I didn't get very far. Next up was two drunk blokes in a little border post cabin which was so small they couldn't get in it. It was like one of those border post boxes on the frontier of the Duchy of Fenwick in *The Mouse That Roared* starring Peter Sellars in nearly all the roles. Apart from a blatantly too small cabin, they had a barrier and everything else you'd expect at a border post. They had caps and a uniform each, even if they could have done with a dry clean. They were obviously the real deal, albeit a bit pissed. True to form, it wasn't long before they asked me for some money and although they were bona fide officials, they were only there to supervise the Romanian end of the bridge over the Danube. I told them that I had a VISA card, and would be happy to pay them the money with that, knowing full well they wouldn't have a machine. With that, one of them asks for a go on the motorbike with a look in his eye as to say 'you ain't goin no further if I don't get a go on your Honda'. Disaster. I ended up sort of jogging alongside him for about twenty yards after which he'd had enough thank God. I bade the moonlighters farewell and crossed the Danube into Bulgaria where the whole process started again.

End of digression.

It was a shame to leave Romania but I was on the road and Asia and Africa were beckoning. Four things really stuck in my mind. The beauty of the place and the changing landscapes; the mountains of the Carpathians, the historic castles, the Danube, Transylvania, and the beauty of Bucharest which merits its claim to be 'the Paris of the Balkans.'

Second were the dodgy folk. I was walking around Bucharest with a Canadian bloke one day, on our way to visit the People's Palace which Romanians claim is the second biggest building in the world after the Pentagon. These two 'police officers' came up to us and unrealistically said; 'Hello, we're the money police. There's a lot of fakes going around at the moment so can you show us all of your money so we can check if any of your banknotes are fakes!' Hmm. He said it all serious and while I wanted to laugh out loud, I was also conscious of the fact that we had a good chance of getting mugged or worse, but as we were in the middle of a market I wasn't too worried.

Another pretty special moment was meeting the former President, Ion Maurer, at his house in a leafy suburb of Bucharest reserved for the party hierarchy in Communist times. Maurer had realised that Ceaucescu was a bad bastard and handed over power to him after a short time in office. That probably saved his life and those of his family. It was weird meeting somebody who I'd written about in essays at university, having done a module on East European politics and the Communist takeovers after World War Two. On my way down through Europe on the Transalp I'd dropped in to see my best mate from school, Yorkie, who was living in Stuttgart, only to find out that he was stepping out with the grandaughter of the ex-President of Romania! He's a boy. She was also very good looking and the one time 125th best tennis player in the world. She gave me some photos to take to her grandparents, which I delivered some weeks later. It was good to meet them if a little brief. The ex-president himself was ninety-seven and had had a major stroke so couldn't speak and was just waiting for God basically. He was proper second hand and I would be more surprised to see him alive seven years down the line than I would to see Elvis make a Vegas comeback.

His wife was ninety-four, had also had a stroke, and couldn't speak English. I spoke to her in French and gave her the gist of what I was doing there.

The last thing about Romania to stick in my mind was one of the strangest places to have a piss up. Things which occur in places and at times when they shouldn't tend to do that. It was half past nine in the morning for a start, and in a petrol station in central Romania. I walked into the paying building just like any regular filling station and it was pretty noisy. The reason was a table in the corner. There was only one table in the place and it had a bottle of spirits and a few beers on it. The people round it were obviously pretty well oiled and one of them offered me a drink which I politely declined explaining that I had to ride the bike. I paid for the fuel after which I had a couple of cups of coffee with them. Very nice, affable folks and we had a great laugh. I explained that I was on my way to Australia and one girl gave me her address so that I could send her a postcard when I got there. I don't think she expected to get one but it was one of the first things I did after getting down under. I left them to their drinking and it's to this day the only time I've seen a drinking spree based in a petrol station. I did ask them why they were getting drunk in there but I can't remember what the answer was.

Places to stay – top end

As I've already opined, I think that posh hotels are a bit of a missed opportunity and I hope to never change the way I travel, even on the slim chance that I ever accumulate any money. As this book is aimed at the cheap seats of life and not the corporate hospitality boxes, the subject of posh, expensive hotels will only be lightly touched on.

Some people are in need of all the creature comforts and use the posh places because they can. Some people use posh hotels out of necessity, be it because of old age, having kids with them or whatever. In this respect, at least these people are out there doing and seeing stuff in places of genuine interest, instead of being in Playa de las Americas on Tenerife, even if they're not immersed in the culture and local community as much as they could be.

What is beyond doubt is that mankind has left a lot of very impressive edifices on this planet, and quite a few of them are hotels. Not only are a lot of hotels very beautiful architecturally, but they're designers are the mothers of invention. They have a vested interest in making their creations stand out from the crowd. This can be done in a variety of different ways.

Size. Biggest is best and the current crown holder is the MGM Grand in Las Vegas, weighing in with five thousand six hundred and ninety rooms (and more to come next year). Sheer opulence and luxury currently peaks at the Burj Al Arab in Dubai which is the only 7 star hotel at the moment, although in this world of one-upmanship, I wouldn't have thought it'll be alone for long. Location is another factor with the likes of Macchu Picchu, and the hotels which have featured in Bond films such as at the top of some Swiss mountain or the Lake Palace Hotel in Udaipur which featured in *Octopussy*. This place is made all the more beautiful by the fact that Maud Adams resided there in the film as she is woo hoo!

You can also go underground and find some great hotels, and even underwater with luxury hotels underwater in the Caribbean and one on the way in the Persian Gulf. On top of the water you have ever bigger cruise ships (floating hotels) which compete to provide ever more luxurious services and to out-do each other with the latest onboard activities. A cruise ship has just been finished in Finland which has a surfing pool on it! Surfing on a cruise liner; whatever next?

What you build them out of is another way of making things posh and exclusive. The ice hotel they build in Sweden every year and the salt hotel I visited in Bolivia are other fairly unique ideas.

For notorious, try the Chateau Marmont on Sunset Boulevard where John Belushi died of a drug overdose and quite a few other stars have achieved infamy. For plain scary it has to be the Overlook Hotel in Stephen King and Stanley Kubrick's *The Shining* which is actually the Timberline Lodge in Oregon. I'd say the Black Vulture in Oradea but Kubrick made such a good job of turning King's novel into reality that *The Shining* gets the vote for scariest hotel.

Classics is another way of classifying great hotels what with all the world famous hotels of the big cities of the world.

My dad says that the Raffles in Singapore is the best he's ever stayed in.

The problem is that for the budget traveller this is all beyond your grasp. It's as visible to you as it is to anyone else but if you're going to travel on the cheap, you'll have to find somewhere else to stay. The good bit comes at the end of a trip. You meet quite a few people who will have a tot up at the end of a trip and realise that they've got enough for a last night blow out and stay in a swanky place after months of slumming it. It's a great thing to do, especially if you've not had a hot shower for a while and you haven't seen a bath since leaving home. There's a good chance that you won't have slept in a proper bed for a while as well.

One thing to bear in mind as well is that posh hotels may not be as safe as you think they are. I'm not just trying to put the willies up you and it's not just sour grapes because I don't get to stay in posh hotels very much. While relaxing on the beach and doing very little apart from conducting the Kenyan leg of the Embassy Mild cigarette endurance smoking tour, myself, Simon and Charlie coughed ourselves awake one morning and headed to get some breakfast. We were on the coast of the marine National Park south of Mombasa at a place called Tiwi Beach; that morning the place was alive with gossip from the next beach, Diani, where there was a swanky four star hotel. It turned out that the night before the police were called to the hotel as a load of robbers were emptying the safe. A shoot out followed, the result of which I can't remember, but I don't recall any mention of blood being spilt. The intrigue of the whole thing was that the robbers turned out to be the local off-duty police who ended up having a shooting match with the local on-duty coppers at the poshest hotel in the area. Classy or what? We may have been slumming in our tents a couple of miles down the beach but at least we weren't cowering under a coffee table trying not to get caught in the crossfire.

Market forces dictate that upmarket stuff must be good. That's the way capitalism works. If humans don't want stuff, it stops being produced. Therefore the number of posh hotels and bars around the world, the large business and first class allocations on planes, and the multitude of designer shops on the King's Road would point to posh stuff in general being a big hit with the population at large. It's a moral victory and very satisfying for people like myself, who have a life sentence in the cheap seats, to occasionally experience this other world. Sometimes you're invited in with open arms by lovely people. Most of the time though, you have to breach the gap by using your initiative. You can use a variety of techniques.

1) Have a financial sponsor.

Mine and my brother Charlie's favourite method of getting some legroom on a plane. If someone is desperate enough for you to return from your travels to work for them, they'll buy you a business class plane ticket which is a vast improvement on 'cattle' class. You can get a haircut in the business class airport lounges, drinks and nibbles on the plane before take-off and lots of other nice stuff besides. The best bit though is walking up to check-in where the person manning the desk assumes that you're in the wrong spot. 'Good evening, economy is just along there.' 'We're aware of that but we're travelling business class thank you.' Fifteen-love to the two scruffy blokes with the rucksacks!

2) Don't be afraid to ask.

As happened to me in LA airport (see chapter three), if you don't ask you don't get. Plane upgrades are just one way of giving your global travels a bit of a silver lining. It can also happen in hotels and in all sorts of different situations. If in doubt ask what's going on, and if you're asked by someone in authority, don't be afraid to say yes. For example, should you be staying in a beautiful colonial plantation house in Fiji which has been converted into a backpackers hostel, and the owners happen to mention that you're welcome to go and use the pool facilities at the local five star Warwick resort just down the road, don't say no; say 'yes, okay, thanks a lot' and collect your towel and stuff before pottering down the road.

3) You have a right to go posh and don't forget it.

Should you find yourself in a posh place or outside somewhere famous and you have the financial means for a splurge, don't be afraid to.

Just because you don't do it every day doesn't mean that you can't do it as a once in a while treat to yourself while on your travels. My favourite memory of this was in Monaco. I wasn't really travelling but just on a foray down to the Côte d'Azur in the Communist-era, Czech Army blue Sköda during the Easter break while at university in Grenoble in south-eastern France.

Monaco is an okay sort of place. It has some lovely buildings but also some high-rise architectural monstrosities which are reminiscent of Tower Hamlets in London or Saint Denis in Paris. Beautiful cliffs are a feature of its winding, dramatic coastline. It has a lot of car showrooms, none of which seem to sell anything for under a hundred thousand of any given currency, so as you can imagine, we're talking Bugattis, Ferraris, Lamborghinis and Bentleys, not second-hand Ford Escorts and Chevy Pintos. I didn't see another Sköda in town. Monaco also has its port to its credit which is in a sort of natural geological horseshoe, which makes for a grand setting and a good boat show. You really can smell the money in Monaco and the whole place is paid for by gambling, whether it's the finely tended lawns of the principality's many fine parks, the cliff top castle or the biggest per-resident law enforcement community in the world. Police officers in

Monaco are like rats in London; you're never more than three metres away from one!

It had been a good day with me getting Ellie and Teus, my travel companions, to get an action shot of the 'scud missile' going round the Loews hairpin on the Grand Prix Circuit. Tacky, yes, but has to be done really. We'd decided to have an end of day splash out at the Café de Paris, rubbing shoulders with the rich folk in the square outside the casino. I met Teus and Ellie who were already installed there, and then the waiter turned up. He looked at me in a snobbish, unfriendly, what-are-you-doing-in-here sort of way which amused me. Admittedly I was sporting a pair of well-travelled Portuguese cowboy boots, a pair of jeans and a ponytail, but so what? Isn't human nature interesting and isn't it weird how 'garçons' in posh, famous cafés such as we were in become snobbish and offhand on behalf of their more esteemed and wealthy customers when confronted with someone like me? The rich and famous are fine about it but it's the wannabes you've got to watch out for. He'd been particularly unwelcoming but he wasn't intimidating me. 'Un Pastis s'il te plait,' I ordered, deliberately using the less formal vernacular, and holding his gaze with a tweak of a cheeky smile. His response came when he brought out the drink. 'Quarante sept francs s'il vous plait' he said with emphasis on the 'vous' in a sarcastic sort of tone. If he'd been feeling more polite he could have just left the ticket under the ashtray, which now had one of my hand rolled cigarettes (deliberately rolled fat and cone-shaped to look as much like a joint as possible and wind him up) gently smouldering in one of its grooves. I took the fact that he didn't as an inference that I didn't look trustworthy enough to have a drink without doing a runner. I smiled at him while slowly withdrawing a fifty franc note from my bulging (joke!) wallet, all the while hoping that my shock at having to pay four pounds seventy for a glass of Pastis and water was not showing; that would have moved him a lot closer to victory in our little battle of wills. Four pounds seventy! This was in 1995 and I was spewing.

So, nasty little waiter has his forty-seven francs and what does he do? Gives me a very haughty, insincere and reluctant 'merci' and walks off! At the second time of asking he turned round and returned the ten yards he's made it from the table and which point I asked him for the change from the fifty and then informed him that I would leave him a tip if I felt like it. We were into the last throes of our battle now and the gloves were off. The expression on my face made it perfectly clear to him that a tip was less than likely, but I was pleased to be keeping my cool, a situation he was no longer in. He handed it to me and walked off without a word.

Lucky old him though; he still got a tip. Five centimes! I bet he thought he'd won the lottery. A bit of a strange one really, five centime coins. They were worth half a penny in sterling and I'd often wondered why the French had not taken them out of circulation. Luckily I had one on me and I thought that leaving that would be an even bigger insult than leaving nothing at all. I would have loved to have stayed for another drink just to piss the little bastard off even more, but I couldn't afford another drink at those prices.

The moral of the 'third way' is that you have a right to spend your money just as much as the rich folk do. Just because a Pastis at the Café de Paris in Monaco costs you about a third of your disposable income for that week doesn't mean that you shouldn't go and have one. Forget about the little snob who thinks you shouldn't be there and enjoy the experience. I've had a few credit card splurges around the planet and never regretted it.

4) Prices differ abroad.

Stuff which you wouldn't do at home isn't necessarily prohibitively expensive where you are. The first thing I do in the Third World is give up shaving. Well, I don't give up, but I try and avoid doing it myself. Firstly I'm lazy. Secondly, I'm not very good at it and loathe shaving. A bathroom where I've been shaving quite often looks like an abattoir and there's invariably a chunk of my chin in the bottom of the sink. Third and foremost, there's nothing quite as good as a proper shave by a good barber.

Go to any Muslim country and you get a good coffee and a very relaxing time in the chair with all the hot towels, a bit of a shoulder massage and a shave as close as Siamese twins, usually done with a cutthroat razor. However, having bigged up Muslim barbers, my all-time best shave was in Bolivia. It was also my highest, right up on the altiplano in Uyuni and it was done by a woman. Having gone in for a haircut, the lady asked me if I wanted a shave as well. Why not? I'll tell you why not; because she pulled out a switchblade but one which didn't have a permanent blade. She slid a disposable razor blade into it which transformed it into a very foreboding instrument of death. The shave turned out to be top dollar. My face was smooth as a baby's bum for days after that. I celebrated with a trip round the corner for a dollar fifty bowl of 'tripa dorada' (see food chapter).

Food and drink – food

Your planetary wanderings are going to wear you out physically. Burning calories is a normal part of life and this goes as much for when you're travelling, if not more so. For a start you've got a backpack to haul around with you. The things to see and do chapters are so full of stuff to go and see, to walk up that you're going to have to take a lot of energy on board. For this purpose think of your stomach as being like the flux capacitor on top of the deLorean in *Back to the Future 2*. You can up your energy levels by chucking food in to yourself. Therefore, by eating, you'll have enough energy to carry that rucksack, to walk up hills (and down dales), to go scuba diving, to go out partying all night and to do all the other things you want to do.

The generally good news about the whole food thing is that it's just like being at home and works just the same. If you're hungry, you eat. The difference is what makes things interesting though, and the difference where food is concerned is that you are abroad. This is your gastronomic gateway of discovery to untold delights and I would suggest that you enjoy it to the full.

What makes this planet so interesting is its huge variety, be it geography, people, climate, etcetera and so on. Food is no different. There's a lot to try out there and it's all good. I'm going to have to stop there because I'm sitting in the middle of a park with no food on me. As my tummy is rumbling as much as my lips are salivating just thinking about writing this chapter, I'm going to have to go on a massive restaurant tour to complete it.

The thing is with being British, a lot of people will automatically assume that you hold global cuisine in such high regard because the food you've been subjected to at home is so awful. In Monopoly terms, they'll assume that if you're a Brit like me, you've been gastronomically fated to not pass 'Go', not collect two hundred quid and just go straight to jail. People go straight to the assumption that you'll escape your own shores by any means necessary and eat dog shit on toast for the rest of your life as opposed to remaining at home and eating the slop served up over here in dear old Blighty. Well, I can tell you that that assumption is absolute bollocks. If that word is not in your vocabulary, may I be the first to inform you that you are wrong.

The first reason for this is that British cooking is actually very good. Not the most subtle on the planet but still very good, honest fare. A witty chap on the telly once said that the difference between French 'cuisine' and that of Britain is in the sauces. French food is complimented by dozens of intricate sauces refined over the centuries to bring out the best in the flavours of the dishes they accompany. True enough. In Britain there are two sauces used in cooking, red and brown. Very funny but far from the truth.

Digression no 37 – Brown sauce

Red sauce (tomato ketchup or catsup) is rubbish. I wouldn't put it on my worst enemy's cornflakes. It doesn't even taste of tomatoes and yet it's a huge planetary success. In Britain, the number of people who adopt the Christian-Slater-in *True Romance* method of ketchup application is astonishing. They do literally 'drown it in that shit' as John Travolta says of the Dutch applying mayonnaise to French fries in *Pulp Fiction*. A bloke I milked cows for in New Zealand informed me that they call it 'tucker fucker' over there. Not only does it rhyme but it's an apt nickname as it does just that.

Brown sauce, on the other hand is a beneficial lifestyle choice. For those of you not familiar with it, it gets its name from its looks. It's brown, hence the name, and it tastes lovely with its sugary blend of molasses and spices. No fried breakfast is complete without some wholegrain mustard and a bit of brown. It has a place in the nation's heart.

Despite the obvious merits of brown sauce, it is not the most famous brown substance in the annuls of British eating. There is a more controversial, more infamous brown substance from these fair isles. Marmite. Marmite is Britain's culinary equivalent of cricket. A lot of the planet has heard of it but not a lot know any more about it other than its existence. As the company themselves admit, you either love Marmite or you hate it. One of the best bits of journalism I've ever read was in a feature on the divine substance in the *International Herald Tribune* a couple of years ago on the occasion of Marmite's anniversary birthday. They'd interviewed a good balance of lovers and haters with the best being a hater of Canadian origin. He recounted arriving to study at university in Oxford in the 1950s, and the excitement running through his college at being invited to a garden party at St Hilda's, one of the all-women colleges. All was going well and he couldn't believe his luck at being in the lovely college quad surrounded by a bevvy of lady undergraduates. He was offered a sandwich and bit into it. It was a Marmite sandwich. He was quoted as saying 'I've never tasted anything so repulsive in my life, before or since, and I've never fully recovered from the experience!' That's the black and white reactions that Marmite provokes. Nobody likes Marmite a bit. You either love it or hate it, just like it says on the jar.

Before departing the subject, Marmite is better than Vegemite. Say the word Marmite within earshot of any

Australian and they'll start going on about Vegemite being better. Not so. Not even close. Marmite rules. Fact.

End of digression.

British food is okay. I should know, I'm extremely good at eating and, having eaten my way around the planet several times, I have still yet to find anything that betters my old dear's roast shoulder of lamb with all the trimmings, gravy and mint jelly. Our mother is a wonderful cook and coming home is therefore always gastronomically exciting. Apart from the disappointment of going through the town of Carterton, you know you're going to get home and get to choose what you have for dinner. For me that is always the old dear's roast shoulder of lamb. Also, having been away for a number of months, you know that there's going to a healthy stack of *Hello* magazines you haven't read to leaf through while sitting on the toilet during your post-prandial dump.

It's not just in our house where the food is good either. If you take the time to stop taking the piss out of British food, you'll notice that it's actually very good. For a start you're on an island and a small one at that. You can't get more than seventy something miles from the sea so good, fresh seafood is available all over Britain. You also have the excitement of sampling a good fish supper which is pretty hard to beat. Fish and chips, mushy peas, salt and vinegar and lashings of tartare sauce. Heaven. Middle Street Fish and Chips in Deal, Kent are pretty hard to beat. We used to go to the Golden Grid in Scarborough after a hard day's beach cricket but it's gone right downhill apparently. For sheer quantity I had a fish supper in the Foyle hotel in Moville, County Donegal which was about the size of a basking shark. Sit-down fish suppers are not the same though. If you get the chance – i.e if it's not raining – eat one on a seafront promenade out of a bit of paper with a wooden fork. Keep it real.

It's not just about the fish though. British cooking is about a lot more than just that. As previously conceded, it's often not the most subtle of food but a nation's sustenance is a reflection of the climate and lie of the land. For example, France is widely accepted as being the world capital of cuisine, but you wouldn't know that if you went out for dinner where I live. It's a number of variations on the theme of potatoes, cream, cheese, bacon, onions and garlic. It's all heart attack-on-a-plate, carbo-loaded stodge, basically. The Alps is a cold harsh place to live in the winter and was even more so in the days before the ski industry, when much of it was totally cut off during the winter. The local dishes are a reflection of that and therefore full of the cholesterol and carbohydrates needed to survive up at altitude in the cold.

The same goes for Britain which is home to lots of hearty stews, savoury puddings and pies, and all sorts of other delights. When you've eaten your way through main course, there's also a vast array of desserts amongst which fruit crumble is my favourite and has become fashionable in, of all places, France! If you have any room left for cheese there are hundreds of different types of that around as well. I take great delight in telling French folk who ask me what my favourite cheese is that my preferred nibble is Stilton, a blue cheese from England.

I have to say my personal favourite at home apart from fish and chips is haggis. A sheep's stomach, stuffed with ground up lamb and meal, served boiled with turnips and potato mash is spot on. A bit of whisky sauce is not bad with it either. In true Scottish tradition and in keeping with its status as the world capital of heart disease, you can also get haggis battered in chip shops. Lovely.

The other angle to approach eating out in Britain from is that of a multi-racial community. As with a lot of countries, as the planet gets smaller we have an increasingly multicultural

291

society and with immigration comes different foods. Britain has become a curry heaven in the last couple of generations, with beautifully aromatic and tasty curry houses popping up all over the place. Yes, a lot of the dishes have now been bastardised and many are hybrids of several different regional specialities, but a curry is hard to beat. So much so has curry become a part of our national gastronomic makeup that upon the death of 1950s singer Ruby Murray, despite the fact that her career achievements included being the only artist ever to have five songs in the top twenty simultaneously, obituaries invariably ended by saying that her name would live on into eternity because it is cockney rhyming slang for a curry.

Digression no 38 – The danger of chickpeas

I love chickpeas but they don't half make you fart. Living and working in the most expensive zipcode in the UK a few years ago, my brother Charlie and I found ourselves residing in a five bedroom detached mock Tudor house in Horsley in Surrey. We stayed in the house but it was gutted right down to the carpet underlay. The good news was that the electric and plumbing were still on so we could have a bath, boil a kettle and plug in a fridge. The other good news was the very good butcher's down the road so we had some great BBQs; and there was a really good curry house in the village. We ended up in there one night eating what must have been a lethal combination of foods, although the 'chana daal', a daal made with chick peas has always been my prime suspect as being the main wind generator. After finishing a lovely meal we headed back to our mansion and I was just reading a few pages of Joe Simpson's *Touching the Void* in bed, prior to going kipside, when the farting began. The first one was a good five second cheek rattler which I was very proud of. It sounded even better in the big empty room. Little did I know then that there were about another six hundred more of the same in the magazine that is my digestive system.

I must have farted a good five hundred times that night and at one stage, following a particularly large and long grunt, got the giggles so badly that it made me fart in time with the giggling. I was pretty tired after a hard day's toil in the summer sun and a couple of bottles of rosé, but the flatulence was so prolific that it kept me wide awake for a good long while, and my duvet fluttering like the windsock on the M1 just by East Midlands airport. Chick peas are dangerous; it's official.

Needless to say we had a couple of hot dishes along with the daal. The cost of ordering a hotty is waking up with an arse like a Japanese flag. Ouch!

End of digression.

One last thing worth a mention is the good old traditional afternoon tea. We took the old dear to London for her sixtieth birthday last year and after the London Eye, we went to a posh hotel for afternoon tea before heading into Theatreland to take in a show. It was the whole nine yards. The setting was the inner courtyard atrium of the Landmark Hotel in Marylebone which is pretty special. On the menu was champagne, sandwiches with the crusts cut off, lots of tea, cakes and scones with jam and cream. Give it a go. It's frightfully British.

Outside of these fair isles, the food doesn't get any worse. You don't have to go very far before you get somewhere else worth stopping for a feed. That's because next door is the gastronomic powerhouse that is France. For the French, food and cuisine is a statement of their national identity; a matter of national pride. From the low cost of eating out in restaurants to the beautifully presented meats and cheeses in the supermarché, or patisseries and viennoiseries in the boulangeries, France is a shrine to all things culinary.

In a sentence, the British love eating but the French love food. We have a lot of world class restaurants and London is considered one of the best cities in the world to go out to eat in, but we do not have an eating out culture. You can eat very well in Britain, but you pay for it. The French have more choice and its survival of the fittest. If you're not good enough, not creative enough or too expensive, you'll fail. Laws of the jungle applied to cooking. It takes place at all levels as well, that's how much they care. You'll struggle to get a better meal in France than at a 'Les Routiers' truck drivers restaurant with a packed car park. The truckers all know where the good places to go are so a full car park is a good sign. It won't be the most refined meal you'll ever eat and there'll be a good deal of rowdy conversation, cheap wine and fag smoke, but it'll be good food, arrive quickly and it'll be very cheap. Only in France would you get a cordon bleu chef committing suicide because he'd lost a Michelin star, as did Bernard l'Oiseau in 2003.

I was gunning it up France recently on the Kawasaki GT750 and applied the busy restaurant test to the beautiful town of Troyes in the bottom of the Champagne region. First rule is, stay away from the main squares in the old town where all the tourists and pigeons will be. Then, tour the back and side streets and don't rush your choice. I selected a restaurant which was a bit tatty but had calf's head on the menu as well as lots of local specialities. Just about to go in and the door opens with a hefty lady who tells me they only open in the evenings on the weekend. She did suggest a similar place for me to go a few streets away, though, and it was great. Troyes is the home of 'Andouillette', a sausage made of chitterlings, which to you is pig's guts. Absolutely delicious and totally repugnant and inedible to most Brits, but I got some good experience at an early age. We used to have cow's tongue for school dinners for God's sake!

Digression no 39 – The best day of my life part 4

Upon arrival at work on the evening of the 29th of March 2005 I sent an email to a load of my mates who I knew would be sitting staring at a computer screen in an office. I did it just to get on their nerves really. Judging by the abuse I got in the replies, it worked! The gist of the email was that they'd all probably earned more that day than I had since the start of the ski season in November, but... I'd left work at 9.45 that morning, ski boots already on and skied fresh tracks in waist deep champagne powder snow for three and a half hours with a couple of mates until we could barely stand up we were so tired.

Off-piste skiing is dangerous and tends to get more dangerous in the spring due to milder temperatures. After midday, as the day warms up, the packed snow tends to be more prone to avalanche. As we got to the bottom of the drag lift again we were going to call it a day but decided the skiing was too good to miss. We'd been leaving big wide free-ride tracks on the hill since 10am.

Back at the top of the Combe de Signal, the pitch we were skiing in Val d'Isère, the place was again deserted, as it had been all morning. Ten minutes later and we'd all survived to tell the tale, and by 1.30 were in the Edelweiss restaurant with a bottle of rosé in front of us and a plate of foie gras on the way. That's the best meal I've ever had in France. It wasn't just the great food and drink in a lovely mountain restaurant, catching some rays in good company. It was the elation and the rush of the skiing we'd just done and the prospect of doing the evening show on the radio while not inconsiderably muddled up. The foie gras, followed by seared scallops accompanied by oodles of rosé, had cost me over a week's wages, but so what?

Some things money simply cannot buy and I'd rather have the memories than the money. I may well die on a motorcycle or skiing off-piste as some of my friends and colleagues have done, but when my life flashes before my eyes, I want it to be days like the 29th of March 2005 which are my last conscious thoughts, and not days in the office.

Most importantly was the time the whole lunch took. Ages. Hours. The big advantage the French and a lot of other countries besides have over the Brits is the amount of time they take to eat. With us it's bang out the courses, gobble it all up amidst conversation muffled by mouthfuls of food, get straight up and do the dishes. In sensible countries the courses come out at regular but good length intervals, the wine waiter looks after you in between times and there's no rushing you to get off your table so you know that you're in it for the long haul. Coffee in most countries takes longer than your average meal in Britain.

End of digression.

South America. That answers the question of where to go next. There's so much to say about food that you may as well go back to the bottom after starting locally.

Now don't get me wrong, I'm not going to slag off a continent wholesale for its lack of imaginative food. See the sleeping rough section for a guide to tasty fruit for a start. Despite this, South America isn't a massive gastronomic highlight. There's only so much you can do with rice and chicken and there's only so many times in a row you can eat it. They do vary it by calling it 'Pollo con arroz' and then changing it back to 'Arroz con pollo' from time to time. Any 'menu del dia' in South America is going to be some sort of chicken and rice.

The tedium of this makes the highlights all the more worthwhile. In the market town of Riobamba in Ecuador I had my first bowl of one of the highlights. Yahuarlocro which is a hearty soup of potatoes, tripe and black pudding with some maize lobbed in for good measure. It is really nice. This year has brought Ecuadorian cuisine into the spotlight if only because their footy team had the misfortune to play England in the World Cup in Germany. As is always the case with our dreadful tabloid newspapers, any little facet of a country we are about to face in a sporting fixture is slated as weird or stupid. This was done in the case of Ecuador's national dish, Cuy, which is grilled guinea pig on a stick. It is delightful, unlike a lot of Britain's press, which is shameful at best.

Further down the way, to use a geographical term, you get to the carnivores. It is quite incredible how much meat Argentinians are capable of eating without the accompaniment of any form of vegetable. It is said that the average human has about two pounds, about a kilo, of undigested meat in their stomachs at any one time. For an Argentinian it must be at least triple that. Darwin was driven to write on the subject while in South America so prolific is their consumption. So was mine as it goes. I'll never forget a load of us having a BBQ on a beach in Mar del Plata, home to smelly sea lion colonies (see chapter eight) and haunt of shit American Presidents, on the coast south of Buenos Aires. We dug a hole in the beach and got a big fire going while a couple went off to get the food. The couple came back with the beautiful girlfriend carrying the bits and bobs and her massive boyfriend carrying the cow. He was a professional sailor and had a triangular body in the mould of Mr Incredible. Despite his physique, even he was wincing under the strain of carrying the bags of cow. I say cow instead of beef because I think it was pretty much a whole cow butchered and put into bags. By now the driftwood had become hot coals and we BBQed the meat before having a big bonfire and party. What a memorable, chilled out night.

Mar del Plata was not the first indication of the carnivorous habits of the lower reaches of South America. Up in Bolivia we'd had some great food in many different regions. The diet is very regional with so many variations in altitude but my favourite find was someone's front room in Uyuni up on the Altiplano, the sort of simple place that I love best. They would change the menu every evening, and then back again the next night. The options were either 'tripa dorada' which was 'golden' fried tripe or 'charque kan' which was stringy, dried llama meat. I think they found it a bit strange that I sat there every other night singing 'I Feel For You' but it was the only Chaka Khan song I could remember. Both dishes were fabulous and both dollar fifty a plate. Bargain.

Back to red meat and getting down to the bottom end of Bolivia and things change again compared to up on the Altiplano and down in the Amazon Basin. Travelling down to Tupiza and Tarija, me and my wingman Cockney Bastard were on the trail of Butch Cassidy and the Sundance Kid, who the Bolivian army finally caught up with and killed in those parts. Despite being a chef, Cockney Bastard was disgusted with my high intake of tripe and refused to eat in what he considered the squalor of my favourite Uyunian food outlet. Down south we hit beef country big time. Our first meal down there was a 'parillada', in what appeared to be the railway workers union social club. 'Parillada' turned out to be Spanish for how much beef you can balance on a large plate. They brought it out and I thought it was for both of us, but we got that much each. The only reason the two plates didn't arrive at once was that the chap couldn't physically carry them. This was pretty much the norm for the whole of Argentina which was a couple of hours south.

Talking of Mama and Papa places like that one in Uyuni reminds me of eating in Eastern Europe and more specifically of the place in Budapest where I used to point at the menu with a bread knife due to communication problems. Eastern Europe on the whole is a great place to eat. Hungarian pork is just one of a number of highlights which include fried cheese in the Czech Republic; are they trying to overtake the Scots' heart disease stats? Fried cheese. Definitely to be consumed in moderation.

In Poland they have a great line in vegetarian restaurants which are superb eateries. My other enduring memory was of a bowl of tripe soup called Flaki Walowe.

Digression no 40 – Tripe

Is this bloke some sort of tripe addict/weirdo? That's what you're wondering isn't it? Tripe in France, tripe in Ecuador, tripe in Bolivia, Poland, etc. Well I love the stuff so why not eat it? Just because it's the lining of a cow's stomach and has the same texture of your average car tyre doesn't mean that it's not got potential to be nice to eat. The trouble with a lot of Brits is that they don't eat a lot of stuff because it sounds repulsive. If you're going to kill an animal, you may as well make it worthwhile by eating as much of the unfortunately deceased animal as possible. This is not the attitude adopted in Britain where a lot of offal (the inside bits) are considered to be, well, awful. (Awful, offal; geddit?) Most Brits turn their noses up and wince at the thought of eating liver or kidneys let alone head, brain, trotter, cheek, hoof, tail or tongue.

Even the people trying to flog the stuff to you are very anti-offal. Before a trip a few years ago I'd selected tripe in milk and onions for my last dinner and went to the butcher's to get the tripe. I asked for three pounds and the bloke said; 'you've got a big dog then?' the assumption being that if you're buying tripe and you're British, it must be for the dog. 'It's not for the dog, the dog's dead. It's for me and my folks,'

I said. 'Oh my God!' he said with enough vehemence to require an exclamation mark, as he actually ducked behind the counter a touch as if to defend himself from the presence of a tripe-eater.

The above dish was actually the first thing I cooked after moving into the madhouse a load of us shared in Bondi Junction in Sydney. A couple of the other residents, notably Foxy and Evans were very fussy eaters. They didn't even like cheese! Weirdoes. Needless to say tripe was on that list as well. Despite the fact that the kitchen was in the back of our terraced house and the stereo was on, I clearly heard Foxy holler, 'What the fook is that smell?' in the uncompromising Yorkshire fashion of delivery, as he came in from work.

I love the stuff. Maybe that's where I'm going wrong. I'm now single after being dropped like a bad habit by my latest ex-girlfriend, who used to make me brush my teeth immediately after eating tripe if I ever wanted any chance of kissing her again. Maybe she binned me due to cumulative disgust? If I didn't like tripe would I not now be sitting alone in a house in Bristol with nothing but a computer with a French keyboard?

End of digression.

Asia. The antithesis of the British approach to offal is Asia and especially the Far East. The French are the big offal eaters in Europe but they've got nothing on the Chinese and others in that region who will eat pretty much every bit of every animal. Good on them as well. It's all good stuff and there's no point in turning your nose up at something just because it's a certain bit of an animal.

I hooked up with Foxy and his sister in Malaysia at some point in 1999 and when it got to dinner time, we'd made it into Southern Thailand. They went for a pizza. I'm not overly in favour of pizza at the best of times because it's basically a toasted sandwich in disguise. If I do want a pizza, I'm going to wait until I'm in New York or Italy or somewhere famous for making them. When in Rome and all that. When in Surat Thani, do as the Surat Thanians do. Before you know it I'm in the night market and I've negotiated a bag of weevils which I followed up with some flash-fried whole locusts. When Foxy found out what I'd been eating he was what I can only describe as absolutely distraught, but contrary to what he thought, the whole lot was lovely. It's not just that either; it's the atmosphere in places like that. The bustling claustrophobia, the raw unshuttered glaring light of the bulbs they all have dangling above their stands and the fascination of the locals when they find a tourist prepared to eat the local fare. If it's good enough for the locals, it's good enough for me.

The warmness of the people and the richness of the land contribute to the incredibly diverse experience that is eating in Asia. The diversity comes partly from the sheer size of the continent but the effort and imagination put into the cuisine of every country is a taste sensation not to be missed at any cost. Thailand is a case in point. A very verdant country with lots of cracking spices, veggies and fruits to bung into the pot. The first time you eat a proper Thai curry it's like a culinary starshell going off inside your head. Your brain is registering the fact that your tastebuds are being bombarded with thousands of different pungent aromas, but it's not quick enough to keep up with the onslaught. Highlighting Thailand is not meant to take anything away from other parts of the region. Having never found anything I won't eat from other parts of the globe, it was unlikely to happen in Asia, and needless to say, I love the lot all the way from Japanese yakatori, sushi and gyoza right down to Indonesian nasi goreng.

I really regret not going on a cookery course while in those parts. My cousin Tom did one and found it well worthwhile; I can make a pretty tidy Thai curry but I'd love to get well into the cooking side of things. It's pretty hard to when you don't have a base and one place to leave all your stuff in.

Africa. My favourite place to have a sundowner to date is in Africa. Well, that depends who you're listening to. A lot of people will tell you that Zanzibar is close to Africa and others will say that it's part of Tanzania and therefore in Africa. Whatever geographical status you give to this beautiful archipelago, the Africa Hotel terrace on the edge of Stone Town is the best place to drink a Gin and Tonic I've ever found. Hang on, isn't this the food section? Well, yes it is but that's part of the reason that the Africa Hotel is so good. You can start with sundowners in the worn out old place with the big terrace. It probably used to be a really grand colonial hotel at some point in the past but it's now showing signs of age.

Getting closer to sunset and the stallholders and chess players start to turn up in Jamhuri Gardens which are between the hotel and the sea wall. It's so beautiful just chilling out, leaning on the front rail sipping a gin and tonic while watching the sunset – silhouetted kids diving into the sea off the wall as the gardens get more and more lively. Eventually there are dozens of stalls selling everything from grilled octopus to sugar cane juice so after a few lubrications you just sidle on down and wander around buying stuff to nibble on while soaking up the atmosphere. I'll never forget it and fully intend to return at some point.

We went big whilst in Zanzibar as well. It was one of those times when you feel like a splurge and just go for it. We went to a lovely restaurant and it probably cost us about fifty times what our usual tour of Jamhuri Gardens cost but it's good to go large now and then. I'd never had lobster thermador before so gave it a go. Scrumptious, although I probably enjoyed it more than the lobster.

My first foray into Africa ended with a bang on the culinary front in a restaurant just outside Nairobi. We went to

'Carnivore', which was the only one of its kind at the time. Apparently there's one in South Africa now as well. It was a massive restaurant and nightclub, although the second bit didn't really come into it as we all overdid it in the restaurant. Carnivore is, as the name would suggest, a Mecca for meat eaters. It is red meat central, and I got totally carried away. It's a very simple concept. You get massive racks of spits over hot coals and spit roast loads of animals. Waiters, resplendent in crisp white uniforms then wander around with two badges on their lapel, one with their name on and the other with the type of meat they have on the skewer they're carrying. These include every type of mammal imaginable as well as crocodile and others. I was in heaven and could barely move by the time it was time to go into the nightclub. I felt like Jabba the Hutt and there was no way I was going to be cutting any moves on the dance floor.

Despite parts of Africa being desperately poor it is a great place to eat, not always for the culinary masterpieces that are served up, but for the social side of the eating. Mealie balls dipped in mutton stew and stuff like that make eating so much more social. It's like in Muslim countries when you're all sat around and wrap up stuff in rotis and chapatis and then dip it in some lovely sauce. The same goes for Africa.

Another time which sticks in my mind was having breakfast on the streets of Dar es Salaam which was really special. On the menu was tea, exactly as you don't like it – served very sweet due to large amounts of condensed milk, out of an old vegetable oil can. There were also some random looking pastry type things. But, it kept us going for a while and we had a great laugh with the seller and his mates.

Later on in the decade I was back, this time in Saharan Africa and Egypt, where falafel will allow you to exist for about two bucks a day if you're really skint. Watch out though, they're made out of chick peas. Windsock imminent.

Something which has been touched on and warrants more discussion is the food in the States. In my three visits over the pond I don't think I've ever had a bad meal. The first one I ever had was at the home of the people I went to stay with on scout exchange when I was fourteen. We sent out for pizza (a product which still excited me in my teens) and when it arrived it had roughly the same diameter as Battersea helipad. I was impressed beyond belief; first of all by getting takeaway food delivered, and second by the fact that there were in fact two pizzas the same size. Despite the Witte family being a couple of olds and four kids, there was no way seven of us were going to get anywhere close to finishing the two Frisbees they'd ordered.

The good thing about the States is that there is no need to finish a meal. Why are you under no pressure to do so? Because of the invention of doggy bags. Doggy bags are a prime example of American ingenuity and good service, but also of the fact that theirs is a country largely devoid of airs and graces. They'd rather you had too much to eat and a means of taking the rest home than to go short and leave their restaurant with any room for more. Back in LA in 97 and we were picked up by our hosts outside Universal Studios (a great day out) and taken straight to a Rodeo Drive ribs joint. The doggy bags came into their own because I'm not sure where they got the ribs from but I'm assuming it was an elephant or some other very large animal. In the States their ribs are like their cars were in the 70s, big is good and bigger is better.

That goes for the foot long chilli cheese dogs in Circus Circus Casino in Vegas as well. I'm aware that this type of food has little if any nutritional value and that the bright orange liquid squirt-on cheese that goes on top probably has ingredients in it which you'll also find in some household detergents, but you have to try the local delicacies. I wouldn't like to eat one every day for the rest of my life in the same way as I wouldn't like to eat a doner kebab while sober, but I am proud to say that I've eaten a whole foot long chilli cheese dog in Vegas. I'd do it again as well.

While we're on the subject of 'junk food' may I also sing the praises of hamburger joints. Junk food is not a very endearing term although it does have some merit. Along with Vegas delicacies, it's fair to say that you don't have to look very far and wide to find something to eat which is healthier than a hamburger. However, with that said, hamburgers taste good, in my opinion. They're also not going to kill you if you eat them now and again. The term 'junk food' just gives fat folk an excuse to be fat instead of varying their diet. I love a good cheeseburger – I consider eating a burger without cheese in it to be a bit pointless – but I don't eat nothing but cheeseburgers. There's no point in suing McDonald's and acting all surprised that you're fat if you've eaten burgers every day for ten years. This doesn't mean you have to abstain altogether though. Especially in California, Arizona and Nevada. That's because these three states are home to 'In 'n' Out Burger', my all-time top burger joint. Good old-fashioned burgers at their best.

One of the classiest things I've ever seen was on the toilet at my parents' house. I was in the middle of a post-travelling *Hello!* magazine readathon and was on the Brad and Jennifer's wedding edition. Turning the pages to bypass all the mushy stuff and get to photos of fit guests I arrived at a page with an In 'n' Out Burger mobile catering van! Brilliant. According to their website they're called 'cookout trailers'. I want one. I was instantly hungry. In 'n' Out Burger at your wedding!

Lastly on the eating in the States front is New York. Being a country bumpkin I've never been totally comfortable in the big bad city but I am getting better. The thing is, if you're going to build a city, build it like New York. Do it properly.

Loads of skyscrapers tightly packed together, car horns blowing, underground carriages making the pavements vibrate. New York is a proper, sprawling city with a proper CBD where every building reaches for the skies. Sydney is the same; downtown is all high reaching and impressive. Everyone's in a rush and living fast. That's why I'm not a huge fan of London. It's not high enough and it doesn't have a proper high rise, tight, compact downtown like what cities should do.

I was in New York with my last-but-four ex-girlfriend. I took her there for her thirtieth birthday a few years ago. We had a great time and it was shop-till-you-drop. It was a great culinary triumph as well. I'd met a New York cab driver-cum-photographer in Bolivia a few years previous who would spend half the year cab driving to finance his travels. I asked him for advice on where to take my girlfriend for her birthday dinner and before I'd finished the question Dick said the Gramercy Tavern at 42nd East 20th St. That obviously meant something to him but of course not to me. Anyway, that's where we ended up and he was not wrong. Good wine and great food including melt in your mouth steak and a waitress from Kentucky who couldn't do enough for you. It was a resumé of everything that is good about eating out in the States.

The other highlight in New York was Burritoville. Birthday girl had gone underwear shopping with her sister so I took the opportunity to go and stuff myself with a massive burrito. You get something the size and approximate weight of a house brick for five bucks and it is full of Mexican goodness. Sour cream, grated cheese, guacamole, beans, meat, chilli, the list of ingredients goes on and on. That's making me hungry, I'm off to cook something.

Right, with the stomach now loaded right up to the hilt we can get on with it. Australia; straightforward food, very straightforward, straight talking people and a wonderful part of the world. Simple, straightforward food is great and just as important is the location in which you are eating. Australia and its population are probably world champions in combining the two in the form of the BBQ. Good food eaten in beautiful surroundings, often down at the beach. Australians have completely sussed the whole how-to-live-life thing. They have a voracious appetite for both food and beer, the French attitude to work, the weather for an outdoor orientated lifestyle and the Brazilian enthusiasm for the beach. Combine all this together and you have a large proportion of a nation down at the beach having fun and enjoying themselves. The culinary side of this lifestyle is a very highly developed system of barbecueing.

Don't get me wrong, I love a traditional winter family Christmas as much as the next person because they're so much fun. The popping of crackers, the hats, bad jokes, Brussels sprouts, bread sauce and of course, asking Aunty Peggy if she 'wants stuffing'; snigger, snigger. That's all good and well but Christmas in thirty degrees of heat at Bronte Beach in Sydney, a game of footy and a cricket match is pretty hard to beat. Christmas on the beach in your board shorts, a few tins of booze from the bottle shop and a barbecue. What more could you want? The Aussies have got the art of BBQing at the beach so sussed out that they even have coin operated electric BBQs on some beaches and all you have to do is take your tongs and some dead animal.

Other countries are also great at BBQ. A fourth of July BBQ in the States is pretty hard to beat. The British are on the whole very poor at them. The good thing about BBQ in Britain is that all British men love to think that they know what they're doing. They're all there crowded round the homeowner who is wearing a 'get the chef a beer' apron, getting covered in smoke and giving advice. That leaves a garden full of women for the rest of chaps who are quite happy not getting remotely involved in the cooking side of things.

Liquids

Sitting here in a nice comfortable leather couch in a posh, trendy, open plan pub on Bristol docks, I'm following the same rationale as I have been with the food section. I can't write about alcohol without a glass of something scrumptious to imbibe, obviously. It doesn't come much more scrumptious than Dry Blackthorn cider, one of the world's greatest substances. I'm going to have to do it in stints because I'm not a very fast typer and if I sit here until I'm done with the alcohol section I'll be totally ring-bolted. The first pint is going down very well though I'm pleased to say. If you ever come to the UK, I do strongly recommend, nay insist, that you have a pint of Dry Blackthorn or some other brand of what we like to call 'West Country champagne'. It's like the posh, expensive French stuff but made out of apples, cheaper and tastier; so totally different in other words.

So, if this section is about booze or whatever other slang word you have for alcohol, why is it called the 'liquids' section? I'll tell you. It's because there are substances out there which you can drink which do not have alcohol in them! This may be a distant memory if you're reading this after finishing a university degree; a distant memory as far back in your mind as your teenage acne, but it's true.

Water--

The question you're asking is; 'why is he harping on about all this?' The answer is because it's important. Water is important. Very important. Of course water is important wherever you are, because without it, you die. Dying is bad for you so water is good for you. See? Good. Here, there or anywhere, water is very important to your personal health but this takes on a different level if you're in the Third World or in a very hot part of the world. In the case of the hot spots this is obviously due to the dehydrating effect of the sun and heat. As to the Third World, a lot of it is hot so the previous paragraph also applies. The other relevant bit is right at the start of the book in the 'travel bugs' section. There are a lot more diseases to catch in the Third World than there are in the developed world and taking on plenty of water is essential while you're on your travels to keep your body's natural defences up and at their best. When I was propped against the front of that bus in Bolivia with stuff flying out of both ends of me, my body was losing a lot of fluids and therefore a lot of its essential minerals and stuff. I say 'and stuff' because I'm no doctor, but I do have a basic knowledge of what is good and bad for me.

The bare bones of the matter is that if you go to the Third Word for any length of time you're likely to get the heeby jeebies at some point, but you can minimize these chances. You can do this by having stuff with you to help you get over it should you be unlucky enough to catch something. Some things you'll need in your bag are:

1) Water purification tablets – very handy and just pop one in a water bottle a while before drinking. You've to remember that in a lot of the third world it's not just a question of turning on a tap and out comes clear, sweet agua. Take some tablets with you and then if you're in any doubt as to the quality of the water, drop one in.

2) A water filter – there are some great products out there. I looked on in amazement as a Swedish bloke in Kenya stuck his filter into a very muddy brown puddle, started winding the handle and, albeit slowly, filled his bottle up with clear water. If you want to go for as many safeguards as you can get and guarantee that you'll have something to drink wherever there's a puddle, buy a filter.

3) Rehydration salts – also essential for the calm after the storm. If you do get some form of 'Dehli belly' you will puke or poo out a lot of the minerals your body requires, and they'll need replacing pretty quickly. The best way to do this is with rehydro tablets which contain loads of what you'll be missing. Chuck one in some water and off you go. They're not a taste sensation but they do the job.

4) Flagyl has sorted me out more than once. It's a bit draconian as medicine goes but effective as well. Its long name is Metronidazole, an antibiotic which removes two layers of skin from your stomach lining and basically gives you a flush out. 'Bleach for your guts' as a mate of mine once put it. Ham-fisted but effective when you're in the shit; literally.

5) Drinking nothing but mineral water is an option but doesn't help you develop your natural protection. It also isn't going to be available everywhere you go all of the time. Beware also that if you do take this path, that salad and vegetables won't be washed in mineral water and ice cubes will be made from tap water. The other trouble is that whereas your body gradually builds up an immunity to diseases in the tap water you are drinking, this is not the case if you drink mineral water, so when you do get ill, you'll get really ill. I tend not to drink mineral water for this last reason, and while I have had a couple of pretty unpleasant intestinal experiences, they would probably have been a lot worse if my body hadn't been playing host to some of the local stomach parasites for some time.

NB – The only time when you MUST drink mineral water in the Third World is when you see the locals doing it. I'm sure that given the choice a lot of the population of the Third World would like to drink nice cool bottles of Evian and San Pellegrino. It'd probably come out of one of those huge brushed stainless steel American style fridges it takes four people to pick up as well. Life isn't like that, though. Folk in the Third World have better things to do with their hard earned cash than spend it on mineral water. So, if you do see them drinking it, maybe you should too. It doesn't happen all that often but one instance for me was in the Bolivian silver mining town of Potosi. The water is so acrid that even the locals don't touch it. Something to do with the minerals in the hills or something.

While on the subject of soft drinks, water is not the only one. There's lots of lovely stuff out there from the root beers of North America to Irn Bru in Scotland to L and P in New Zealand. Best of all though is the purple, grape-flavoured Fanta you get in Africa and Latin America. It is officially super-double lovely.

One other thing in passing is that I was amazed to find out while in Peru that there is a substance on the planet with more sugar in it than Coca-Cola. In Peru they drink 'Inca Cola' which is the same colour as urine and its sugar content is about 200% at a conservative estimate. Not only is it revolting but the Peruvians drink it by the crate. To make things worse, they drink it without refrigeration so it doesn't even quench your thirst. Yuck.

Alcoholic beverages –

It's now tomorrow and yesterday's Blackthorn-fest down at the Bristol docks seems less of a good idea. Bit of a headache. Nothing fifteen cups of tea won't sort out, though. A bit fragile but nothing compared to my worst hangover ever. That was on New Year's Day 1998 in San Agustín in Colombia. New Year's Eve had been great. Festivities were well underway with lots of fireworks, music and dancing by the time we arrived. As a non-beer drinker, I was on the local firewater of a large part of South America which is called Aguardiente. The last thing I remember saying to Tom was 'I just can't get pissed on this stuff.' Then all of a sudden it was daylight and I was being woken up by my brother who had found me in a pothole in the middle of a dirt road; everything in between is a blur. Not the safest place you can choose to fall asleep, the middle of the road, especially a Colombian road. Idiot. I repaired back to the scary-French-woman-with-too-much-plastic-surgery's place (see places to stay chapter) and fell asleep. I woke up at ten o'clock at night and assumed that I was dying of a brain haemorrhage. The slightest movement of any limb, eyelid or anything put me straight into extreme pain. Never again. Yeah, right.

Local brews are more often than not pretty lethal. This goes for at home as well as abroad. On a day off from work one summer, a few of us were sitting in one of Somerset's rougher pubs drinking a lunchtime pint. Not being the sort of establishment you'd expect to see tourists in, imagine our surprise when a family of Americans walked in. The father asked for some advice on what to select and told us he wanted a 'glass of real apple cider'. Before he knew it he had a pint of Burrow Hill farmhouse cider from Kingsbury Episcopi in his hand, a fairly innocuous looking dull, light brown opaque sort of substance not dissimilar to dishwater, or cold, weak tea with very little milk in it. Half an hour later he was weaving out of the door walking like a newly born calf with his family propping him up. How we laughed!

I've done it again since as well, in the Marina del Rey area of Los Angeles in a restaurant called The Library. It was in 97 when cigar smoking was all the rage and the place was a swanky restaurant with a big fumador; allegedly a favourite haunt of the now governor Arnie Schwarznegger. We were guests of some fabulously rich American friends of Charlie's parents, and they were being as hospitable as Americans invariably are; that is to say very. They were so kind to us which is all the more admirable considering that they'd met

312

Charlie once about ten years previous and didn't know me from Adam.

Talking of Adam, that was the name of their pretty straight laced son, a lovely chap who took us to Universal Studios and a Six Flags theme park with a dozen rollercoasters. I was very surprised to find Perry on the drinks menu and asked for a pint of it. Adam asked me what it was and I told him it was cider made from pears, that it was delicious, and how surprised I was to see it on the drinks list. He said he's have one as well.

Well, my first one departed at a speed he was quite surprised at, and he was obviously struggling. I was quite surprised that he joined me when I asked for a reload. After three he was in quite serious difficulties and nursed a glass of wine for the rest of the meal. Americans don't seem to be able to cope with anything stronger than Lite 'training' beer.

The boot was on the other foot in Egypt though. I was well pleased to have made it through Eastern Europe alive after several encounters with the local go-go juice, a plum brandy called Slivovitz, which my dad had warned me about. Now at Aswan in Egypt, I find out that one of the other people on the felucca trip I took back up the Nile, Jurij, was Slovakian. On the first night, we were sitting under the stars and talking about his homeland when he pulled a bottle of Slivovitz out of his bag and that stuff gets you muddled right up, I can tell you. If presented with a bottle of novelty alcohol or 'boom boom' as John Lee Hooker calls it, always allow the person who's produced it have the first glug. Needless to say, we got spangled.

Fiji: I told you we'd be back there at some point. You may remember that their national drink, Cava, doesn't contain any alcohol; but is a natural amphetamine, made from some sort of root. Other stuff comes out of Fiji which definitely has alcohol in it though. Fiji Bitter is widely considered by beer drinkers to be a pretty good beverage but the best was saved until last. On our way through Nadi, Fiji's international airport, for a flight to LA, Charlie and I were in duty free. Fiji gin, two pint bottle, ten Fijian dollars. Sold. Two pints of gin for a couple of pounds sterling! At prices like that you can't really afford to stay sober! We purchased a bottle each.

As previously recounted, one bottle made it to Vegas only to be mixed with a 64 ounce super slurp. The other bottle got the good news on our first night in LA. Day two saw us promoted to the luxury of Pacific Pallisades and the massive house our benefactors lived in. For the first night we stayed in the much more lowly, but very lively and world famous Venice Beach, complete with rollerbladers, police cruisers and 'don't feed the animals' signs on Muscle Beach. We were in a hostel called Jim's or something and ended up sharing a room with a couple of Swedish lads. The Fijian gin was unleashed and before you know it we were well worse for wear and heading out on the town. Except for one of the Swedes who had to remain in his billet due to being too top heavy. A big surprise that was because Swedes tend to be pretty big movers in the drinking stakes and this bloke was a right thumper as well; not dissimilar to the much younger really muscly bloke called 'Swede' Clint Eastwood beats up to inflate his ageing ego in the film *Heartbreak Ridge*. It was 'goodnight Vienna' for him but I don't think the rest of us lasted a lot longer either.

Next stop on the alcohol tour of the world is Thailand where they've got some proper dangerous stuff which comes under a variety of names. Mekong whisky, Sang Tip rum and Sang Som rum are all lethal. If there is any difference between them it's not overly discernible and they're all pretty much just a load of floor sweepings distilled with some sort of novelty alcohol-based stuff and bottled up. For good measure it is said that the bottles are topped up with amphetamine and you can't take a bottle home with you because it contains ten banned substances!

I thought that this was a blatant exaggeration until one morning after a full moon party on the island of Ko Pha Ngan. There was Foxy still dancing in the sea at ten in the morning. I paddled in to see him and asked him how it was going. After taking several seconds to recognise me, he said he was fine except that his shoulders hurt a bit. I had to explain to him that it was ten in the morning and that he was getting sunburn at which point he declared that he hadn't noticed it had changed from night to day! Maybe those stories about the ingredients of Thai spirits are true after all.

Getting back to the flux capacitor in *Back to the Future 2*, first visited in the last chapter. Remember how Doc Brown goes round collecting some worthwhile bits of food to stick in it to start with? That's the food. Then he tops up with the crappy old juices he finds in the bottom of a few cartons in the trash to top the system up. That's the alcohol of time travel. The rubbish you chuck in to test the system. In fact, in the first of those films when the deLorean requires much more specific fuel, Doc Brown could probably have bypassed years of painstaking research by using any home-grown alcoholic spirit from Thailand.

Last but not least in the alcohol section is the most impressive Super Mario lookalike I've ever met and the greatest drinking at breakfast feat I've ever witnessed.

Wars get in the way of everything and this includes my motorbiking and sightseeing. I'd got down to southern Turkey on the Honda Transalp and was looking forward to visiting the Crusader forts and fortifications of Syria and the Lebanon before heading into Israel. This was thwarted by a major ding-dong between Turkey and Syria who were close to war at the time. Instead I had to get a boat to Rhodes and wander around the world heritage site that is Rhodes old town. Very

315

impressive. From there another ferry went to Haifa in Israel via the Cypriot port of Limassol. Cyprus is a very beautiful island nation and this was the second time I'd visited it for less than half a day. With its winding coastline and backbone of mountains, I'll be back for a longer visit at some point.

Digression no 41 – interesting Cyprus fact

Cyprus is the only country in the world which has a map of itself on its national flag.

End of digression.

Alighting for a few hours in Limassol, I had an unexpected treat in the form of a proper fried breakfast. Egg, bacon, sausage, black pudding and all the trimmings; a taste sensation I'd not enjoyed since leaving home some six weeks earlier.

That's where I met Super Mario. Can't remember his actual name but he was a great chap. A retired civil servant of about sixty, he was tucking into a plate of olives as I sat down. Also on his table was a quart bottle of some sort of brown liquid which as we got talking turned out to be Cypriot brandy. You know, one of those 1/3 bottles of spirit that fit in your back pocket. I went off to the loo and checked the watch. 10.30 in the morning and he'd just about cracked a third of a bottle of brandy! Top bombing. When I got back he had! The remnants of the bottle was in his glass. Then the waiter came back with another quart bottle! My eyebrows were right up there by now as Super Mario went up in my estimations as quickly as he headed for the alcohol hall of fame. Well, you wouldn't read about it; by the time I'd finished my fried breakfast he was well on his way through his third bottle of brandy of the day. I bade him farewell saying that I needed to get back to my Israel-bound boat. The reality was that I had lots of time but I wanted to have a look around the town. I also wanted to avoid having to nurse a chunky Cypriot who'd drunk a bottle of brandy before midday. He was a lovely bloke, very interesting and actually showed few effects from his pre-yardarm piss-up, but I thought I'd better do the off before I had to help peel him off the terrace.

That pretty much concludes the alcohol section. Not everybody's cup of tea I know, but I've spent many a night in all corners of the planet having a great time getting bevvied on a number of potions. There are many that I wouldn't recommend to my worst enemy, the worst I've come across being 'Suze'.Suze is French, made out of God knows what and should be banned. Apart from this and other Suze-like concoctions, it's all good fun. Don't overdo it though. It's important to allow a bit of blood into your alcohol stream from time to time.

Back to healthier stuff and don't forget that consuming soft drinks doesn't mean a compulsory sugarfest. If you fancy something more natural try any of the fresh pressed fruit juices the pick of which for me is the 'jugo de melocotones' (melon juice) you get in Latin America. Not that you need to go that far. A mango milkshake in the Lahore Karahi curry house in Southall, London takes some beating.

On the caffeine front, I never drink coffee in Britain. The explosion of 'proper' coffee shops has improved the quality, there's no doubt, but they're just not really my thing. I'm used to living in France where you can expect to get a proper cup of coffee for under three quid and without the poncy surroundings. The other scourge of British coffee drinking is the cafetière. What the hell is a cafetière when it's at home? I've never seen one in another country and the coffee they produce is rubbish. Us Brits are being conned by a glass jug with a plunger that's been given a foreign-sounding name.

Out there in the rest of the world, the coffee is great. As I said, Venezuela is the big boy on the block if you want a serious rush. If you want it cold I would recommend South East Asia and any Muslim country for the best iced coffee going.

As to other caffeine, you'll not find a better cup of tea than a good old cup of PG Tips builder's strength with a bit of sugar and plenty of milk. You can look for better, but you'll die of old age first.

Toilets

Toilets and what goes on in them is a source of fascination to every member of the male gender of the human race. See, I'm going on about members already! We can't help ourselves. On the other hand, getting girls interested in a conversation about anything relating to poo, or even just farting, is nigh on impossible.

Our generation's involvement with shit started at an early age. From very early on, whenever we were at the grandparent's house, me, Charlie and Tom would all sooner nip out of the small windows at the back of the living room and go and have a dump or pee in the bushes rather than walk to the other end of the house and go in the outdoor bog by the larder. Why I don't know, but we were all into 'extreme pooing' from an early age. It transpires, following a damning admission a few years ago, that Tom used to get so worried about missing a single second of his favourite programmes that he used to lie on his side and piss underneath the antique bureau desk no one used in the back corner of the grandparent's living room! It took them a while to work out why the carpet had rotted so badly, but that was the cause.

It wasn't just our own shit which interested us either. Cow shit was of equal interest to us and we used most of the red Chinese 'pétards' bangers we smuggled back from France to blow up sloppy cow shit. Now don't ask me why but in those days we used to think it was good fun to light the fuse and all crowd around the cowpat in question till the banger blew up. The winner was the one with the most cow shit on them. Twenty-five plus years on and it seems like a strange activity but at the time it seemed like a good idea. The rest of the bangers were used for scaring 'old' people with; that is to say anyone over fifteen.

Toilets are a fact of life. Whether you're interested in them, and even more so talking about them, is irrelevant. You have to use them. This is a cause of major strife to a lot of posh people who prefer to completely disavow the existence of defecation and the facilities which go with it. Posh people quite often complain about being able to 'see the toilets' at our flower show in the summer which must be awful for them! Posh or not, toilets are a fact of life.

When travelling this can be more of a problem than at home because you'll often find that toilet hygiene is of a lower standard than you would have hoped. Add to the quest for a clean toilet the fact that you could well have the 'two bob bits' a fair bit of the time and toilets tend to become a fairly major part of your life. It's true, even women start talking about toilets when away travelling. As previously discussed, word of mouth is where you will glean a lot of the information from about the places you're going to visit. Swapping information with like-minded backpackers is the best way of getting up to date information on your next destination. This applies as much to toilets as any other aspect of travelling. You hear people discussing the best toilet venues of a town.

This is one sense in which US commercial globalisation can be seen in a positive light. Okay, so the Styrofoam containers McDonald's use are not good for the environment. It's also said that their farming techniques have a pretty negative effect on the Amazon jungle and other sensitive ecosystems. All of this planet raping may cumulatively lead to the ultimate demise of the planet and the wiping out of the human race but, if you go into a McDonald's 'restaurant' anywhere on earth, it will have a decent toilet. Believe me, if you're on the road and you have got a bit of intestinal bother, the fate of the planet is much lower on your list of priorities than having a good quality, trouble-free turn out on a comfortable seat.

Before further discussion of the hygienic pitfalls you may encounter while travelling, it is important to stress that being in the developed world does not guarantee that you're going to get to perform your ablutions in a high quality cubicle. There's a time honoured piece of advice which goes like this; never go to Belgium because you get the French toilets and the German sense of humour. This is a very inaccurate piece of advice. I've already opined that the Germans are not as bad a bunch as a lot of people make out and all of our rubbish British newspapers would have you believe. It's also untrue to say that you shouldn't go to Belgium. A life which ends without going to Bruges or Liège is a life unfulfilled.

As to the French toilets, I couldn't agree more. France has the fourth largest economy in the world but is about 200th out of 207 nation states in the global bad toilets league. You would expect a country capable of organising itself into an economic powerhouse to be able to get its bogs right; right? Wrong. Why can the French not sort their toilets out? One of the great mysteries of the modern world. The French themselves, or at least the men, get around this problem by only using toilets when they need to poo. One of the great things about France is that it's acceptable for men to piss just about anywhere, which I think is the way it should be.

Mind you, I didn't think that one day when I was having a picnic at the top of a chair lift in Tignes. I was with my then-girlfriend and we were right on the edge of the piste with our legs dangling over the edge of a small cliff. This French bloke came off the chairlift with his family and took his skis off about ten yards away from us. He stomped over and stood right next to us. By right next to us I mean two feet away. I couldn't believe it. He had the whole of a 400 km ski area to select somewhere to have a piss, thousands of acres of Alps, and he

321

chose to stand right next to a couple of people eating their lunch. After he'd finished, tucked himself in and walked off I looked over my shoulder to see him putting his skis back on and he had a big damp patch on the front of his ski suit! Didn't get much right really, did he?

The Tignes incident happened about three years ago by which time I'd been having trouble with French toilets for a good two and a half decades. It started at school in Brittany when I was seven. Imagine my surprise to go into the bogs at school for the first time to find a cistern and a hole in the ground. As my French was still not very good I chose to run all the way home without telling the teacher and use our proper loo complete with porcelain and plastic seat. What is it with Turkish toilets? What's the point? I never ever did use those bogs except for going for a pee. Three full years of education without going for a dump at school. My next problem with French bogs was about a year later at a wedding in Le Mans.

I was sitting on a long drop at the hippo-watching mecca, Lake Boringo in Kenya, having a bit of a reminisce amongst all the flies. A long drop is a hole in the ground with a toilet seat plonked on top of it basically. You just bung a bit of chemical blue down the hole every now and then as far as I can work out. If you're on a long drop in a hot place like Kenya, there are invariably a lot of flies about as well. In 95 up at Lake Boringo in Kenya, I finished up and came out into the sunlight, squinting like Steve McQueen coming out of the cooler in *The Great Escape*, to see Charlie and Simon walking towards me. 'What are the bogs like?' Charlie enquired nervously. 'Not bad,' I lied, telling Charlie what I thought he wanted to hear as he walked nervously towards the long drop. 'This won't last long,' I said to Simon, knowing well that Charlie had a pretty low toiletry tolerance level. With that the door of the long drop flew open and a retching Charlie burst out into the sunlight amidst a swarm of flies. Needless to say, giggling and chortling was as much sympathy as Simon and I could muster. Oh well, that's the perils of life in the cheap seats isn't it? A few more quid and he could have been staying in the posh place down the road with the flushing bogs.

Anyway, back in Le Mans and I was sitting on my first long drop. The thing was, I didn't even know it was a long drop. That didn't matter though, it was doing the job. What did matter was that at that point the door opened. 'Bonsoir,' said the big moustachioed chap in the moonlight as he shut the door. 'Bonsoir,' I replied with a quivering voice as the chap unzipped his trousers in the renewed darkness. I was so scared. Who was this bloke undoing his trousers in my bog? I knew I should have given more thought to why there was no lock on the door. With that, my stable mate sat down and lit a cigarette at which point I could breathe a sigh of relief. The flare of the match gave me the time to see that we were in a three seater long drop and his presence was totally justified. All I had to worry about now was whether or not the naked flame was going to combine with the methane of the long drop and blow us to high heaven.

It's quite extraordinary how bad some French bogs are. I met up with a girl in Lyon a few years ago for a dirty weekend. It wasn't all that dirty but it was good fun and well worth it. France's second city is a joy to visit, not only because it is the proud holder of the title of culinary capital of the most culinary country on earth, but also because it has a lovely old town. We were in a tiny bar and after a couple of bevvies, the lady in question decided that she needed the loo. The patronne gave her a key and sent her up to the top of the courtyard where the 'facilities', as my gran calls them, were located. She came back a couple of minutes later looking a bit green around the gills and said we had to leave. It turned out that she still needed the loo having been unable to bring herself to use the ones up in the courtyard. Bearing in mind that this is someone who spent a lot of her early life living in India and you can start to imagine how bad the bog must have been to make her refuse to use it. I nipped up for a look out of curiosity and it has to be said that it was not dissimilar to the 'worst bog in Scotland' featured in *Trainspotting*. Not good at all.

Getting back to the fact that French men often don't even bother waiting till they find a toilet, my toilet troubles continued even after moving back to the UK. On a visit to go and see some of our old school mates, Eric Le Texier's dad took us to Rennes to see what was my first ever game of professional football. I can't remember a thing about the game but I do remember the fence behind the main stand at the end of the game. An angled concrete path ran from the fence back down to the main flat path behind the stand and it was full of men having a post-final whistle pee. Trouble was, with the pitch towards the path, their collective evacuations streamed down onto the flat bit and we were walking through a sea of urine as we made for the exit. I was so far up on my toe tips that I must have looked like Nuryev. Only in France.

On our foray round South America, so obsessed did Tom get about a subject which has always captivated him, he actually wrote a song called 'The South American Bog Seat Song'. I didn't mind there being no bog seats. It's just one of those creature comforts that you realise you don't need after a while. Like bog paper really; nothing wrong with a left hand swipe as practiced by large parts of the world's population. Much more hygienic than bogwrap for a start. Incidentally, Tom's only other musical scrawling on that trip was a tune called 'Does Peter Beardsley's Mum Cut Your Hair?' Neither has yet made the charts, surprisingly enough.

Last but not least on that fair continent, the efforts of Paul the plumber are worth a mention. He's the unfortunate chap whose wife threw up on him, quite a few chapters ago, half an hour into a 24-hour bus trip. Well, on the Inca trail he totally excelled himself at a rest stop where Charlie had nipped behind some rocks for a poo. 'Extreme pooing' is the avoidance of using a toilet altogether, and on the Inca trail that's the only way to go because it is the middle of nowhere. You could at least get off the trail though, like Charlie did. I turned round to find Paul crouched about a foot off of the edge of the beaten track curling one down. Shocking. The end product was such a stack that I can only describe it as a steaming cairn. I know Paul's a big unit of twenty-something stone, but that was the largest pile of crap I've ever seen produced by a non-quadruped. Far too much information.

Holland – great country but pretty strange toilets quite frankly. Most of them have an 'inspection shelf' as perfectly horizontal as the country itself. It is onto this shelf that you deposit your offering so that when you turn around it's just sitting there on the shelf, all static and brown. Then you flush hoping that the pile is going to get shifted by the water flow but, as often as not, it isn't budged. Then the toilet brush comes into its own. To quote a very good, humorous American publication on life in Holland, 'the brush in a Dutch toilet is always wet but never mentioned'.

It doesn't get any better at work in the summer either. Having worked in events for the last fifteen years I've seen the legends of the mobile toilet industry as well as the many victims. An elderly lady and her daughter turned up to an event at which I work near London about twelve years ago and were very understanding under the circumstances which took place. Somewhere, someone turned a tap the wrong way and to his horror, the chap servicing some of the chemical toilets was confronted by this poor lady staggering out of one of the toilets after being bodily lifted off the toilet she was on by a high powered jet of chemical toilet 'blue', as the disinfecting product is known. Nowadays with the ambulance-chasing compensation culture we live in the incident would have

325

finished up in court. As it happened, she had a bit of a scrub up and someone took her into Kingston-upon-Thames to get a new frock.

As for 'blue wings' earned for courage in the face of blocked event toilets, the original master is Dave 'Blue Knuckles' French, who used to run a laughably shoddy mobile toilet company staffed by himself, a Toyota Landcruiser full of toilet roll, and a load of fragile students who were totally afraid of digested food. Not so for Dave who would walk into a mobile toilet unit rolling up his sleeves as the students scattered, vomiting as they went, after witnessing the horrors of the malfunctioning 'facilities'. He'd emerge five minutes later having not bothered adorning the rubber gloves his employees deemed necessary, and declare the problem to be solved and the crisis over. Then he'd return his attentions to his favourite habit; biting his nails!

Sorry, am I still talking shit? Further reading on the subject should be conducted at the paragraph below and in the antipodean publication mentioned.

Of course it's not all that long since everyone was in the same boat, in the days before toilets were plumbed in anywhere. In this respect I would highly recommend anyone to read Clive James' account of growing up in Australia. They used to have a 'dunny man' who'd come round to collect a stainless steel tub of their digested offerings once a week and there's an hilarious account of what happened when a young Clive left his push-bike out in the drive for the bloke with the bucket of mabonga to trip over. Maybe that's just a bloke thing though? Would a woman find it funny or just something not worth mentioning?

The Future

The question is, what to do next? Haven't got a clue to be honest. I'm thirty four and sitting in my parents' kitchen drinking about twenty five cups of tea a day and going for a ride on my dead grandad's push-bike every time I've had enough of staring at my computer screen. I've just finished a 'gap decade' and am strongly considering taking another. A lot of people take a gap year but in the realms of one-upmanship, I've decided to go one better and go for the decade. Since graduating in 96, I've been about the place a bit and had some great times. I've seen some great places, climbed up stuff, made some great friends and laughed a hell of a lot. So why not do it again? I may regret it in my mid-sixties when I'm forced to live in a cardboard box under some motorway flyover, but at least I'll be able to look back on a life fulfilled. Besides, there's nothing wrong with being in the gutter, as long as you're lying on your back looking at the stars. Let's face it, the alternatives to continuing on the same tack are pretty bleak. Work and an M40 traffic jam before and after.

Digression No42 – The M40 'protest fence'

Whether or not it has an official name I don't know. I call it the 'protest fence' because it is exactly that. Heading into London on the M40, some time after High Wycombe, you'll be on a hill and see a big field on your left with a fence across the top end of it. Written along a hundred or so yards of it in six foot letters is the question 'Why do I still do this every day?' Good question. The word 'still' was added after the original question, 'why do I do this every day?' was scrubbed out. I've always wondered how many motorists it has inspired to 'do a Michael Douglas'; as in emulating his character in Joel Schumacher's film *Falling Down*. He's in a traffic queue in LA and just gives up, gets out of his car and walks off, disgruntled with life. Let's hope that there are plenty of Brits inspired to do the same by the 'protest fence', although you'd hope none of them end up pulling a gun in a burger joint because they're three minutes too late for the breakfast menu, like Michael Douglas did.

End of digression.

Apart from mulling over the possibility of another ten years off, I've got lots else on. Planning for the future is pretty much a waste of time as I keep telling my increasingly worried mother. She's obsessed that me and my brother need to keep paying National Insurance contributions so that we get a state pension. Anyone in their right mind knows that there'll be nothing left in the kitty in thirty years' time so our generation is going to get stitched right up. I just ignore it.

Why is planning for the future such a waste of time? Because you never know what's going to happen next. If I hadn't been dumped by my latest ex-girlfriend this summer, I would have spent the summer on the beach in Hossegor in south-west France. Lovely part of the world. Unfortunately, following an unexpected stitch up and dumping which made Prime Minister Harold MacMillan's 'Night Of The Long Knives' look no fiercer than a Women's Institute 'Bring and Buy' sale, I've ended up elsewhere.

I'm contemplating this sitting in a restaurant in the middle of the Atlantic Ocean which is owned by a Frenchman who was separated at birth with Zinédine Zidane. The seared tuna is top notch and to add to the bizarreness of the situation, we're sitting eating with a French spear fisherman who is the life double of octogenarian blonde-locked DJ, Jimmy Saville. Best of all is the live acoustic guitar which is being played by a bloke who is pretending to be a local Cape Verdean but I'm convinced is actually Derek Griffiths, the former presenter of the BBC's legendary kids programme *Playschool*, trying to escape his fame on this lovely archipelago. His moustache is a vast caterpillar. He's getting paid in beer and after a few more he starts performing a bit more like the Kazak journalist Borat than Derek G, and the bum notes become a bit more frequent, but we clap the songs nonetheless. I was thinking 'is this really happening?' in the same way I was at the military Morris Dancing in Peru. You literally couldn't make it up. Surreal sandwiches all round.

Despite the futility of planning, you can aspire to doing things. In my case those include; canoeing down the Thames with my brother, taking my gran to New York on the Queen Mary II, learning to play the piano, sailing across the Atlantic, climbing Kilimanjaro, visiting every country in the world, having a lot more sex and eventually some kids, and owning a metallic lime green Triumph T509 Speed Triple motorbike. These are but a few of the things which are currently on the list, the most important elements of which are getting rid of leaf blowers and terrace heaters. Oh yes, and getting a job commentating on 'Test Match Special', the only job I would really like to do.

Digression No 43 – leaf leaf blowers, terrace heaters and chelsea tractors

Can someone please enlighten me, because my brain can't cope. On a planet running out of oil and gas, are we seriously going to use the last few barrels to fill leaf blowers up with fuel, heat the sky outside pubs, and navigate our way to schools on pothole-free tarmac roads in Porsche Cayennes and Jeep Cherokees? Is it a big wind-up or is this all really happening?

Former favourite song lyrics; 'the traffic lights turn blue tomorrow'; Hendrix

Current favourite song lyrics; 'leaf blowers, the futility of it all.' William Shatner

End of digression.

What I do instead of planning ahead is stick to some rules, some of which have been proven over the decades and centuries and some of whose common sense will save you a lot of ball ache . Mine are as follows;

Rule No1) It's better to burn out than to fade away; take risks. Furthermore, if in doubt, do it. It's easier to beg for forgiveness than to ask for permission.

Rule No2) Never invade Russia in the third week of June. I haven't got an army but if I did have and harboured ambitions to own Russia, I'd invade before June. Invade in late June and you'll never make Moscow before the cold snap. You need to make your big push over the river Neman a good month earlier, just ask Hitler or Napoleon 1er. They went for it on the 22nd and 24th respectively; that'll teach 'em, it all ended in tears.

Rule No3) Never eat yellow snow, it's invariably got piss in it.

Rule No4) Never invade Afghanistan full stop, even if you've got a really hard army. Considered by many people to be the most beautiful country in the world, Afghanistan has never been rumbled by the many warmongers who've tried.

Rule No5) Take a camera and binoculars if you can, but if it's a choice of either or, take the binoculars. If others want to go and see something they can jolly well go themselves!

Rule No6) Don't lick stamps in Romania; they taste absolutely revolting and don't stick properly anyway. Fortunately help is at hand in the form of the European Union.

With Romania about to join the world's most ridiculous bureaucracy, the EU is sure to have diktats covering the ingredients and taste of stamp glue which will have to be rigidly enforced. That's probably why they're joining. If you read the Daily Xenophobe in the UK you'll mistakenly think that they want to join so that they can come over here stealing all our jobs. In actual fact it's so that they can get some tastier stamps.

Rule No7) Remember, it's a small world. I once came out of the toilets at the campsite in Threeways, Northern Territory, Australia to find myself standing in front of Keith Towell who I used to go to scouts with. What are the odds? Both half a planet from home in what must be one of the most remote campsites on the planet. Imagine how many people you nearly bump into as well. We very nearly spent a night fifty yards apart in the same campsite without knowing it.

Rule No8) Always backwash your pint a bit; no one is going to minesweep a pint with bits of crisps floating in it.

Rule No 9) Never go out on the piss with your passport in your pocket! My cousin once met a bloke in Australia who had gone out one evening to buy a packet of fags in Warrington (the one in Cheshire in the UK), and somehow ended up at the Australia v England rugby test in Sydney, New South Wales. Adding to his woes, he was AWOL so was in for a good bollocking from his wife when he got home.

Rule No 10) If you're really unpopular, get your marketing done by the same people who doves employed. No, not the English alternative band who are quite deservedly anything but unpopular, I'm talking about the birds.

Pigeons are not very popular birds, and for pretty good reason. So how is it then, that doves, which are just white-feathered pigeons, have managed to become regarded as the global symbol of peace?

Rule No11) Last but not least, the best bit of advice you'll ever get; always point a wheelbarrow in the direction you're going to push it in before filling it.

I hope you've made it this far, and if you have, thanks for reading. That's the end of the book.

P.S. The author is aware that Tony Blair is no longer the Prime Minister and that Margaret Beckett is not now the Foreign Secretary. Similarly, Arnie and George W have also left their posts. As you will have surmised, these and other inaccuracies are due to a significant hiatus between the writing and publishing of this book.

Have fun!

This book is dedicated to Jamie Purvis and Lionel Hichens, both of whom expired in 2010. Lovely men.